The Agricultural Economy of Manitoba Hutterite Colonies

John Ryan

The Carleton Library No. 101

Published by McClelland and Stewart Limited
in association with the Institute of
Canadian Studies, Carleton University

Library
I.U.P.
Indiana, Pa.
338.109712 R955a
c.1

The Canadian Publishers
McClelland and Stewart Limited
25 Hollinger Road, Toronto

Printed and bound in Canada

CONTENTS

DIAGRAMS

MAPS

PLATES

TABLES

PREFACE

Hutterite colonies are no longer isolated and rather mysterious phenomena; their presence is now felt to a greater or lesser extent in almost all major agricultural districts of Manitoba. The colonies are unique features of the agricultural landscape, and partly because of the different basis of operation, there has been controversy regarding their economic and sociological impact on both the local and the provincial scene. An analysis of the Hutterite contribution to Manitoba is long overdue; in preparing this study I have attempted to meet this need.

An undertaking of this type would have been quite impossible without the co-operation of the Hutterite colonies themselves. The research has been based almost entirely on data and information obtained by interviewing the management and the workers of the colonies. At the end of 1971 there were 48 colonies in Manitoba, spread out over most of the southern part of the province. My first task was to convince the management personnel of each of these colonies that my study would be objective and useful both to them and for purposes of scientific inquiry. Once having established a rapport and reached agreement that such a study would indeed be worthwhile, I received the most complete co-operation and friendly assistance that I could ever hope for at each and every colony. It would not be quite correct to refer to my visits to the colonies as formal research interviews. I have eaten meals on almost every colony and after the first visit was always accepted as a friend and received with appropriate hospitality. It was in this spirit that I compiled the data on the colonies. The questionnaire on each of the colonies was so lengthy and detailed that it was almost embarrassing to ask these people to give up to it so much of their obviously busy time. It took several visits to each colony to compile all the data. Not once was any of the information given in an impatient or grudging manner. In addition to the data that I obtained at the colonies themselves, I had permission from each colony to obtain copies of their official financial statements, dating back to 1961, from their accountant's office in Brandon.

For their splendid co-operation I owe a great debt of gratitude to the management personnel of every colony, but I am especially indebted to Reverend Jacob Kleinsasser of Crystal Spring Colony. I have visited Jake, as he prefers to be called, on a great many occasions over a four-year period. He has been my major source of information on the many aspects of colony life. In addition, he spent many hours examining the raw data I had accumulated on all the enterprises for each of the colonies for possible inconsistencies. Because of his efforts, a number of omissions were noted and a few minor errors in the data were corrected. However, it was most gratifying to have his assurance that the bulk of the data were complete and accurate. When this study was almost completed, Reverend Kleinsasser read the original manuscript, corrected or improved a number of interpretations, and offered numerous helpful suggestions. His continued interest in the project has added immeasurably to the value of this work.

I am grateful to Mr. Dave Norris, the accountant employed by the Hutterites, for his analysis of many problems and for arranging to have his office staff provide me with copies of the voluminous financial reports on each of the colonies. Also gratefully acknowledged is the advice on statistical procedures provided by Mr. Metro Daciw, Agricultural Statistician of the Manitoba Department of Agriculture.

I wish to express thanks to my colleagues, Dr. Brian M. Evans and Dr. James M. Richtik of the Department of Geography at the University of Winnipeg, for their valued comments and suggestions on the improvement of several sections of the study. I am also indebted to Geoffrey R. Thomson, the cartographer at the Geography department, who drafted most of the final maps.

I wish to extend special thanks to Dr. Trevor Lloyd, of McGill University, who provided encouragement throughout the study and invaluable assistance with the revision of the manuscript. And finally, I have very much appreciated the interest, the concern, and the many helpful suggestions of my wife, Marie.

This study was originally done as a Ph.D. dissertation in geography for McGill University. The text was written in 1972 and it is based on field work conducted between 1968 and 1971, using 1968 as the base year for most of the data. To bring the study up to date would require a total duplication of all the field work that was conducted during this four-year period. However, the basic nature of Hutterite agriculture has not changed since the time of writing, and more recent data would in all likelihood not alter the major conclusions of this study. Hence, the study is published as it was originally written, except for the addition of an epilogue. The epilogue discusses the events and changes that have occurred up to 1976.

This study was financed by research and publication grants from the Canada Council, the Secretary of State, the Manitoba Department of Agriculture, and the University of Winnipeg, for which I am grateful and appreciative.

John Ryan,
University of Winnipeg,
March 1976

INTRODUCTION

Nature of the Study

This is a pioneer study of the agricultural economy of Manitoba Hutterite colonies. Although agriculture is a vital feature of Hutterite life, very little has been written on this topic *per se*.

Literature on the Hutterites is quite extensive, but most of it is from the viewpoint of demography, history, religion, psychology, and sociology.[1] Furthermore, the bulk of the literature deals with the Hutterites in the United States, whereas the majority of them live in Canada. The most authoritative account of the Hutterites in Manitoba is by Victor Peters in his M.A. thesis and in his book *All Things Common*.[2] However, his prime concern is not agriculture and he deals with this topic briefly and in a very general way. John W. Bennett (1967 and 1969) presents the most detailed account available of Hutterite agricultural operations, but it is based on colonies in Saskatchewan.[3] He provides a general discussion of the agricultural practices of six colonies, but does not analyze the subject systematically. Marvin P. Riley (1970), in a brief but informative booklet, describes the Hutterite farming practices in South Dakota.[4] Several other writers have dealt with limited aspects of Hutterite agriculture, but they are not applicable to Manitoba.[5] And finally, in recent years a few articles dealing with certain Hutterite enterprises have appeared in magazines and newspapers.[6] Although these are informative for the general reader, they are too brief to be of any consequence. So far as the writer has been able to learn there is no other literature on Hutterite agricultural operations applicable to Manitoba. Before the present study was begun there were in Manitoba no data on Hutterite agricultural operations or production. In view of this the present study is a pioneer one.

The main purpose of this study is to present a comprehensive account of how the Hutterites utilize their farmlands and how their operations compare with those of other Manitoba farms.[7] Specifically, the study examines each of the major Hutterite agricultural enterprises, and a comparison is made with the Manitoba farm average in regard to scale of operations, output, and productivity. In addition, the study examines the Hutterite contribution to the Manitoba agricultural economy in relation to the amount of land that they operate. It would be premature to advance major theories or hypotheses regarding Hutterite agriculture, but many explanations and interpretations of various aspects of Hutterite activities are put forward. It is hoped that one contribution of the study will be to provide and interpret essential basic data on Hutterite enterprises so as to prepare the way for future more detailed studies of specific aspects of Hutterite agriculture.

To understand and appreciate these agricultural operations is difficult as they cannot be considered in isolation, apart from the whole Hutterite way of life. In many ways, agriculture is the core of the daily routine on Hutterite colonies. To be able to view the role of agriculture in proper perspective, it is necessary to examine Hutterite colonies themselves and the characteristics of Hutterite people, hence several chapters are devoted to this.

The Hutterites practise a form of communal living which is unique on the North American continent. The need for periodic colony expansion should be appreciated, as well as the process and significance of colony division. It is also necessary to know how Hutterite colonies spread into the various parts of Manitoba, to examine the type of land settled, and the factors involved in the selection of land for new colonies. The total number of people involved, and the quality, experience, and training of the labour force are also significant. Since this is a communal way of life, it is essential to understand how the colony operates administratively and how decisions and policies are formulated. Only through understanding how the colonies function is it possible to achieve some appreciation of Hutterite agriculture as a whole.

Early in the study a decision was made to conduct a complete census on the operations of every colony. Since there were not many colonies, this was considered to be preferable to resorting to a sampling process. Furthermore, it would make available complete data on Hutterite agriculture, without the need for estimates. In this way more reliable comparisons could be made with operations on Manitoba farms. Data were systematically collected on each colony, and afterwards as the colonies were revisited for further information, the questionnaires were double-checked. The most serious drawback to such a procedure was that, because of the need to establish a proper rapport with the colonies, the writer had to conduct all the field work himself. This proved to be far more time-consuming than was anticipated.

Although the lifestyle of the Hutterites and the essential background material applies to the year 1971, the base year for Hutterite production data and for comparison with Manitoba farms is 1968. It would have been preferable to use 1971 alone as the base year, but this proved to be impossible for two reasons. Firstly, there had not been sufficient time to compile data on the Hutterites for 1971, and secondly, at the time of writing, the 1971 census material for Manitoba had only just begun to be released. There were other reasons for using 1968 as the base year. The most complete and thoroughly verified data available for the Hutterites were for 1968. Also for purposes of comparison with Manitoba farms, 1968 was better than either 1969 or 1970. The latter two years were for several reasons far less representative of average agricultural conditions in Manitoba than 1968. Mainly as a result of low prices, lack of markets, and government restrictions, wheat production on Manitoba farms was reduced drastically during these two years.[8] There were other readjustments as well, so that by 1970 the Manitoba net farm income dropped to less than one-half of the five-year average ending in 1968.[9] However, there were hardly any production changes on the Hutterite colonies during these two years, and in regard to net income, the colonies were not as adversely affected as other Manitoba farms. Consequently, it was decided that a 1968 comparison would be far more indicative of average conditions than either of the two later years.

One of the difficulties that this study encountered in comparing Hutterite operations with those of Manitoba farms was the lack of completely comparable data in certain instances. Fortunately, these cases were very few and actually involved only the number of farms in Manitoba on a district basis and their acreage. Data on Manitoba farms on a district basis were available for 1966 only, whereas Hutterite data were for 1968. In such instances, it was necessary to make the appropriate comparisons even though the dates differed. However, it was felt that since there was only a two-year difference, the results would not be seriously affected. Production data were not involved in these comparisons, but only the number of farms on which certain enterprises were conducted. Nevertheless, this was another reason for selecting 1968 as the base year. If a more recent year had been selected, valid comparisons could not have been made using any of the 1966 data.

Relevance and Significance of the Study to the Field of Geography

In a broad sense the object of this study from the viewpoint of geography has been to elucidate the effects of the Hutterite phenomenon on the Manitoba landscape. More specifically, the study provides a knowledge and appreciation of the Hutterite contribution to Manitoba's agricultural geography and to the province's rural settlement pattern.

A review of the literature of agricultural geography has led the writer to agree with Gregor that there is almost unanimous agreement that the primary object of this discipline is the study of the areal variation of agriculture.[10] For example, Reeds states that, "Agricultural geography in its broadest sense seeks to describe and explain areal differentiation in agriculture . . ."[11] However, there is less agreement about the context in which these variations should be studied. Agricultural geography deals with a wide range of phenomena, some of which are also studied in other disciplines such as agricultural science and economics. There is also an overlapping between agricultural geography and other aspects of geography, e.g., with settlement and cultural geography. Recognition that it is a conceptual impossibility to separate the agricultural landscape from the cultural landscape has encouraged a more liberal view of the relationships between agricultural geography and the related disciplines. As Otremba has pointed out, agricultural geography is one of the "typical boundary and correlative sciences," and that "it is neither wise nor necessary to draw sharp subject boundaries."[12] Some further indication of what is comprehended within agricultural geography may be obtained from the contributions made to it. Indeed, as Gregor points out, "many would argue that these materials are even better indicators of what geographers think agricultural geography is."[13] An examination of a wide range of recent material in "agricultural geography" convinces the writer this is indeed a border discipline, and that Otremba's view is valid.[14]

Surprisingly, agricultural geography in Manitoba is still at an early stage of development. Geographers have neglected it, for although there are of course many studies of various aspects of Manitoba agriculture, practically all of them approach it from the viewpoint of agricultural science or economics. The material that can be considered as agricultural geography bears little if any relationship in content and approach to a study of Hutterite agricultural practices.[15] Hence the present study is a pioneer venture not only in regard to Hutterite farming, but to some degree also with regard to agricultural geography as a whole in the province.

The continuing geographical theme throughout this study is the areal variation of agriculture. Specifically, the main objective is to examine how the Hutterites utilize their farmlands and how the various operations compare with those of other Manitoba farms. However, it is impossible to isolate just the "agricultural aspect" within the Hutterite milieu, and even if this were possible, an adequate explanation of their agricultural operations could not be provided without reference to the whole Hutterite culture. Hence this study involves the total spectrum of agricultural geography, including the overlapping areas in agricultural science and economics as well as settlement and cultural geography.

As Gregor points out, "Systematic field work has long played a particularly prominent role in agricultural geography,"[16] and in this the present study has proved to be no exception. Since there were no data of any kind available on the agricultural operations of the Manitoba Hutterites, the writer had no choice but to resort to intensive field work. As mentioned earlier, most of the data were collected from personal interviews and recorded in detailed questionnaires. Additional data were obtained from Hutterite farm records and from the accounting firm employed by the colonies. Data on Manitoba farms were obtained from official publications, for instance, the census, agricultural year-books, and various government publications. Hence a major part of the research project was necessarily devoted to the accumulation of raw statistical data.

The remainder of the study was taken up with the processing, organization, and analysis of this wide range of materials, that is, filled-out questionnaires, farm records, inventory reports, financial statements, records of interviews, and so on. The main purpose was to organize the material in such a way that basic comparisons could be made between the Hutterite and other Manitoba farms. By processing the material from the individual colonies and organizing it in tabular form, along with comparable data for Manitoba farms, it was possible to draw many comparisons, for instance, scale of operations, farm output, productivity, and the overall Hutterite contribution to the Manitoba agricultural economy. In addition, the Hutterite share of production could be shown in relation to the amount of land that they operated.

With the large amount of systematized data and the analysis of it that the study now makes available, it should be possible to launch more detailed studies, involving possibly computerized techniques.[17]

It is worth emphasizing that the writer during the course of the study established a remarkably close rapport with each of the Hutterite colonies. This is a significant contribution in itself, and should make it possible for other research workers to build on this spirit of good will. The importance of a proper rapport with the Hutterites should not be underestimated, since if this is lacking, serious research becomes almost impossible.

Hutterite Communal Farming Compared to Other Communal Farming Systems

Hutterite colonies are one of many instances in the world where agricultural operations are conducted on a communal basis. This form of social organization has, of course, deep roots in history. While it has been superceded in, for example, western Europe, and was never adapted widely when the farmlands of North America were opened up, there remain significant present-day evidences of communal or co-operative farming elsewhere in the world. While these have had no influence on the practices of the Manitoba Hutterites, they may be cited in passing.

The world's major communal farming systems today include the following: collective and state farms in the U.S.S.R. and to a varying extent in the socialist countries of eastern Europe and in Cuba; the communes in China; the kibbutzim and other co-operative farming systems in Israel; and the ejidos in Mexico. Although there are many differences between these types, all have something in common, and on this basis they may be compared to Hutterite colonies.

The essential similarity between the Hutterite colonies and other communal farming systems is the communal operation of the farmland. Although the organization and farming procedures differ, the collective approach is the unifying feature. Another similar feature is the village-type settlement pattern. However, the Hutterite village is derived directly from the traditional agricultural villages of eastern Europe. Likewise it should be noted that the present day kolkhoz or collective farm of the U.S.S.R. is in many cases a lineal descendant of the old estate surrounding a typical village.

Probably the most basic distinction between the Hutterite colonies and all the other communal farming systems is in their raison d'être. Whereas political philosophy and economic considerations have been responsible for the formation and continuation of the other communal forming systems, the raison d'être for the Hutterite colonies is religion. At the root of the Hutterite system is the early Christian idea that people should hold all things in common. Hence, while agriculture forms the economic basis for the colonies, the agricultural operations are only a means by which the Hutterites are able to maintain their religious communal way of life.

Another difference that distinguishes the Hutterite system from other communal farming systems is the political and economic setting. The individual Hutterite colonies in Canada and the United States can in a sense be viewed as little "socialist" oases surrounded by a broadly capitalist economy. On the other hand, most of the other communal farming systems, with the notable exception of Israel and Mexico, are located in socialist countries.

A further difference between the Hutterite colonies and other communal systems is the size and scale of farming operations. Almost without exception, the Hutterite colonies are appreciably smaller than the farm units in other communal systems.

Notes and References

1. Marvin P. Riley, *The Hutterite Brethren: An Annotated Bibliography with Special Reference to South Dakota Colonies*, Rural Sociology Department, Project 255 (Brookings: South Dakota State University, 1965). This publication lists most of the literature available on the Hutterites.
2. Victor Peters, "All Things Common—The Hutterians of Manitoba" (unpublished Master's thesis, University of Manitoba, 1958); Victor Peters, *All Things Common: The Hutterian Way of Life* (Minneapolis: The University of Minnesota Press, 1965).
3. John W. Bennett, *Hutterian Brethren: The Agricultural Economy and Social Organization of a Communal People* (Stanford: Stanford University Press, 1967); John W. Bennett, *Northern Plainsmen: Adaptive Strategy and Agrarian Life* (Chicago: Aldine Publishing Company, 1969).
4. Marvin P. Riley, *South Dakota's Hutterite Colonies: 1874-1969*, Rural Sociology Department, Bulletin 565 (Brookings: South Dakota State University, 1970).
5. The following are some of the publications that deal with Hutterite agriculture, but none of these have any significant bearing on the Manitoba colonies: Joseph W. Eaton, *Exploring Tomorrow's Agriculture* (New York: Harper and Brothers, 1943); John A. Hostetler and Gertrude Enders Huntington, *The Hutterites in North America* (New York: Holt, Rinehart and Winston, 1967); Saul M. Katz "The Security of Cooperative Farming" (unpublished Master's thesis, Cornell University, 1953).
6. An extensive file of magazine and newspaper clippings on the Hutterites is available at the library of the Manitoba Department of Agriculture in the Norquay Building, Winnipeg.
7. This study accepted the *1966 Census of Canada* definition of a farm, i.e., ". . . an agricultural holding of one acre or more with sales of agricultural products, during the 12-month period prior to the census, of $50 or more." This same definition is accepted by

the *Yearbook of Manitoba Agriculture*, which appears annually. Most of the comparisons in this study are based on data from these two sources.

8. Wheat production dropped from an average of 85 million bushels for the five-year period ending in 1968 to 64 million in 1969 and 30.5 million in 1970 (*Yearbook of Manitoba Agriculture*, 1970, p. 77).

9. The average total Manitoba farm net income for the five-year period ending in 1968 was 160 million dollars, but this dropped to 117 million in 1969 and to 79 million in 1970 (*Yearbook of Manitoba Agriculture,* 1970, p. 77).

10. Howard F. Gregor, *Geography of Agriculture: Themes in Research* (Englewood Cliffs, N. J.: Prentice-Hall, Inc., 1970), p. 2; *International Geography 1972 La géographie internationale* (Papers submitted to the 22nd International Geographical Congress, Canada. Edited by W. Peter Adams and Frederick M. Helleiner. Volume 2. Toronto: University of Toronto Press, 1972), pp. 695-787.

11. L. G. Reeds, "Agricultural Geography: Progress and Prospects," *Canadian Geographer*, Vol. 8 (1964), p. 51.

12. E. Otremba, *Allgemeine Agrar- und Industriegeographie* (Stuttgart: Franckh, 1953), pp. 19f., cited by Howard F. Gregor, *Geography of Agriculture: Themes in Research* (Englewood Cliffs, N. J.: Prentice-Hall, Inc., 1970), p. 7.

13. Gregor, *op. cit.*, p. 16.

14. *International Geography 1972, op. cit.*, pp. 695-787; Bruce Proudfoot, "Agriculture," *The Prairie Provinces* (Studies in Canadian Geography. Edited by P. J. Smith. Published for the 22nd International Geographical Congress, Montreal 1972. Toronto: University of Toronto Press, 1972), pp. 51-64; Leslie Symons, *Agricultural Geography* (London: G. Bell and Sons, Ltd., 1967).

15. The following deal to some extent with the agricultural geography of Manitoba.

   ● J. S. Dunlop, "Changes in the Canadian Wheat Belt, 1931-1969," *Geography*, Vol. 55 (2), April 1970, pp. 156-168. Although this study deals with aspects of Manitoba agriculture, none of the Hutterite colonies are located in the "wheat belt." Furthermore, the paper's broad view of wheat production changes on the prairies is not applicable to a detailed study of Hutterite agricultural operations.

   ● Richard C. Fordham, "The Structure of Manitoba's Agricultural Geography, 1951-1964" (unpublished Master's thesis, The University of Manitoba, 1966). The study deals with types of farming in Manitoba, the relative efficiency of different areas, and possible future production changes. This is a statistical study based entirely on income and expense census data for census divisions. Its focus is the large scale statistical region, hence its approach is not applicable to a study which involves individual farming units.

- John Friesen, "The Manitoba Sugar Beet Industry—A Geographical Study" (unpublished Master's thesis, The University of Manitoba, 1962). A detailed analysis of the sugar beet industry in Manitoba, but it is not applicable to a study of Hutterite agriculture because none of the Hutterite colonies produce sugar beets.
- John Ryan, *Mixed Farming Near Carman, Manitoba* (Toronto: Ginn and Company. 1968). A case study of an average, successful mixed farm in Manitoba. The study is useful for comparison purposes with Hutterite colonies, especially with regard to scale of operations. While preparing this publication, the author became thoroughly familiar with many mixed farms in Manitoba, an experience which proved of considerable value during the Hutterite study.
- J. Warkentin, *Manitoba Settlement Patterns* (Papers published by the Historical and Scientific Society of Manitoba. Series 3, No. 16. Winnipeg, 1961), pp. 62-77. Deals primarily with settlement geography although some reference is made to Manitoba agriculture.
- J. Warkentin, "Mennonite Agricultural Settlements of Southern Manitoba," *Geographical Review*, Vol. 49 (1959), pp. 348-368. A paper on settlement geography with some reference to agriculture, but it is concerned primarily with Mennonite settlements.
- John H. Warkentin, "The Mennonite Settlements of Southern Manitoba" (unpublished Ph.D. thesis, The University of Toronto, 1960). A study of Mennonite settlement in Manitoba. Although it deals with their agricultural practices, it is primarily from the viewpoint of cultural and settlement geography.

16. Gregor, *op. cit.*, p. 17.
17. On several occasions during the course of this study the writer discussed possible alternative ways of analysing the data collected with Mr. M. Daciw, Agricultural Statistician of the Manitoba Department of Agriculture. In Mr. Daciw's opinion the writer followed the most logical and worthwhile approach at this stage of research on the Hutterite colonies. He feels that the contribution made by this study will now enable other research workers to use it as the basis for more detailed studies, especially in the area of cost-accounting.

CHAPTER 1

HISTORICAL BACKGROUND AND MAJOR CHARACTERISTICS OF HUTTERITE COLONIES

Historical Background of Hutterian Brethren[1]

The Hutterites, or the Hutterian Brethren which is their full title, had their origin in Central Europe at the time of the Reformation. In their history of almost 450 years these people have been subjected to periodic persecution which invariably resulted in migration. These migrations have led them from Moravia, Slovakia, Transylvania, Tsarist Russia, the United States, and eventually to Canada.* At the present time there are over 19,000 Hutterites**—more than two-thirds of them live in Manitoba, Saskatchewan, and Alberta, while the remainder are in the United States, mainly in South Dakota and Montana.[2]

Throughout their history the Hutterites have practiced a way of life which clearly distinguished them from the surrounding society, and this has largely been the cause of their persecution.

This unique way of life had its formal beginnings in Moravia in 1528 when a group of about 200 Anabaptists banded together in the face of religious persecution. Under the leadership of Jacob Huter and later Peter Riedemann, they worked out the basic tenets of Hutterian beliefs which have been followed with little deviation to the present day.[3] These beliefs, based on early Christian teachings, include a form of communal living, communal ownership of all property, non-violence and opposition to war, adult baptism, and the practice of a fundamentalist religion. In addition, they have retained the dress, the customs, and the simple, austere manner of living of their early ancestors. They have managed to preserve and maintain their traditional ways by living in colonies in rural areas and practicing agriculture for a livelihood. Agriculture to the Hutterites is more than an occupation or means of livelihood—it is a way of life sanctioned by religion.

Until relatively recent times the Hutterites were subjected to persecution mainly because of their insistence on practising their own form of

*See Map 22, page 272.
**The total North American Hutterite population in 1974 was 21,521 (Hostetler 1974).

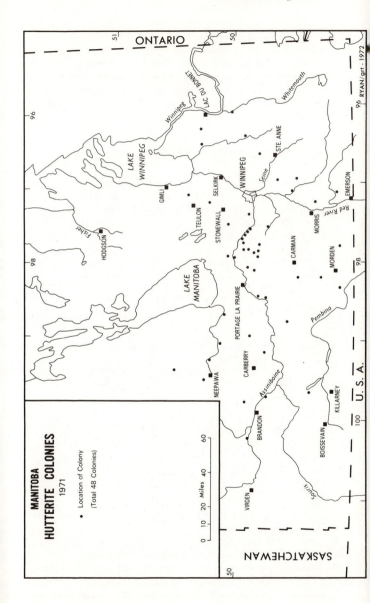

religion and because of their refusal to be inducted into military service. For instance, their migration to Canada from the United States in 1918 was the result of persecution during World War I because of their refusal to participate in military operations. Among the problems that they have faced in Canada have been the attempts to prevent them from purchasing land in large blocks and from establishing colonies wherever they desired.

Major Characteristics of Hutterite Colonies

At the end of 1971 there were 48 colonies in Manitoba, located in various parts of the province as shown on Map 1. The total Manitoba Hutterite population at the end of 1970 was 4,666.[4] In recent years the population of the colonies has varied from about 50 to 160. When a colony acquires a population of over 125 or when labour considerations present problems, plans are made for the establishment of a new colony. Once the land for a new colony is purchased and buildings are constructed, the parent colony splits in half. Typically, colonies have been branching out approximately every 14 years.[5]

Most colonies in Manitoba have a land area of between 3,500 and 4,500 acres. Although this may seem to be large, on a per family basis the acreage is smaller than the provincial average. Most Hutterites would like to operate larger units, but for a variety of reasons, they face difficulties in obtaining larger tracts.

Although the Hutterites lead a very simple and austere life, they nevertheless utilize the most modern implements and machinery available. Indeed, the Hutterites try to employ the most technically advanced methods for all farm operations.

Hutterites operate a basically mixed farm economy, and in this sense their practices do not differ materially from those of other mixed farm operators. Wheat, oats, barley, and hay are their main field crops. On practically all colonies hogs are far more important than cattle, and most colonies keep large numbers of laying hens, turkeys, ducks, and geese. Consequently, most of the grain that is produced is used for feed, and in fact, most colonies buy additional grain for feed purposes from local farmers. Hence government quotas on grain shipments are of little consequence to them.

To some extent Hutterite colonies are self-sufficient units. They have men highly skilled in metal work and machine repairing, electrical work, plumbing, carpentry, construction work, and so on. In addition, most of their clothing is homemade. The colonies, however, do make a very substantial contribution to the local economy. Large sums are spent annually in nearby towns and villages on agricultural machinery, gas and oil, lumber, cement, groceries, dry goods, hardware, etc. In addition, most colonies purchase certain supplies such as feed concentrate, fabrics, some clothing, and other goods on a wholesale or bulk basis in Winnipeg.

The Hutterite Way of Life

Although Hutterite farm operations do not differ basically from those of other farms, the Hutterite way of life as such is completely different. As has already been pointed out, they are a deeply religious people who believe in communal living. Each family occupies separate living quarters, but all meals are eaten in the communal kitchen. All property is owned collectively. No member is paid any wages, but the basic wants and needs of all are looked after. No one receives any preferential treatment; great pains are taken to treat every family and every individual equally. No individual may choose his own job, but skills are usually recognized and a person is assigned with this in mind. The majority viewpoint rules and the minority willingly adapts itself to the majority's wishes. Each member endeavours to do his part to the best of his abilities. There is complete security in this way of life and experience shows that there is very little psychological pressure.

Mainly because Hutterite farming is on a fairly large scale it has not been affected as severely as the typical farm by market fluctuations. However, even the Hutterites have faced severe problems with certain enterprises, for instance, egg production has suffered from low prices. Economic matters apart, the Hutterites have been under pressure from the outside world in a number of ways. Municipalities have attempted to prevent Hutterites from expanding their farm holdings and from purchasing land wherever they desired. This has not been particularly successful in Manitoba because although the previous governments had given passive support to the municipalities, they did not enact official legislation against the Hutterites.[6] This was done in Alberta, however, and government restrictions were enforced. Other problems that the Hutterites have encountered include the attempts by certain Manitoba school districts to force Hutterite children to attend regular schools rather than colony schools. The Hutterites realize that if this should occur, it could very easily lead to their total disintegration within a short period of time. Consequently they have resisted all such attempts to interfere with their educational system. Finally, the indirect pressures from the modern outside world are a constant threat to the Hutterites. Although the colonies do not own radios, television, or ordinary cars, the young people are not unaware of the outside world. In certain colonies as many as 20 percent of the young people between 19 and 24 may leave the colony but until now it seems that about 85 percent of them eventually return to the colony.[7] One factor contributing to the high rate of return seems to be that after being reared on a colony, the outside world presents too many pressures and problems for the average Hutterite. Another factor seems to be that after experiencing the outside world, and comparing the two ways of life, the majority of the Hutterites decide in favour of colony life. This seems to be the case especially in instances where some Hutterites have returned to colony life after extensive travel and years of success at high-paying jobs.

In spite of the various problems encountered by Hutterites, in Manitoba it is apparent that the colonies are well established and they provide an ever increasing amount of agricultural produce for the Canadian economy.

Notes and References

1. This introductory chapter on the history of the Hutterites and their major characteristics is based primarily on information obtained from discussions with Reverend Jacob Kleinsasser of Crystal Spring Colony and other Hutterite ministers and colony managers. In addition, reference was made to relevant sections in the following: John W. Bennett, *Hutterian Brethren* (Stanford: Stanford University Press, 1967); John A. Hostetler and Gertrude Enders Huntington, *The Hutterites in North America* (Toronto: Holt, Rinehart and Winston, 1967); Victor Peters, *All Things Common* (Minneapolis: The University of Minnesota Press, 1965).

2. Ben J. Raber, *The 43rd Year of the New American Calendar 1972* (Baltic, Ohio: published by Ben J. Raber and printed by the Gordonville Printshop, Gordonville, Pennsylvania, 1972), pp. 4-5. This annual publication, printed in German, deals primarily with Amish news and events but a section is devoted to the Hutterian Brethren. It lists the 1971 Hutterite population as being 5,900 in the U.S.A. and 13,554 in Canada, making a total Hutterite population of 19,454. These data were apparently compiled by Mr. Raber from the reports of Hutterian Senior Elders, and this is probably the most accurate population estimate to date. The Canada *Census* does not classify the Hutterites either as a separate ethnic group nor as a religious denomination. In the first instance, they are included in the German category, and in the second, they

are included with the Mennonites. Hence, there are no published census data available on the Hutterites.

3. Jacob Huter organized the various Moravian Anabaptist groups into well unified community-congregations, and was largely instrumental in resolving initial internal disputes and unifying the whole movement. He was captured and burned at the stake in 1536, and thenceforth the group of community-minded Anabaptists took their name from this leader and called themselves the Hutterian Brethren (Peters 1965).

4. The 1970 Manitoba Hutterite population data were compiled from the Hutterite Income Tax records by Dave Norris, the accountant employed by the Hutterite colonies. These records are unquestionably the most reliable source of information on Hutterite population. New reports are prepared each year, as of December 31, on a per colony and per family basis, listing each Hutterite individual, including the birthdate. However, the total population data are not tabulated unless the colonies make a special request to have this done. Furthermore, although each colony keeps its combined financial and income tax records at the accountant's office in Brandon, these are made available for research purposes only upon the written permission from each colony.

5. This is based on data compiled from field investigation by the writer.

6. According to Reverend Jacob Kleinsasser of Crystal Spring Colony, in 1957 Premier Campbell strongly urged the Hutterites to sign a ''gentlemen's agreement'' with the Union of Manitoba Municipalities which would put restrictions on future Hutterite land purchases. Facing the likely prospect of restrictive legislation, the Hutterites signed the agreement on April 12, 1957, and abided by it until 1971. In that year, contrary to the agreement, they purchased the land and buildings of a former airbase owned by the provincial government. In reply to the protests of the Union of Municipalities, Premier Schreyer's government went on record opposing any restrictions on the Hutterites. As a result, the Hutterites now consider the 1957 ''gentlemen's agreement'' to be null and void.

7. This is an estimate made by Reverend Jacob Kleinsasser of Crystal Spring Colony.

CHAPTER 2

HUTTERITE SETTLEMENT AND COLONY EXPANSION

The Colony Settlement[1]

As a result of their belief in communal living, Hutterites establish a village-type settlement, or *Bruderhof*, on each colony farm. This settlement includes not only their living quarters but all the structures and facilities associated with the farm economy. Since the population of colonies varies from about 50 to 160 and the structures required for a mixed farming economy are numerous and usually extensive, the average colony settlement is indeed a significant feature of the landscape. Together with the colony garden and shelter belts, the settlement may occupy an area from 20 acres to as much as 150 acres.

Considerable care is taken in selecting the site for the settlement. In their attempts to keep the outside world from infringing on their way of life, the settlement is usually established some distance from towns and if possible away from main traffic arteries. However, the relocation of the Trans-Canada Highway west of Winnipeg in 1956 placed it within only a few miles of several Hutterite colonies. Almost every colony settlement in Manitoba has been established near a river or creek. This is largely to ensure a convenient water supply for the geese, ducks, and livestock. On the other hand, this means that in most cases a considerable amount of land near the water course may be unsuitable for cultivation. However, little of this is wasteland because most of it is used for pasture or hayland.

It is often pointed out that the layout plan and the orientation of buildings on a Hutterite colony differ significantly from those of an average farmstead. As a general rule an average individual farmer plans his farmstead in such a way that his house and lawn face the road or at least serve as the entrance to the farm. In the case of an average Hutterite colony, however, the residential quarters which are the most aesthetically pleasing section of the colony invariably serve as the core of the settlement. In other words, the appearance of an average colony from the main entrance road is usually unimpressive, almost as if by design. On entering a colony one is apt to first encounter implement sheds, barns, or some other structures not particularly noted for their aesthetic qualities. After winding his way through this section, the visitor then enters the usually well designed and attractive residential core of the settlement. On most colonies the central part of the settlement has well tended lawns, flowerbeds, numerous shade trees, and in general has a peaceful, relaxed, park-like atmosphere. In contrast to the first impressions from a distance and from the entrance way, this change of scene at the heart of the colony comes as a pleasant surprise.

The explanation for such an orientation plan is based on practicality and function. An average farmer does not have very many barns or structures and therefore he can easily arrange to have his house and lawn at the entrance to his farm. In the case of a Hutterite colony with its many enterprises, the buildings are so abundant that the most functional and practical plan is to build them around the periphery of the residential area. Furthermore, some of the buildings require a large surrounding yard of several acres, for instance, the turkey and geese facilities. In the case of the hog and chicken enterprises, the large structures require space and because of the undesirable odours, these enterprises are usually built at some distance from the residential area. In any case, the residential section is invariably located at the core of the settlement and the various farm enterprises are functionally arranged around the periphery.

The layout of buildings and various facilities on typical Hutterite colonies appears in Maps 2, 3 and 4, and Plates 1, 2, 3, and 4. These colonies demonstrate how the residential core is not the first section of a colony to be encountered from the main entrance. Furthermore, these colonies illustrate how the basic layout plan is very similar on all colonies, regardless if they were established about 50 years ago or very recently.

An attempt is always made to place the community dining hall at the very core of the settlement. This is because of the obvious need for a central location, since all the members of the colony assemble there at least three times daily.

About half of the colonies have a separate church building but many colonies use the dining hall for church services. On some colonies the school may be used for this purpose. It should perhaps be pointed out that the use of the dining hall as a place of worship is not inappropriate or unusual in any sense. For Hutterites the taking of nourishment is in itself a form of religious service. While in our society eating is a routine function, for them it is an expression of worship as the entire community gathers in the dining hall to partake of a meal in almost complete silence.

Len Boszko (1971)

PLATE 1. *Blumengart Hutterite Colony*, established 1922, and located 10 miles southeast of Winkler. In a typical manner the residential core is surrounded by the buildings and facilities of various enterprises.

PLATE 2. *Bloomfield Hutterite Colony*, established 1955, and located along the Whitemud River 25 miles northwest of Portage la Prairie. Residential section in the foreground, granaries are top-right, 3 large chicken barns top-centre and top-left, cow barn top-left near river, and 3 hog barns top-left off the picture.

Len Boszko (1971)

PLATE 3. *Hillside Hutterite Colony*, established 1957, and located 12 miles northeast of Brandon. Residential section centre-foreground, chicken barns on right, hog barns top-centre, and cow barn top-left off the picture. Close-up of large two-storey single-family dwelling in bottom-centre is shown on Plate 6.

Len Boszko (1971)

PLATE 4. *Parkview Hutterite Colony*, established 1964, and located 6 miles east of Riding Mountain National Park. Residential section consisting mainly of 3- and 4-family dwellings in centre-foreground, hog barns top-left, and chicken barns to the left off the picture.

Len Boszko (1971)

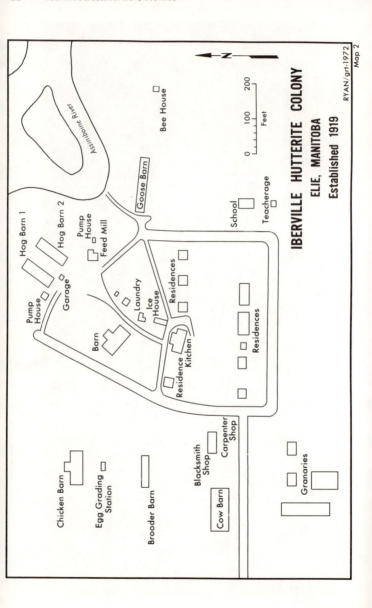

IBERVILLE HUTTERITE COLONY
ELIE, MANITOBA
Established 1919

RYAN/grt-1972   Map 2

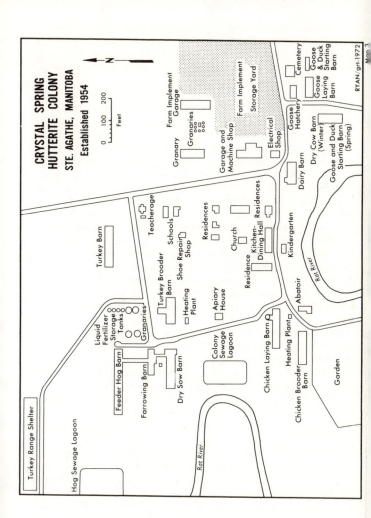

CRYSTAL SPRING
HUTTERITE COLONY
STE. AGATHE, MANITOBA
Established 1954

0 100 200
Feet

RYAN/grt-1972
Map 3

The structure that houses the dining hall is an exceptionally large building because it also contains the colony kitchen (as elaborately equipped as that of a large restaurant), and the cold storage and refrigeration area. In addition, on some colonies this building also houses the colony laundry facilities.

The residential buildings are spaced around the colony dining hall. The number of these buildings depends on the size of the colony and on the type of residential structures. In addition to single family dwellings, Hutterites often build multiple family structures. Some of these are duplexes, some are three-family units, and some are designed for four or more families. The main reason for multiple family dwellings is the saving in cost, but it is also partly because of tradition. However, a change in style appears to be developing because many of the newer colonies have placed an emphasis on duplexes and three-family dwellings rather than on larger structures typical of the older colonies. Furthermore, some of the new colonies have a number of single family dwellings which can easily be moved when the colony subdivides. In addition, many colonies will have at least one very conventional single family dwelling. Invariably, this is a house that was built by the original farmer from whom the Hutterites bought the land. Often the interior of such a house is remodeled and the kitchen is removed because there is no need for this facility in a Hutterite home. Various types of Hutterite dwellings are shown on Plates 5, 6, 7, 8, 9 and 10.

The kindergarten building, the school, and often a small house for the teacher are also located within the residential complex. The kindergarten is usually not far from the dining hall because youngsters from two and a half to five years of age eat their meals in the kindergarten under the supervision of their teacher and her assistants.

All Hutterite colonies have one- or two-room schools. Even though some School Districts have recently begun to withhold school grants in an indirect attempt to force the Hutterites to send their children to large district schools, the Hutterites are adamant on this issue and continue to operate their own schools. They realize that once their children attend outside schools, this will undoubtedly undermine the entire Hutterian way of life. Therefore, if need be they are prepared to pay the full educational costs themselves. This is a major problem for all the Hutterite communities; they have by no means resigned themselves to give way to such outside pressures. How the issue will be resolved still remains to be seen.

Beyond the residential complex are the numerous buildings and facilities associated with the farm economy. Every colony is involved in the production of hogs and for this enterprise two or three large structures are required. Usually these are some distance from the

RYAN/grt-1972
Map 4

RIDGELAND HUTTERITE COLONY
ANOLA, MANITOBA
Established 1967

Sow Shed

Dry Sow Barn

Hog Brooder Barn

Hog Feeder Barn

Grain Elevator

Engine Garage

River

Cow Shed

Cow Barn

Egg House

Chicken Laying Barn

Granaries

Chicken Brooder Barn

Boiler Room

Root Cellar

Wash House

Freezer

Carpenter Shop

Radial Saw Shop

Bulk Milk Shop

Garage

Machine Shed

Dwellings

Kitchen

Dwelling

Dwelling

Dwelling

Teacherage

Bee House

Dwelling

Dwelling

Kindergarten

School

0   100   200
Feet

N

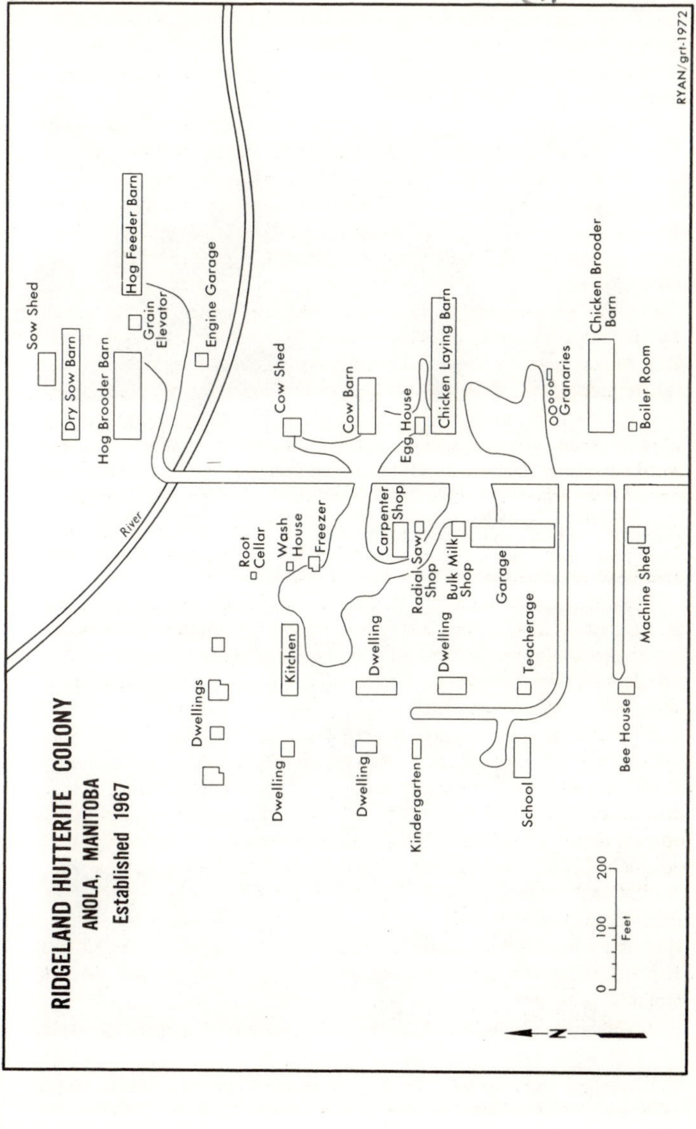

J. Ryan (1972)

PLATE 5. *Single-family Hutterite dwelling* at Suncrest Colony located 6 miles north of St. Pierre. The house was built in 1965 at Crystal Spring Colony, and when the colony subdivided in 1969 to form Suncrest, four such houses were moved to the new colony. Single-family Hutterite dwellings have the advantage of portability. Until relatively recent times most colonies had no single-family dwellings, and they were unable to move the large multiple-family dwellings. This meant that when a colony subdivided, the parent colony was left with considerable vacant housing for a number of years.

J. Ryan (1969)

PLATE 6. *Single-family remodelled home* of original farmer from whom the Hutterites purchased the land. The house is about 50 years old and is located at Hillside Colony near Brandon (Plate 3). Aside from removing the kitchen, the Hutterites made few alterations to it.

J. Ryan (1972)

PLATE 7. *Modern two-family Hutterite dwelling* at Suncrest Colony. Three such houses were built in 1968, the year before the colony was founded.

J. Ryan (1969)

PLATE 8. *Modern three-family Hutterite dwelling* at Rock Lake Colony located about 20 miles northwest of Winnipeg. It was built in 1968 and is typical of the modern three-family units on many colonies.

J. Ryan (1969)

PLATE 9. *Traditional style four-family dwelling* at Rock Lake Colony. The structure was built in 1947, the year that the colony was founded. The entire colony settlement is well landscaped and has a park-like appearance.

J. Ryan (1972)

PLATE 10. *Traditional style six-family dwelling* at James Valley Colony located 5 miles south of Elie. This is one of the original multiple-family dwellings built in 1918, the year that the Hutterites first moved to Manitoba. These houses had very small living quarters per family, and some have now been remodelled by adding a full second storey. On this house the original wood siding has been replaced by stucco. The large trees and the old style buildings give this colony an air of permanence and tradition.

residential area because of the odours. The chicken enterprise involves two or three buildings depending on the extent of the colony's involvement. Colonies that keep turkeys, geese, and ducks will have the appropriate buildings for these plus several acres of yard space. Most colonies will have some provision for cattle, but there is a wide variation from colony to colony. Some specialize in beef cattle and so will have a feed lot and an appropriate shelter for the animals. Those that are involved in dairying will have a standard type of dairy barn with all the associated facilities. In general though, most colonies are not too deeply involved in raising cattle. In addition to the buildings already mentioned, each colony has numerous granaries, a grain elevator, large implement sheds, a repair garage and blacksmith shop or machine shop, a slaughterhouse, honey processing facilities, a shoe repair shop; some may have a goose and duck hatchery, plus other structures such as a freezer plant, a root cellar, etc.

Although the basic pattern of life is practically the same at all the colonies, each functions as a completely independent economic unit. Furthermore, the tastes of the different groups of people differ, and consequently it is possible to detect variations from colony to colony. Some are kept very neat with all their buildings well-painted and in excellent repair, while others may tend to neglect this. Some have neat shrubbery, lawns, and flowerbeds; at other colonies these may be almost totally absent. As would be expected, the older colonies differ considerably from the very recent ones. Most of the older colonies, some dating back over 50 years, have an air of permanence and character to them. In contrast, some of the recent colonies with the lack of trees and shrubbery have an uncomfortable resemblance to a newly established urban district.

The Need for Colony Expansion

The need for Hutterites to establish new colonies continually is basically because of population increase. Although a typical colony can support a population somewhat in excess of 150, in most instances serious consideration is given to the establishment of a new colony once the population exceeds 125. In addition to the basic economic problem of dealing with an increasing population on a non-expanding resource base, the larger population in itself begins to pose administrative and social problems. A larger population tends to weaken the familial atmosphere of a colony; sub-groups or cliques may develop, supervisory duties increase, and various other problems come to the fore. A very practical problem is of course the gradual development of a surplus of labour, especially in recent years with the advent of more and more labour saving devices. Hence there comes a time for every Hutterite community when it will face the process of establishing a new colony.

Once a colony is established the Hutterites are always on the alert for the possiblity of purchasing land for a new colony. Usually it takes years before a suitable area of land can be located and purchased. However, if an exceptionally good land deal presents itself, the Hutterites may decide to go through with the purchase and to establish a new colony several years before this would normally be done. On the other hand, if new land cannot be readily purchased, or if population pressure is not great, a colony may not subdivide for a much longer period of time than is usual. By way of illustration, a number of colonies have subdivided within 10 years of formation, but in one instance a period of 27 years elapsed before subdivision took place.[2] It should be pointed out, however, that some colonies prefer to wait for a longer period of time as a matter of principle. Such colonies feel that they should build up their financial reserves as much as possible before they subdivide, and this may take as long as 15 to 20 years.

An examination of the dates of subdivision of the 42 colonies that have been established in Manitoba since the formation of the original 6 in 1918 shows that the median year for subdivision is 14.[3] With the exception of several colonies that were formed almost immediately after 1918, the period for subdivision has been from 8 to 27 years. It is widely assumed that Hutterite colonies have been subdividing more and more frequently as the years have gone along. However, the record does not indicate any such trend (Appendix A and H). The overall median is 14 and the median for the last 10 years is also 14. Furthermore, for the six new colonies that are now being founded the median is almost certain to be about 14 years.

The Process of Colony Division[4]

Before a colony can proceed to buy land for purposes of eventual colony division, permission to do so must be granted by a majority vote of all Hutterite colonies in Manitoba. This is largely a precaution to prevent any colony from making a hasty decision on such a major course of action. In essence this makes certain that the need to subdivide is fully considered along with the full economic and financial implications. The other colonies have a legitimate interest in any colony's decision to subdivide because if the move should prove to be a financial disaster, the other colonies would need to render assistance.

During the 1950's an important change occurred in the process of colony division. Formerly, when sufficient land was purchased, the colony assets were divided and a decision was made as to who would move to the new colony. The move was made almost immediately and the group moving would be fully responsible for building up the new colony. During the 1950's this procedure was changed, and since then, colony division has followed a different pattern. When land is now purchased, the decision regarding the division of both colony assets and population is not made for a number of years. During these years the new colony is built up by the efforts of the entire labour force of the parent colony. The parent colony assumes the full financial responsibility for the land payments and the construction of all buildings and facilities on the new colony. Only when all the major facilities on the new colony are almost completed, is the decision on colony division made. Prior to this time, no one on the colony knows if he or she will be moving to the new colony or staying on the old. Under these conditions, most colony members work diligently to build up the new colony because there is a possibility that they may live there. If the new colony is some distance from the old, a small group may actually live there during the construction period.[5] However, the old colony continues to be used as the real base of operations. This newer procedure has eliminated the hardship that used to occur in the past when division took place immediately and the new group had to carry out the construction unaided.

The decision regarding who moves to the new colony and who stays on the old is made by lot on a family basis. However, groups of families are paired with one another beforehand to make certain that the two colonies retain an approximately equal sex and age distribution.

The economic and financial division is carefully worked out, and the final financial statement is prepared by a professional accountant. The total assets of the old and the new colony, including all buildings, equipment, machinery, livestock, etc., are considered so that there can be a completely equal financial division. This means that after the division, each colony must have equal assets. In this way, neither the old nor the new colony is financially or economically at a disadvantage. It also means that there is no decline in the standard of living on either colony.

Some colonies have agreed on a 40:60 division of all assets and population rather than the traditional 50:50 division. This has occurred twice at Milltown Colony—in 1942 when Sunnyside Colony was established and in 1966 when Glenway was established. In both cases there was a 40:60 division of population and assets, with the smaller proportion going to the new colonies.[6]

Because of the need for periodic colony division each colony goes through a cyclical economic and financial development. Although at the time of division both the parent and the offspring colony are on an equal financial basis, both colonies are often in debt because of the costs involved in purchasing the land, machinery, equipment, and the construction costs of establishing the new colony. It takes a number of years of successful operations for both of these colonies to once again build up their economic and financial resources. However, as soon as their resources are built up, it is almost time for colony division to take place again. Therefore, although most of the colony enterprises are profitable and successful operations, and even though the Hutterites live a thrifty and relatively austere life, because of periodic colony division, no colony is in any way really wealthy with large sums of cash on hand.

Factors Involved in Selecting Land for New Colonies[7]

The factors involved in selecting and purchasing land for a new colony include the following: 1) the ability to purchase a large and preferably contiguous block of land, 2) the fertility and productivity of the farmland, 3) the price of land, 4) proximity to the home colony, 5) formal restrictions imposed on Hutterites regarding the establishment of new colonies. All these factors, with the exception of the last one, have always been of significance in selecting land for a new colony. The last factor has only been of significance in Manitoba since 1957. Not all the factors are of equal importance, however, and the significance of each will vary from case to case.

It is always a major problem to purchase 3,000 to 5,000 acres, preferably in a contiguous block. There is difficulty in finding several farmers with adjoining lands who are prepared to sell—not only to sell, but to accept a reasonable price for their land. It is not uncommon for some farmers to ask an unreasonably high price for their property once they realize that the Hutterites are buying land in their neighborhood. For this reason alone it may take years to complete certain deals and sometimes the entire proposal is abandoned because of the unreasonableness of one or more farmers.

The quality of the farmland is naturally an important consideration. Since the Hutterites operate a mixed farm economy it is not essential for them to have all the land suitable for cultivation because some land can always be used for pasture. Soil fertility, good drainage, lack of stones, and a reasonable frost free season are factors of major importance. Often Hutterites try to purchase some land that has a river or a creek going through it so that there is a convenient water supply for ducks, geese, and livestock. If there is a stream on the property the Hutterites will almost always establish the colony settlement somewhere along the water course.

Under ordinary circumstances the price of land should reflect its quality. The Hutterites are always prepared to pay a fair and reasonable price, but as has already been mentioned, sometimes farmers try to exact a higher price than they could ordinarily hope to obtain. A strong point in their favour in bargaining however is that often Hutterites are able to pay all or a major part of land cost in cash. There are not many buyers who can do this, so the Hutterites are often able to get an exceptionally good deal because of this. Furthermore, the Hutterites have excellent credit rating at banks, so if need be they are in a good position to finance their major capital expenditures.

Proximity to the home colony is very desirable but it is only rarely that land can be purchased nearby. If land can be purchased reasonably close, say, within 20 miles or so, the parent colony may be able to carry on farming operations from the original home base without the necessity of purchasing a great deal of extra machinery or starting a building programme immediately. In such a case the building programme and the purchase of much of the new machinery can be delayed until the colony has had time to build up its financial reserves following its expenditure on land. While this would appear to be a most important consideration, yet, of the 42 colonies that were established since the founding of the original 6, only 13 have been within a distance of 20 miles. Furthermore, 5 of these 13 were established within the first few years of development. It is noteworthy that 20 of the new colonies were established over 50 miles from the home colonies, and of these, four were over 100 miles away. Although proximity is a significant factor it is not often that the Hutterites have been able to take advantage of it.

For reasons that will be considered in some detail later, various municipalities in Manitoba have attempted to impose restrictions on the expansion of Hutterite colonies and on land purchases. However, the Manitoba Hutterites have been far more fortunate than those in Alberta where restrictive government legislation has been enacted. Although the municipalities in Manitoba were unable to secure official government support, they did manage to get the Hutterites to sign a "gentleman's agreement" in 1957 which in effect established certain restrictions.[8] The Hutterites signed this agreement because they believed that if they opposed all restrictions the government would pass restrictive legislation against them. Under the agreement the Hutterites accepted three basic conditions: 1) that they would limit the landholdings of each new colony to 5,120 acres, 2) that they would limit the number of colonies per municipality to two, unless the municipality itself was willing to accept more colonies, and 3) the new colonies would be at least 10 miles from each other. The Hutterites believed that such restrictions were basically undemocratic and hoped that in time, the agreement would be annulled. However, for the following 14 years the Hutterites kept the agreement and the restrictions had considerable influence on the establishment of new colonies.

As the years passed, the Hutterites realized that for the colonies to remain economically viable they would eventually have to be larger. Furthermore, the restrictions occasionally forced them to pass up good land deals. Faced with the complete refusal of the Union of Municipalities to even discuss revision of the ''gentleman's agreement,'' the Hutterites in 1971 decided to ignore the agreement and put in a bid to purchase the land and buildings of the former McDonald airbase. The Manitoba government ignored objections of the Union of Municipalities and sold the property to the New Rosedale Colony in that same year. The Hutterites are convinced that the municipal restrictions against them are undemocratic and they now feel confident that the Manitoba government will not enact legislation against them. Consequently, it appears that the 1957 ''gentleman's agreement'' is now a dead letter, and that from now on the Hutterites intend to exercise the same rights as other citizens. This undoubtedly means that in the future they will consider themselves free to purchase land wherever they wish.

The Establishment of the Original Colonies in Manitoba[9]

From the time of their arrival in the United States in 1874 until the First World War, the Hutterites found life satisfactory on their colonies in North and South Dakota. However, during these war years, their refusal to participate in any type of military service resulted in such animosity, intolerance, and persecution that continued life in the United States became intolerable. Following a friendly reception during discussions with Canadian immigration officials, the Hutterites sold their property, and with the exception of a single colony, emigrated en masse to Canada in 1918. Initially, they all settled in two provinces— Manitoba and Alberta.

Those who wanted to settle in Manitoba had the immediate task of purchasing large blocks of suitable farm land. After examining various areas they decided to purchase several blocks of land owned by Senator Aimé Benard in the Elie district, in the rural municipality of Cartier. They purchased approximately 9,000 acres in this district, and by the end of 1918 had set up six colonies, all within ten miles of one another (Map 5). These were the colonies of Bon Homme, Huron, James Valley, Maxwell, Milltown, and Rosedale (Map 6).

In the years that followed, in addition to founding new colonies in Manitoba and Alberta, some were founded in Saskatchewan and some were re-established in the United States.

Historical Development of Colonies in Manitoba

The decision to purchase land in the Elie district and to found the original colonies in this area set the basic pattern for Hutterite settlement in Manitoba. In the years that followed additional colonies were set up in the immediate region. However, as has already been pointed out, proximity is not the only factor of significance, consequently Hutterite settlement has now spread to almost all parts of the province. Nevertheless, the original settlements provided the core of Hutterite settlement in Manitoba.

Almost immediately after the six original colonies were established there was pressure to found other colonies. Some of the first colonies were overcrowded from the time of their formation because the Hutterites had not been able initially to purchase sufficient farmland. They had been short of funds because in their haste to move from the United States, they had sold their properties at depressed prices, and meantime, the price of land in Canada was relatively high. Nevertheless, two colonies were able to purchase nearby land within the first two years. Iberville was established in 1919 only three miles from its parent colony, Rosedale. In 1920 Barickman was established only two miles from its founding colony, Maxwell. However, as additional land nearby was too expensive, in 1922 Milltown established a daughter colony, Blumengart, 70 miles away in the southern part of the province. In 1929 Huron Colony branched out and formed a colony west of Carman at Roseisle. A series of crop failures eventually forced the Hutterites to abandon this colony and in 1937 a former colony site was repurchased in South Dakota. Hence, Huron's first daughter colony moved back to the United States. Map 7 shows the distribution of colonies at the end of the first twelve years in Manitoba.

Six new colonies were established during the 1930's. Map 8 shows the distribution of the colonies at the end of this decade. Unfortunately, Maxwell's 1932 offspring met the same fate of Huron's first new

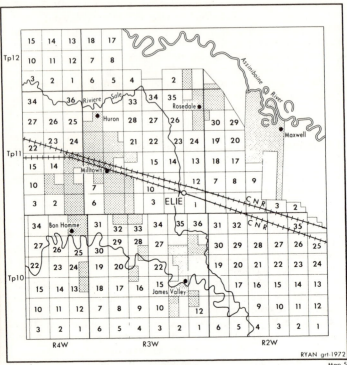

RYAN grt-1972

Map 5

MANITOBA

**ORIGINAL HUTTERITE LAND TRACTS
PURCHASED IN 1918**

Hutterite Land Tract

●   Site of Colony Settlement

0 1 2 3 4 5 6

Miles

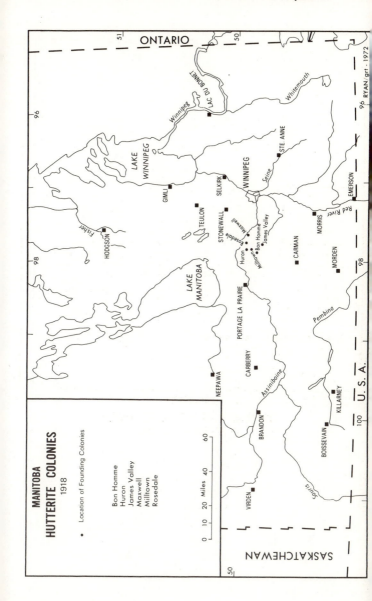

MANITOBA
HUTTERITE COLONIES
1918

• Location of Founding Colonies

Bon Homme
Huron
James Valley
Maxwell
Milltown
Rosedale

0   10   20   40   60
        Miles

RYAN /grt - 1972

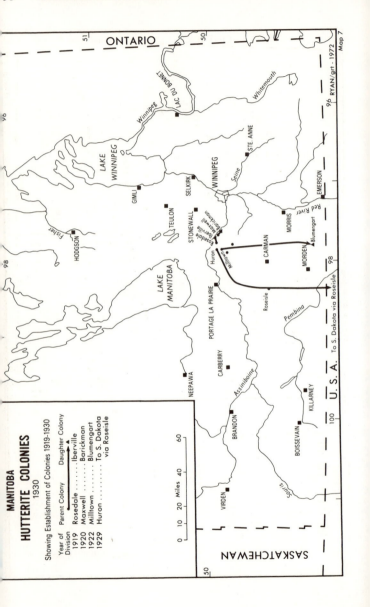

MANITOBA

HUTTERITE COLONIES

1930

Showing Establishment of Colonies 1919-1930

Year of Division	Parent Colony	Daughter Colony
1919	Rosedale	Iberville
1920	Maxwell	Barickman
1922	Milltown	Blumengart
1929	Huron	To S. Dakota via Roseisle

0   10   20   40   60

Miles

Map 7

RYAN/grt - 1972

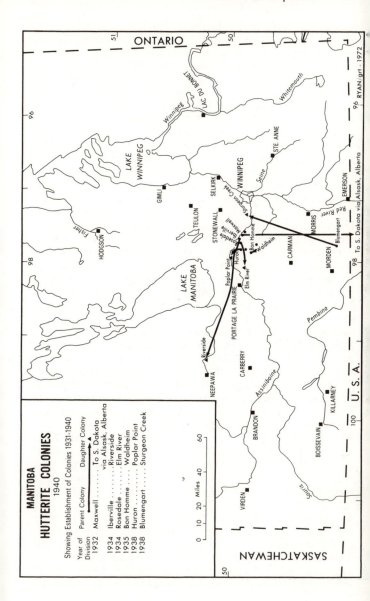

MANITOBA
HUTTERITE COLONIES
1940

Showing Establishment of Colonies 1931-1940

Year of
Division   Parent Colony   Daughter Colony
1932   Maxwell ....   To S. Dakota
                            via Alsask, Alberta
1934   Iberville ....   Riverside
1934   Rosedale ....   Elm River
1935   Bon Homme ....   Waldheim
1938   Huron ....   Poplar Point
1938   Blumengart ....   Sturgeon Creek

0   10   20   30   40   60
                    Miles

96 RYAN. grt - 1972

colony. Maxwell's 1932 colony had been established at Alsask in Alberta, but crop failures led to its closing and in 1949 it too reestablished itself in South Dakota. In spite of such difficulties, because of their basically self-sufficient economy, the Hutterites managed to survive the depression years far better than typical farmers. This placed them in a relatively good position to purchase land during this period, and three colonies bought large blocks of nearby farmland. In 1935 Bon Homme established the colony of Waldheim only one mile away. In 1938 Poplar Point was established 8 miles from its founding colony, Huron. Rosedale in 1934 established its second daughter colony, Elm River, within a reasonable distance of 18 miles. The two remaining colonies that were established during this period were at a considerable distance, both because of favourable land purchases. In 1934 Iberville established the colony of Riverside on good farmland near Arden, but this was 80 miles away. In 1938 Blumengart set up the colony of Sturgeon Creek near Winnipeg and near the original core of Hutterite settlement, but this was 65 miles away from the founding colony.

The 1940's proved to be an interesting period for Hutterite expansion—six new colonies were established in Manitoba and four were founded in the United States (Map 9). The main reason for movement to the United States was the availability of large blocks of land at relatively low prices. Barickman set up a colony in South Dakota in 1942, and Huron, Bon Homme, and Milltown also set up new colonies there in 1949. Proximity was a factor in three of the colonies founded in Manitoba. In 1947 Maxwell established Lakeside at a distance of only three miles, Milltown founded Sunnyside 15 miles away in 1942, and Iberville set up the colony of Rock Lake about 20 miles away in 1947. This period marks the beginning of fairly steady Hutterite expansion to other regions mainly because land became more and more difficult to acquire in the core area. The move to the southwest of Portage la Prairie was begun in 1944 by Rosedale when it founded the colony of New Rosedale at a distance of some 40 miles. James Valley purchased land 80 miles away and set up the colony of Riverdale in 1945 northwest of Portage la Prairie. The first move east of Winnipeg was made by Poplar Point when it founded the colony of Springfield in 1950. This colony is about 30 miles east of Winnipeg and over 70 miles from its founding colony.

At the end of 1950 there were 20 colonies in Manitoba, but within the next decade this increased to 32 (Map 10). During this period only one colony was established in the old core area—in 1959 Bon Homme founded Grand Colony only 3 miles away. In that same year, Fairholme was established 6 miles from its parent colony, New Rosedale. However, with the exception of these two cases, all the colonies during this

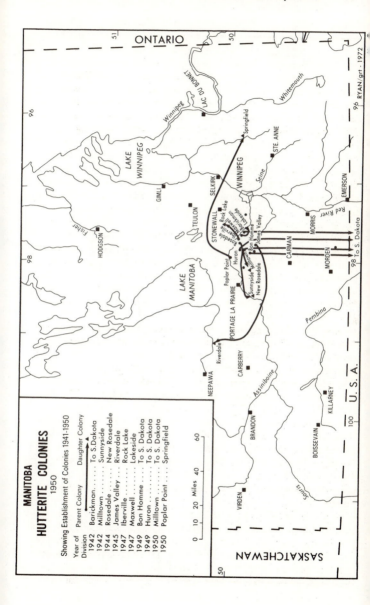

MANITOBA
HUTTERITE COLONIES
1950

Showing Establishment of Colonies 1941-1950

Year of Division	Parent Colony	Daughter Colony
1942	Barickman	To S. Dakota
1942	Milltown	Sunnyside
1944	Rosedale	New Rosedale
1945	James Valley	Riverdale
1947	Iberville	Rock Lake
1947	Maxwell	Lakeside
1949	Bon Homme	To S. Dakota
1949	Huron	To S. Dakota
1950	Milltown	To S. Dakota
1950	Poplar Point	Springfield

0 10 20 Miles 40 60

RYAN/grt - 1972

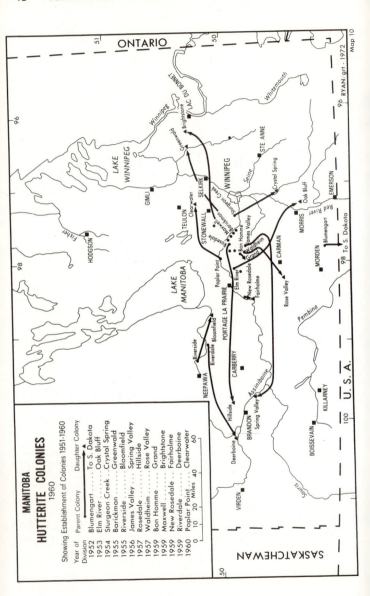

MANITOBA
HUTTERITE COLONIES
1960

Showing Establishment of Colonies 1951-1960

Year of Division	Parent Colony	Daughter Colony
1952	Blumengart	To S. Dakota
1953	Elm River	Oak Bluff
1954	Sturgeon Creek	Crystal Spring
1955	Barickman	Greenwald
1955	Riverside	Bloomfield
1956	James Valley	Spring Valley
1957	Rosedale	Hillside
1957	Waldheim	Rose Valley
1959	Bon Homme	Grand
1959	Maxwell	Brightstone
1959	New Rosedale	Fairholme
1959	Riverdale	Deerboine
1960	Poplar Point	Clearwater

0 10 20 Miles 40 60

RYAN grt - 1972   Map 10

period were established at a considerable distance from their parent colonies. As it becomes more difficult to acquire a large block of productive land at a reasonable price, proximity is a factor that has to be sacrificed.

Unable to purchase land in Manitoba, Blumengart founded a colony in South Dakota in 1952. This was the seventh and last group of Hutterites to move back to the United States until the present time.

The Hutterites entered the area directly south of Winnipeg with the introduction of Oak Bluff Colony in 1953. Its founding colony was Elm River some 75 miles away. A year later Crystal Spring became the second colony in this area—it was 45 miles away from its founding colony, Sturgeon Creek. In 1955 Bloomfield became the third colony in the area northwest of Portage la Prairie. It was founded by a colony in the same area, Riverside, some 28 miles to the west. Rose Valley became the second colony in the area southwest of Winnipeg. It was founded in 1957 by Waldheim which was 45 miles to the north. Barickman established the colony of Greenwald in 1955 in the marginal lands northeast of Winnipeg. Four years later Brightstone was set up still further to the east by Maxwell. The Brandon area acquired Spring Valley in 1956, Hillside in 1957, and Deerboine in 1959. The founding colonies were about 100 miles away—James Valley, Rosedale, and Riverdale, respectively. The last colony to be established during this period was Clearwater in 1960 in the productive southern part of the Interlake area. Its founding colony was Poplar Point about 45 miles away.

A total of 16 new colonies were established in the 1960's. The expansion took place in districts that already had Hutterite settlements. No single factor was outstanding in colony development during this decade but because of the number of new colonies involved, this period can be divided into two parts. Map 11 shows the distribution of colonies up to 1965.

Interlake Colony was founded in 1961 by Rock Lake and it became the second colony in this area. In 1962 Whiteshell Colony was founded on the edge of the Shield by Iberville. Also in 1962 Pembina was established by Blumengart and Homewood by Lakeside. Homewood is located 15 miles from its founding colony and this is the only instance in this period when a colony was established reasonably close to the parent colony. Three colonies were established in 1964—Rainbow, Springhill, and Parkview. The founding colonies were Elm River, Huron, and Sunnyside, respectively.

Map 12 shows the distribution of colonies at the end of 1970. In 1966 Miami was established by James Valley in the area southwest of Winnipeg, and Glenway was founded by Milltown in the southern part

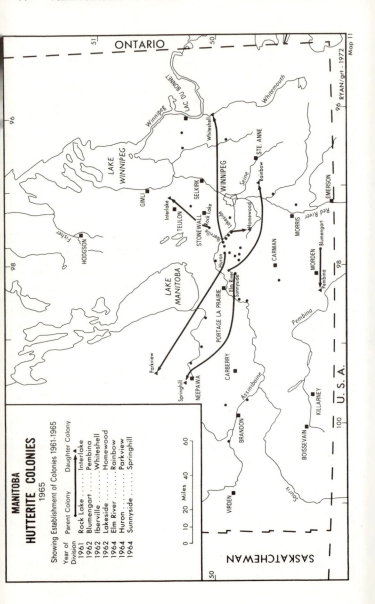

MANITOBA
HUTTERITE COLONIES
1965

Showing Establishment of Colonies 1961-1965

Year of Division	Parent Colony	Daughter Colony
1961	Rock Lake	Interlake
1962	Blumengart	Pembina
1962	Iberville	Whiteshell
1962	Lakeside	Homewood
1964	Elm River	Rainbow
1964	Huron	Parkview
1964	Sunnyside	Springhill

RYAN/grt - 1972   Map 11

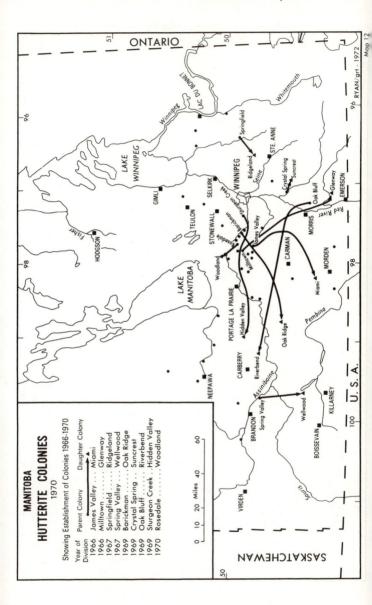

MANITOBA
HUTTERITE COLONIES
1970

Showing Establishment of Colonies 1966-1970

Year of Division	Parent Colony	Daughter Colony
1966	James Valley	Miami
1966	Milltown	Glenway
1967	Springfield	Ridgeland
1967	Spring Valley	Wellwood
1969	Barickman	Oak Ridge
1969	Crystal Spring	Suncrest
1969	Oak Bluff	Riverbend
1969	Sturgeon Creek	Hidden Valley
1970	Rosedale	Woodland

0   10   20   Miles   40   60

RYAN/grt · 1972   Map 12

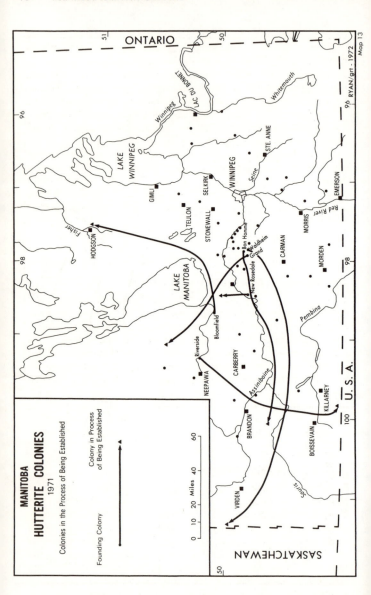

RYAN/grt · 1972

Map 13

MANITOBA
HUTTERITE COLONIES
1971

Colonies in the Process of Being Established

Founding Colony

Colony in Process
of Being Established

Miles

0   10   20   40   60

of the province. Ridgeland and Wellwood were established in 1967—the first by Springfield and the second by Spring Valley. In 1969 the following colonies were established (the founding colonies are in parentheses): Oak Ridge (Barickman), Hidden Valley (Sturgeon Creek), Riverbend (Oak Bluff), Suncrest (Crystal Spring). The distances between the new colonies and the founding colonies varied from 8 miles in the case of Suncrest to 120 miles in the case of Riverbend. Finally in 1970 Rosedale established the most recent colony, Woodland, in an area just to the north of the old core region.

Map 13 shows that six colonies were in the process of formation in 1971. With one exception the new colonies are at a considerable distance from the founding colonies. Furthermore, three are being established in new areas. Although New Rosedale plans to subdivide and to establish the new Airport Colony in 1972, the others will be established later.

The names of all the colonies and their dates of formation are listed in Appendix A.

The Hutterite Settlement Pattern

At the end of 1971 there were 48 Hutterite colonies in Manitoba; their pattern of distribution is shown on Map 14. Although their growth and evolution was discussed on a decade by decade basis in the preceding section, their present-day pattern of distribution should also be examined. On the basis of location and physical environment, the Hutterite colonies can be grouped into eight fairly distinct regions (Map 15).[10] An analysis of the colonies shows that each regional group has several common characteristics. Although most of these are due to the physical environment, which is discussed in a separate chapter, others and the distinctive features of each region should be presented here.

Area I—Assiniboine Region

The Assiniboine region contains the original 6 founding colonies plus another 12 established subsequently. This region includes more than one-third of all the colonies in the province, and it forms in many ways the core of Manitoba Hutterite settlement. The evolution of the colonies in the area has already been discussed, but it should be emphasized that all of them, except three, were founded over 25 years ago. Hence these colonies have an air of permanence, stability, and tradition. As most of them are close to one another there is an especially intimate relationship between them and ideas pass very readily from

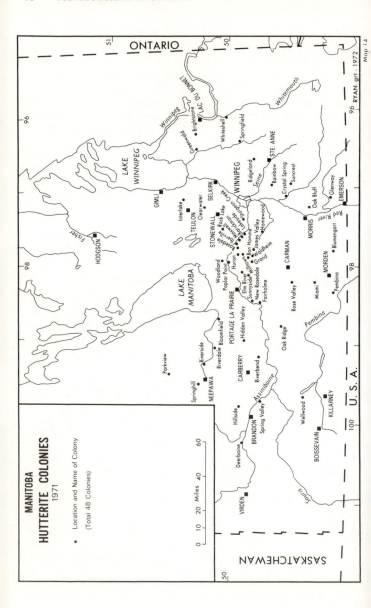

MANITOBA
HUTTERITE COLONIES
1971

• Location and Name of Colony

(Total 48 Colonies)

0   10   20   40   60
Miles

Map 14

RYAN grt - 1972

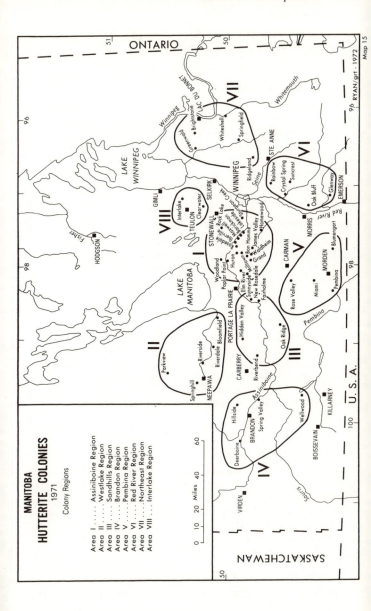

MANITOBA
HUTTERITE COLONIES
1971
Colony Regions

Area I .... Assiniboine Region
Area II .... Westlake Region
Area III .... Sandhills Region
Area IV .... Brandon Region
Area V .... Pembina Region
Area VI .... Red River Region
Area VII .... Northeast Region
Area VIII .... Interlake Region

Map 15

9/6 RYAN/grt - 1972

one colony to another. Therefore, it is not surprising that the agricultural enterprises of all the colonies are very similar.

Area II—Westlake Region

Four of the 5 colonies in this region are along the Whitemud River or its tributaties; the remaining one is to the northwest near Riding Mountain National Park. Hutterites first moved into this area in the 1930's, but the last 2 colonies are recent arrivals. Although these colonies are not located near one another, they differ from the colonies in the Assiniboine core area by being more highly specialized in the chicken enterprise, while none have a turkey enterprise.

Area III—Sandhills Region

This is a region where large-scale Hutterite settlement is relatively new, although the first colony, New Rosedale, was established near Portage la Prairie in the 1940's. The main unifying feature is the location of the colonies in predominantly sandy, rolling terrain.

Area IV—Brandon Region

Three of the 4 colonies in this region were established in the 1950's, and, before the Sandhills region was settled by Hutterites, they were more or less isolated from the other Manitoba colonies. Although quite widely dispersed, they maintain close contact with each other mainly because of their distance from other colonies. Their agricultural enterprises follow the basic Hutterite pattern, with perhaps a particularly strong emphasis on hogs.

Area V—Pembina Region

The Hutterites made their presence felt in this part of Manitoba almost 50 years ago with the establishment of Blumengart Colony near Winkler. Three other colonies are more recent. Largely because of its older status, Blumengart has a full range of enterprises very similar to most of the colonies in the Assiniboine core area, but the newer colonies are noticeably less diversified.

Area VI—Red River Region

This is a relatively new area of settlement for the Hutterites, the oldest 2 colonies having been established in the 1950's. Although most of the colonies have the usual range of Hutterite enterprises, there seems to be less conformity to traditional practices and more inclination to experiment, especially at Crystal Spring Colony.

Area VII—Northeast Region

Here on the edge of the Canadian Shield, is one of the poorest agricultural areas in Manitoba. Nevertheless, the Hutterites have managed to establish their colonies on relatively good soils, although great effort was needed to drain the land and clear it for farming. Because good land is scarce these colonies have only about two-thirds of the average acreage of Manitoba Hutterites. Therefore, the activities of all the colonies in this region are smaller than usual. Just as the Brandon region was noted as being relatively isolated to the west, this area is as remote in the east.

Area VIII—Interlake Region

There are at present only 2 colonies in this region, but a third is in the process of being established in the northern area near Hodgson. This region is not generally noted for agricultural productivity, but the Hutterite colonies are located on relatively good soils and are average colonies in every respect.

An overview of the Hutterite settlement pattern shows that most of the early colonies were relatively central in the Manitoba farming belt, but with the passage of time a greater number of colonies were established in peripheral areas. At first some of these new colonies, for instance, the ones near Brandon or the Lac du Bonnet area, were remote in terms of their association with other Hutterite colonies. However, of those that are now in the process of formation, some are not only far from other colonies, they are in truly remote areas and far from Winnipeg, for instance, north near the Fisher River, southwest near the United States border, west near the Saskatchewan border (Map 13). For these colonies, a trip to Winnipeg with a load of hogs will be a far different matter than it is for a colony near Portage la Prairie. In other words, marketing will be more expensive in terms of both time and transportation costs. Perhaps even more significant is the fact that although the Hutterites have tried to select the best land in these remote districts, the quality of the farmland does not compare with the land in the central farming belt. Hence it seems that some of the new colonies may find it more difficult to operate as efficiently as the older colonies.

Notes and References

1. This section is based primarily on information compiled by the writer from field work which included numerous visits to all 48 colonies in Manitoba from the fall of 1967 to the beginning of 1972. Reference was also made to the works of Bennett, Hostetler, and Peters.
2. James Valley Colony was established in 1918, but its first subdivision took place in 1945—after a period of 27 years. When established, the colony had a small population and few young people, hence its population increased slowly.
3. Data on dates of subdivision were compiled from enquiries by the writer. All Manitoba colony division dates are listed in Appendix A and H.
4. The basic information on colony division was obtained from discussions with Reverend Jacob Kleinsasser of Crystal Spring Colony and Mr. Dave Norris of Brandon, Manitoba, the accountant employed by the Hutterite colonies.
5. An example of this at the time of writing is Bloomfield Colony near Gladstone, Manitoba, which is in the process of establishing a colony near Hodgson, Manitoba—a distance of about 180 miles away. Commuting is out of the question and therefore a group of about 35 people have been living on the new colony for the past year or so.
6. This information was obtained from Reverend Mike Waldner of Milltown Colony in an interview on April 22, 1972.
7. This section is based on material that the writer compiled from discussions over the years with numerous Hutterite ministers and colony managers.
8. The ''gentleman's agreement'' was signed on April 12, 1957, and a number of colonies have copies of the document. Reverend Jacob Kleinsasser provided the writer with a copy.
9. The material on the growth and spread of Hutterite colonies in Manitoba was compiled from field work by the writer.
10. For the purposes of this study, the Hutterite regions have been assigned names on the basis of location or customary local usage.

CHAPTER 3

PHYSICAL ENVIRONMENT OF HUTTERITE FARMLAND

In discussing the physical environment of Hutterite farmland the main factors that will be considered are landforms, surface deposits, drainage, soils, and climatic elements.[1] As indicated on Map 15, it is possible to group the Hutterite colonies into eight district regions. Consequently a regional analysis seems to be the most appropriate procedure.

Although the regions in which the Hutterite colonies are located are spread across most of the southern part of the province, the variation in the physical environment between them is not great. Since the agricultural productivity of the land is of prime concern in this study, the various aspects of physical geography will be considered from this viewpoint. It should also be noted that the precise location of Hutterite farmland in any particular region is very important. The physical characteristics of a favorable location may vary considerably from those of the region in general. This is significant because the Hutterites always try to select the most productive land that they can afford. Hence they are very likely to have above average farmland in most regions. So in addition to the general characteristics of the region, the specific location of Hutterite farmland is of significance.

The eight different regions and the colonies involved are located on Map 15.

Area I—Assiniboine Region

This area between Winnipeg and Portage la Prairie is an almost level lacustrine plain. Its fine sediments, mainly clay and silt, were deposited over glacial drift when southern Manitoba was covered by glacial Lake Agassiz. The only exception to this type of landform is the land immediately bordering the meandering Assiniboine River. Several Hutterite colonies are situated along the river, so some of their river land is waste or is used for pasture. The extreme flatness and the fine texture of the clay and silt of the region have given some farmlands drainage problems, especially during spring run-off. Many drainage projects now largely alleviate the problem, but some of the area is still subject to occasional flooding from the Assiniboine River.

All the colonies in the region, except Poplar Point and Woodland, are underlain by black fine-textured soils. The lush cover of grasses that made up the natural vegetation helped to produce an A horizon well supplied with organic matter. This horizon has a depth of 6 to 12 inches and has a granular structure. These are very fertile soils and form some of the best agricultural land in Manitoba. The colonies of Poplar Point and Woodland have black medium-textured soils. These soils are better drained than the fine-textured soils and the A horizon is deeper. Here these soils are even more productive than the fine-textured soils.

The Canada Land Inventory maps show that half of the colonies in this region are located on Class 1 soils and half on Class 2 soils. This means that the former have no crop limitations while the latter have only minor limitations. In any event, the colonies are located on the best soils in the region.

The average annual precipitation for this area is 20 inches, with the months of May, June, and July getting over 7 inches. The growing season varies from 111 frost-free days near Winnipeg to a high of 127 frost-free days at Portage la Prairie. These climatic conditions are probably the most favorable for agricultural production of any in Manitoba.

This region, containing more than one-third of the Manitoba colonies, has a physical environment well suited to agricultural production, and is in fact one of the best agricultural regions in the province.

Area II—Westlake Region

The Westlake area of Manitoba has a gently undulating till plain with local relief under 25 feet. Glacial Lake Agassiz covered this region for only a short period so much of the area does not have appreciable deposits of lacustrine clay. However, four out of the five colonies in this region are in fact located on clay deposits. The one exception, Riverdale, is on sandy loam glacio-fluvial deposits.

Although the whole region is within the black soil zone, the Canada Land Inventory has placed most of it in Classes 3 and 4, thus indicating certain crop limitations. This is justified in the case of Bloomfield Colony where the soil of part of the farmland has an alkali content which limits productivity. Riverdale Colony, being on sandy loam deposits, has black coarse-textured soils which are subject to wind erosion. Such soils are better for stock raising than grain production, and the colony has encountered problems because of this. Riverside, Springhill, and Parkview are located on black medium-textured soils which can be highly productive with good management. The colonies are on sites with better than average soils for the area and so have managed to maintain high crop yields.

The average annual precipitation in the areas of Bloomfield, Riverdale, and Riverside colonies is about 20 inches or slightly more. Springhill and Parkview are somewhat drier with between 18 and 19 inches. Bloomfield and Riverdale have a frost-free season of about 110 days, while Riverside, Springhill and Parkview have a shorter season of about 100.

Area III—Sandhills Region

This is an area of sand plains which were formed as the main glacial streams began to abate and coarse to medium textured sediments were laid down in the glacial valley of the Assiniboine and on the adjacent flood plains. Subsequently winds created dunes over an extensive area resulting in the present sand-hill topography. The colonies in this region are located primarily in areas of sandy loam deposits. All of them, with the exception of Oak Ridge, have black coarse-textured soils. Although the A horizon is fairly deep (6 to 15 inches), its structure is poor and the soil tends to erode easily. This problem is particularly serious at Hidden Valley because much of this colony's land is very hilly. Fortunately, the mixed farming economy practiced by the Hutterites is well suited to these soil conditions. Oak Ridge Colony is in the transitional zone between black and grey wooded soils. The fertility of these grey-black soils is relatively high, but a few hundred acres of the colony are hilly and heavily forested and so may not be used for agricultural production.

The Canada Land Inventory has placed the soils suitable for agriculture in most of this area mainly in Classes 3 and 4. However, with the exception of Riverbend, the colonies are located on better than average soils. Much of Riverbend's farmland is very sandy with a low moisture-holding capacity.

The area around Riverbend Colony has an annual precipitation of about 20 inches while the other colonies have slightly more than 20 inches. All have a growing season of about 110 frost-free days.

Area IV—Brandon Region

The colonies in the Brandon area are located in a region of undulating to rolling till plains. The local relief varies from 25 to 50 feet. Wellwood Colony, near Pelican Lake, is on a morainic upland, where the local relief is slightly greater. At Spring Valley and Deerboine the ground moraine was covered by gravel-type, coarse-textured glacio-fluvial deposits. In the Wellwood and Hillside areas the surface deposits are medium-textured and nearly stone-free glacial drift.

The Canada Land Inventory maps show Hillside Colony as located on Class 2 soils. These are the best in the region. Wellwood Colony is on relatively productive Class 3 soils. Deerboine Colony is in a hilly area along the Assiniboine River and its farmland varies. Some soils are in Class 2, but a considerable part of the colony has soils in Classes 4, 5, and 6. Consequently, about one-fifth of this colony remains in wooded pasture. Spring Valley's farmland is very sandy, and although part of the colony has Class 2 soils, most of the farmland is in Classes 3, 4, and 5.

The area surrounding Hillside Colony has an average annual precipitation of 20 inches while the other colonies have between 18 to 19 inches. All have a growing season of approximately 100 frost-free days.

Area V—Pembina Region

Blumengart, Rose Valley, and Miami are on the former Lake Agassiz lacustrine plain. The Blumengart area is extremely level and has a surface deposit of clay, while those of the other two colonies are gently undulating with sandy loam deposits. Pembina Colony is on a morainic upland which is overlain by medium-textured glacial drift.

Practically all of Blumengart's farmland is on the productive black medium-textured Class 1 soil. Miami and Pembina are on almost equally productive Class 2 soils. Part of Rose Valley's land is on Class 2 soils, but most of it is on Class 3. However, this is still productive land.

All the colonies receive slightly more than 20 inches of precipitation annually. Blumengart has about 120 frost-free days and the other colonies about 115.

Area VI—Red River Region

The colonies in this area are located on an extremely level lacustrine plain which is composed of clay and silt with black fine-textured soils. The physical geography of this area, including climatic elements, is almost identical with that in the Assiniboine Region. However, there are no Class 1 soils, most of the area being in Classes 2 and 3. Practically all of the Hutterite land is on Class 2 soils, so the colonies have better than average conditions.

Area VII—Northeast Region

The colonies in this area, with the exception of Whiteshell, are located on the gently undulating eastern margin of the Lake Agassiz lacustrine plain. Whiteshell Colony is on the edge of the Shield, and lies along the Whitemouth River in an area of undulating till plain. The colonies of Greenwald and Brightstone are in an area of poorly drained clay and silt deposits. Ridgeland, Springfield, and Whiteshell are in an area of high lime glacial drift.

Greenwald and Brightstone colonies have grey-black soils which were produced under a natural vegetation of grasses and mixed forest. Although the fertility of these soils is considered high, the region at one time suffered from serious drainage problems and peat covered many areas. To make the land suitable for farming the peat had to be stripped off and burned and drainage ditches dug. Brightstone Colony has been exceptionally well located because most of its soils are in a Class 2 category. Greenwald, however, has mostly Class 3 soils and some in Class 6. The latter soils are very sandy and are more suited for forage crops than grain production. Whiteshell Colony has mainly Class 3 soils. Springfield and Ridgeland colonies have a mixture of soils mainly in Classes 2 and 3, but there are drainage problems, especially at Springfield.

This area receives an average annual precipitation of about 21 inches, and has a growing season of about 110 frost-free days.

In general this is a region of marginal mixed farming and only selected areas are relatively productive. The Hutterites secured some of the best land in this district, but nevertheless, the colonies have encountered farming problems.

Area VIII—Interlake Region

The two colonies in this southern part of the Interlake area are located on the gently undulating Lake Agassiz lacustrine plain. The surface deposits are of clay and silt and there are transitional grey-black soils. Both colonies are located on some of the best land in this region. Most of the soils are in Classes 2 and 3 and are very productive. This region receives about 20 inches of precipitation and it has a growing season of about 110 frost-free days.

In summary, it should be said that in all eight regions, the Hutterite colonies have been located on better than average farmland. Although purchase of this land has been more expensive, it is in keeping with a basic Hutterite policy of attempting to establish colonies on superior farmland. As a long-term policy this is unquestionably sound economically.

Notes and References

1. It has not been the intention to provide a detailed account of the physiographic environment of the Hutterite farmland. One of the main objectives has been to provide a general statement which would indicate the relative quality of land that the Hutterites selected in each region. The main sources of reference have been the text and the maps in the *Economic Atlas of Manitoba* (1960), and the *Soil Capability Classification for Agriculture* maps prepared by the *Canada Land Inventory* (1969). In addition, the writer relied on information acquired from the Hutterites during his field work.

CHAPTER 4

POPULATION CHARACTERISTICS AND LABOUR FORCE

Colony Population and Family Structure

At the end of 1970 the total population of the 48 colonies in Manitoba was 4,666 people.[1] The colony with the smallest population was Interlake which had 48 people, while Bon Homme was the largest with a population of 161. Interlake is to some extent an exception because several years ago a number of families left the colony as a result of an internal disagreement. Glenway was the next smallest colony with a population of 55, but Glenway is exceptional as well because when the colony was established in 1966 only 40 percent of the founding colony's population settled at the new colony. [2] In 1970 the median colony population was 95 and the mean was 97 which were represented by Rainbow and Barickman, respectively. The population of all the colonies for 1968 and 1970 is listed in Appendices B and C.*

Family data are unavailable for 1970, but in 1968 the 48 colonies had a total of 635 families.[3] In that year the median number of families per colony was 14 and the mean was 14.8. This varied from Interlake Colony with 4 families to Sturgeon Creek with 24. Considering the possible bias of Interlake, the colony with the next smallest number of families was Spring Valley with a total of 8.

In 1968 the average number of family persons per household was 6.9. This of course is based on an average which ranges from newly wed couples to mature families where no further children are expected and where none have yet left to form households of their own, and it includes retired couples, and widows or widowers who maintain separate households. In contrast, in 1966 the average number of family persons per household in Manitoba was 3.2 and it was 3.8 for the farm population.[4]

Data are not available for the average number of children per Manitoba Hutterite family, but according to a study of all Hutterites in Canada

* For 1975, see Appendix I.

and the United States the median number of children per married Hutterite woman in 1950 was 10.4.[5] There does not appear to have been any appreciable change in the Hutterite mode of life in the past 20 years and since the colonies outside of Manitoba are basically the same, this figure is still probably valid today.

Marriage is not permitted until both partners are baptized, and this occurs only after the age of 19. Hutterites usually marry between the ages of 20 and 25. Few persons remain unmarried, and unmarried life is considered almost abnormal. Marriage is a very stable institution and there are no cases of Hutterite divorce in Manitoba.

Age and Sex Structure of Hutterite Population[6]

There is an amazing uniformity in the age and sex structure of Hutterites on all colonies. There is a fairly even distribution of both males and females in all age groups on any colony, whether the colony is one of the oldest in the province or one of the newest. The explanation for this is based on the method by which colonies divide. Colonies split vertically through the generations, and therefore a new colony will possess a population pyramid practically identical to that of its parent. The division of a colony is very carefully planned and takes into consideration the size of families, the number of males and females, and an approximately equal number of young and old couples. This means that the new colony is in effect an extension of the old, and it helps to account for the social and economic stability evident in all the colonies. As would be expected under these conditions, the relationship between the new colony and the parent colony remains exceptionally close for a decade or so, and often until the new colony subdivides itself.

Specific examples of the population structure of Hutterite colonies at different stages of development are shown in Tables 4-1, 4-2, 4-3, 4-4, and 4-5 and Diagram 4-1. Crystal Spring Colony is shown at the time of its formation in 1954 (Table 4-1), at the time just before subdivision in 1969 (Table 4-2), and immediately after subdivision in 1969 (Table 4-3). Suncrest Colony, which was formed as a result of the subdivision of Crystal Spring, is shown at the time of its formation in 1969 (Table 4-4). In addition, James Valley is shown as an example of a colony that has subdivided several times (Table 4-5). Diagram 4-1 shows the population pyramids for each of these colonies and, for comparison purposes, shows the population structure of Manitoba and Canada.

The first thing that should be noted is the basic similarity of the population structure on Hutterite colonies, regardless of their stage of

TABLE 4-1

CRYSTAL SPRING HUTTERITE COLONY
STE. AGATHE, MANITOBA

DISTRIBUTION OF POPULATION BY AGE GROUPS AND SEX, 1954

(At the time of its formation as a result of
the subdivision of Sturgeon Creek Colony)

Age Group	Male Population		Female Population		Total Population	
	No.	%	No.	%	No.	%
0 - 4	6	8.8%	13	19.1%	19	27.9%
5 - 9	5	7.3%	3	4.4%	8	11.7%
10 - 14	4	5.9%	0	-	4	5.9%
15 - 19	3	4.4%	5	7.3%	8	11.7%
20 - 24	3	4.4%	3	4.4%	6	8.8%
25 - 29	4	5.9%	4	5.9%	8	11.8%
30 - 34	5	7.3%	2	3.0%	7	10.3%
35 - 39	0	-	1	1.5%	1	1.5%
40 - 44	0	-	0	-	0	-
45 - 49	0	-	1	1.5%	1	1.5%
50 - 54	1	1.5%	1	1.5%	2	3.0%
55 - 59	2	3.0%	1	1.5%	3	4.5%
60 - 64	0	-	0	-	0	-
65 - 69	0	-	0	-	0	-
70 - 74	1	1.5%	0	-	1	1.5%
75 - 79	0	-	0	-	0	-
80+	0	-	0	-	0	-
Total	34	50%	34	50%	68	100%

Source: Data compiled by J. Ryan from the Crystal Spring
Colony population records.

TABLE 4-2

CRYSTAL SPRING HUTTERITE COLONY

STE. AGATHE, MANITOBA

DISTRIBUTION OF POPULATION BY AGE GROUPS AND SEX, 1969

(At the time just before subdivision
to form the new colony of Suncrest)

Age Group	Male Population		Female Population		Total Population	
	No.	%	No.	%	No.	%
0 - 4	12	7.3%	14	8.5%	26	15.8%
5 - 9	17	10.3%	18	10.9%	35	21.2%
10 - 14	17	10.3%	14	8.5%	31	18.8%
15 - 19	5	3.0%	15	9.1%	20	12.1%
20 - 24	5	3.0%	6	3.6%	11	6.6%
25 - 29	4	2.4%	3	1.8%	7	4.2%
30 - 34	3	1.8%	3	1.8%	6	3.6%
35 - 39	3	1.8%	5	3.0%	8	4.8%
40 - 44	4	2.4%	4	2.4%	8	4.8%
45 - 49	5	3.0%	2	1.2%	7	4.2%
50 - 54	0	-	1	.6%	1	.6%
55 - 59	0	-	0	-	0	-
60 - 64	0	-	1	.6%	1	.6%
65 - 69	1	.6%	1	.6%	2	1.2%
70 - 74	1	.6%	1	.6%	2	1.2%
75 - 79	0	-	0	-	0	-
80 +	0	-	0	-	0	-
Total	77	46.7%	88	53.3%	165	100%

Source: Data compiled by J. Ryan from the Crystal Spring
Colony population records.

TABLE 4-3

CRYSTAL SPRING HUTTERITE COLONY

STE. AGATHE, MANITOBA

DISTRIBUTION OF POPULATION BY AGE GROUPS AND SEX, 1969

(At the time immediately following its subdivision
to form the new colony of Suncrest)

Age Group	Male Population		Female Population		Total Population	
	No.	%	No.	%	No.	%
0 - 4	6	7.2%	9	10.9%	15	18.1%
5 - 9	6	7.2%	12	14.5%	18	21.7%
10 - 14	11	13.3%	6	7.2%	17	20.5%
15 - 19	2	2.4%	9	10.9%	11	13.3%
20 - 24	1	1.2%	1	1.2%	2	2.4%
25 - 29	3	3.6%	3	3.6%	6	7.2%
30 - 34	1	1.2%	0	-	1	1.2%
35 - 39	1	1.2%	3	3.6%	4	4.8%
40 - 44	3	3.6%	2	2.4%	5	6.0%
45 - 49	2	2.4%	0	-	2	2.4%
50 - 54	0	-	1	1.2%	1	1.2%
55 - 59	0	-	0	-	0	-
60 - 64	0	-	0	-	0	-
65 - 69	0	-	1	1.2%	1	1.2%
70 - 74	0	-	0	-	0	-
75 - 79	0	-	0	-	0	-
80 +	0	-	0	-	0	-
Total	42	50.6%	41	49.4%	83	100%

Source: Data compiled from the Crystal Spring Colony
population records.

TABLE 4-4

SUNCREST HUTTERITE COLONY

ST. PIERRE, MANITOBA

DISTRIBUTION OF POPULATION BY AGE GROUPS AND SEX, 1969

(At the time of its formation as a result of
the subdivision of Crystal Spring Colony)

Age Group	Male Population		Female Population		Total Population	
	No.	%	No.	%	No.	%
0 - 4	6	7.3%	5	6.1%	11	13.4%
5 - 9	5	6.1%	12	14.6%	17	20.7%
10 - 14	6	7.3%	8	9.8%	14	17.1%
15 - 19	3	3.7%	6	7.3%	9	11.0%
20 - 24	4	4.9%	5	6.1%	9	11.0%
25 - 29	1	1.2%	0	-	1	1.2%
30 - 34	2	2.4%	3	3.7%	5	6.1%
35 - 39	2	2.4%	2	2.4%	4	4.9%
40 - 44	1	1.2%	2	2.4%	3	3.7%
45 - 49	3	3.7%	2	2.4%	5	6.1%
50 - 54	0	-	0	-	0	-
55 - 59	0	-	0	-	0	-
60 - 64	0	-	1	1.2%	1	1.2%
65 - 69	1	1.2%	0	-	1	1.2%
70 - 74	1	1.2%	1	1.2%	2	2.4%
75 - 79	0	-	0	-	0	-
80 +	0	-	0	-	0	-
Total	35	42.7%	47	57.3%	82	100%

Source: Data compiled by J. Ryan from Suncrest Colony
population records.

TABLE 4-5

JAMES VALLEY HUTTERITE COLONY

ELIE, MANITOBA

DISTRIBUTION OF POPULATION BY AGE GROUPS AND SEX, 1969

(Originally founded in Manitoba in 1918 and subdivided to form new colonies in 1945, 1956, and 1966)

Age Group	Male Population		Female Population		Total Population	
	No.	%	No.	%	No.	%
0 - 4	11	12.9%	9	10.6%	20	23.5%
5 - 9	7	8.2%	7	8.2%	14	16.4%
10 - 14	3	3.5%	4	4.7%	7	8.2%
15 - 19	5	5.9%	1	1.2%	6	7.1%
20 - 24	2	2.4%	3	3.5%	5	5.9%
25 - 29	4	4.7%	4	4.7%	8	9.4%
30 - 34	7	8.2%	5	5.9%	12	14.1%
35 - 39	1	1.2%	3	3.5%	4	4.7%
40 - 44	0	-	0	-	0	-
45 - 49	1	1.2%	1	1.2%	2	2.4%
50 - 54	0	-	0	-	0	-
55 - 59	2	2.4%	1	1.2%	3	3.5%
60 - 64	0	-	2	2.4%	2	2.4%
65 - 69	1	1.2%	0	-	1	1.2%
70 - 74	0	-	0	-	0	-
75 - 79	0	-	0	-	0	-
80 +	1	1.2%	0	-	1	1.2%
Total	45	52.9%	40	47.1%	85	100%

Source: Data compiled by J. Ryan from the James Valley Colony population records.

DIAGRAM 4-1a

PERCENTAGE DISTRIBUTION OF POPULATION BY AGE GROUPS AND SEX

CRYSTAL SPRING COLONY, 1954
(At time of formation)

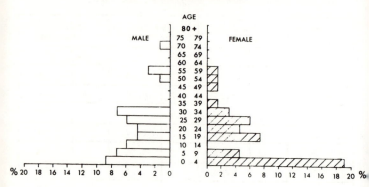

CRYSTAL SPRING COLONY, 1969
(Before subdivision)

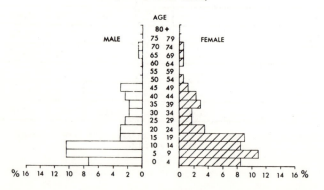

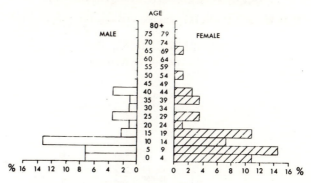

CRYSTAL SPRING COLONY, 1969
(After subdivision to form Suncrest Colony)

Source: Data compiled by J. Ryan from the population records
at Crystal Spring colony

DIAGRAM 4-1b

PERCENTAGE DISTRIBUTION OF
POPULATION BY AGE GROUPS AND SEX

SUNCREST COLONY 1969
(At time of formation)

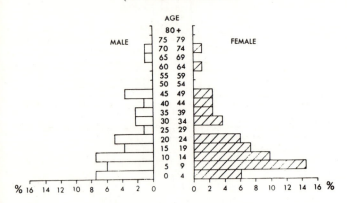

JAMES VALLEY COLONY, 1969
(3 years after third subdivision)

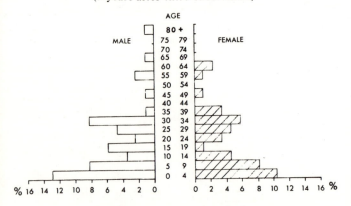

Source: Data compiled by J. Ryan from the population records
at Suncrest and James Valley colonies

DIAGRAM 4-1 c

PERCENTAGE DISTRIBUTION
OF POPULATION
BY AGE GROUPS AND SEX

MANITOBA, 1966
(Total population)

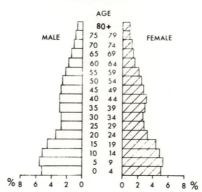

CANADA, 1966
(Total population)

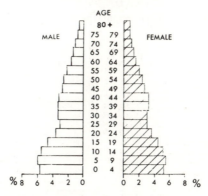

Source: 1966 Census of Canada

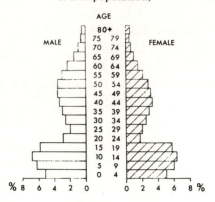

MANITOBA, 1966
(Farm population)

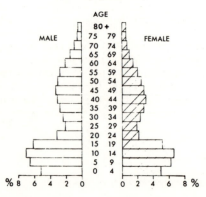

CANADA, 1966
(Farm population)

development, and the great contrast with the population of Manitoba and Canada. Whereas about 37 percent of the Manitoba farm population was under 15 years of age, on the Hutterite colonies shown in the tables, this group ranged from 45 percent to 60 percent. Hence, Hutterite population is remarkably youthful. At the other end of the scale, about 6 percent of the Manitoba farm population was over age 65, but this group ranged from 1.2 percent to 3.6 percent on the Hutterite colonies.

A detailed examination of the tables and the diagram will illustrate how closely the subdivision principles have been followed. The first thing that should be noted is that when Crystal Spring subdivided in 1969, the division was made as equal as possible, that is, out of the total population of 165, one colony was allotted 82 people and the other 83. The attempt to have an almost equal number of males and females at the time of a colony's formation was achieved by Crystal Spring in 1954 and in 1969, and it was probably close for James Valley in 1966. However, when Suncrest was formed, somehow it was allocated a significantly larger number of females than males. On the other hand, this is probably balanced by the fact that Suncrest acquired a larger male labour force between the ages of 15 and 54 than Crystal Spring, that is, 16 males as compared to 13 at Crystal Spring. In regard to the male labour force between the ages of 15 and 54, it should be noted that this group forms a relatively small proportion of the total population on all colonies. In the case of Crystal Spring this group formed 24 percent of the population when the colony was formed in 1954, but by the time the colony was ready to subdivide in 1969 it dropped to 18 percent, and it was only 16 percent after subdivision. At Suncrest the male labour force totalled 20 percent and it was 24 percent at James Valley. One final point that should be noted is that although James Valley was formed in 1918 and has gone through three subdivisions, its population structure is not significantly different from that of Suncrest which was formed in 1969.

A point not brought out by the tables is the fact that the composition of colonies is not static. Many marriages take place between members of different colonies and this results in the movement of women from one colony to another, including those in the United States. This is a very significant exchange of female colony members, but in the long-run it balances out and the population structure is not changed basically.

Birth Rate, Death Rate, and Natural Increase of Hutterite Population

A sufficient amount of data on the Manitoba Hutterite population are unavailable for purposes of computing birth rates, death rates, and natural increase. However, the demographic study of all Hutterites in Canada and the United States by Eaton and Mayer (referred to in a previous section), is probably still valid even though it is dated. According to this study the Hutterite birth rate during the five year period of 1946 through 1950 was 45.9 per 1,000 population.[7] At that time the birth rate in Canada was 27.4, but by 1970 it dropped to 17.4.[8] However, it is unlikely that the Hutterite birth rate has changed significantly during this period because their families appear to be as large now as they were then, and there has been no noticeable change in their overall mode of life. At that time the Hutterite death rate was 4.4 per 1,000 per year, as compared to 9.3 for Canada. In 1970 the death rate in Canada was 7.3, but there is no evidence to suspect a significant change in the Hutterite rate.[9]

Since natural increase is the balance of births over deaths, according to the Eaton and Mayer study the Hutterite rate of natural increase for the decade 1941-1950 was 41.5 per 1,000.[10] Table 4-6 shows how this compares with the natural increase of the population in Manitoba, Canada, the United States, and several countries with the highest reported rates. The table indicates that Hutterite natural increase is extremely high as compared to other populations. However, even though Hutterite demographic rates have apparently been stable, the fact that these data are about 20 years old should be duly considered.

According to the Eaton and Mayer study, the total Hutterite population on December 31, 1950 in both Canada and the United States was 8,542.[11] These writers calculated that the true rate of natural increase for the Hutterites was 4.1 percent per year and that the population doubled in about 16 years.[12] On this basis they made a projection that by 1970 the total Hutterite population would be 19,200.[13] In a 1972 publication, Ben J. Raber reported that the total Hutterite population in Canada and the United States was 19,454 in 1971.[14] Raber's data were apparently compiled from colony reports submitted by Hutterian Senior Elders, and on this basis these data should be authentic. If Raber's data are indeed accurate, the Eaton and Mayer projection is almost incredible. To support their hypothesis that Hutterite population doubles in about 16 years, Tables 4-1 and 4-2 show that the population at Crystal Spring Colony increased from 68 in 1954 to 165 in 1969. This is an increase of 143 percent in 15 years. In any event, the demographic data compiled by these writers still appear to have a high degree of validity at the present time.

TABLE 4-6

BIRTH RATE, DEATH RATE, AND NATURAL INCREASE

OF SELECTED POPULATIONS

Population	Year	Birth Rate (per 1,000)	Death Rate (per 1,000)	Natural Increase (per 1,000)
Hutterites[1] (Canada & U.S.A.)	1946-1950	45.9	4.4	41.5
Manitoba[2]	1946-1950	25.9	9.0	16.9
Manitoba[3]	1970	18.6	8.0	10.6
Canada[4]	1946-1950	27.4	9.3	18.1
Canada[5]	1970	17.4	7.3	10.1
U.S.A.[6]	1948	24.2	9.9	14.3
U.S.A.[7]	1970	18.2	9.4	8.8
Costa Rica[7]	1965-1970	45.1	7.6	37.5
Kuwait[7]	1965-1970	43.3	7.4	35.9
British Honduras[7]	1968	40.2	6.1	34.1
Columbia[7]	1965-1970	44.6	10.6	34.0
Iraq[7]	1965-1970	49.3	15.5	33.8
Algeria[7]	1965-1970	49.1	16.9	32.2

[1] Eaton and Mayer (1954)

[2] *Canada Year Book 1970-71*

[3] Statistics Canada (1972)

[4] *Canada Year Book 1970-71*

[5] Statistics Canada (1972)

[6] Eaton and Mayer (1954)

[7] *United Nations Demographic Yearbook 1970*

Health of Hutterite Population

The entire Hutterite population that lives on colonies in North America stems from about 50 families or a reported total of 443 individuals who were part of a larger group that migrated from Tsarist Russia.[15] In spite of the small founding group, there are apparently no inbreeding problems. Hutterites allow marriages between second and third cousins but marriage between first cousins has never been permitted. This is consistent with Canadian mores and laws. The Hutterites have nevertheless considered the possibility of a problem of inbreeding and have consulted medical authorities on this issue. However, they have apparently been assured that they have no cause for concern because the Hutterite population is sufficiently large to permit healthy mate selection.[16]

On the basis of medical studies conducted on the Hutterites, their general physical and mental health is considered to be better than the national average, although these comparisons were not made with Manitoba farm families.[17] Their way of life provides their men, women, and children with a healthy outdoor environment, plenty of exercise, wholesome food, and an apparent total lack of tension and stress. An observer cannot fail to be impressed by an average Hutterite's self-confidence, good humour, and poise.

Education and Training of Labour Force[18]

The Hutterites very early in their history recognized the need for a sound and practical elementary education. This was primarily to enable their members to read the Bible and thereby become better Christians. They maintained their own schools in order to emphasize religious instruction and to keep out the undesirable influences of the outside world. By the end of the sixteenth century the Hutterite schools were considered to be superior to any others in southern Moravia. [19]

Although the Hutterites recognized the need for an elementary education, they rejected all forms of higher education. The leaders felt that secular higher education was irrelevant to their way of life and that furthermore it would introduce undesirable ideas that might undermine their egalitarian community system. This attitude toward higher education has remained with the Hutterites to the present day. However it must be emphasized that the Hutterites place high regard on literacy and on what they consider to be practical education. The ability to read and to possess a good vocabulary plus a sound knowledge of arithmetic and accounting techniques is essential for their leaders and farm enterprise managers. The Hutterites realize that unless a colony has a competent core of managers, it is courting economic disaster. Consequently, in addition to elementary education, a number of Hutterites have taken university extension courses on poultry and livestock nutrition plus veterinary science, mechanical, and electrical courses. Furthermore, some Hutterites have taken high school correspondence cources and one colony has its own teacher.

Throughout the years the colonies have been adamant in refusing to send their children to outside public schools. Instead they have maintained their own schools on the colonies and these follow the standard school curriculum and are thereby accepted by the government. In addition to the elementary public school, the colony education includes kindergarten, German school, Sunday school, and an informal apprenticeship programme with the various colony enterprises.

1. Kindergarten

Youngsters from the ages of two and a half to six attend kindergarten. It operates from early spring to late fall, and is headed usually by a middle-aged woman. To allow her time for her own housework, she is assigned an alternate for certain periods during the week. In addition, she has the help of two or three assistants, girls of 18 to 20.

The kindergarten building is an attractive structure and the yard has a sandbox, swings, and other playground equipment (Plate 11). The building has washroom facilities, a classroom with appropriate tables and chairs, and a special bedroom.

The children attend kindergarten from eight o'clock in the morning until five in the afternoon. They eat their meals at kindergarten and they also have a long nap in the afternoon. Instruction is informal, but they are taught songs, prayers, and have Bible stories read to them. Throughout the day lessons are interspersed by active games.

Hutterians are trilingual. They speak English, German, and a Tyrolese dialect that they use only among themselves. Small children speak the Tyrolese dialect only, and kindergarten is conducted in this vernacular. They gradually become familiar with German by learning songs and Bible stories. At most colonies English is now introduced at the senior kindergarten stage.

There is no doubt that kindergarten has a profound effect on the youngsters. This is the first time that they have been away for any period of time from their home environment, and the first time that they really experience colony discipline. In the course of lessons, songs, and

J. Ryan (1969)

PLATE 11. *Kindergarten children* with Reverend Jacob Kleinsasser at Crystal Spring Colony.

games the youngsters undergo an intensive socialization process. A-social behaviour is punished, and they gradually learn that obedience, submission, and acceptance is the best policy. These early years are fundamental in setting the life style for a Hutterite.

2. The Public School

After leaving kindergarten the Hutterite youngsters start attending the public school located on their colony. They are required by law to attend the public school until the age of 16. In general most youngsters show good progress in school and many are now completing Grade X. In addition, on a few colonies some of the young men are taking correspondence courses with the intention of completing Grade XII and becoming teachers on the colonies.

All the Hutterite public schools follow the programme of studies prescribed for the province, and most colonies now have properly qualified teachers. However, in recent years since the introduction of the large school divisions and consolidated schools, some Districts have terminated the government grants to the colonies. This is an attempt to force the Hutterites to send their children to the large consolidated schools. The Hutterites have refused to do this and in all these instances are financing their own school operations. In the meantime they have made appeals to the government to try to get their grants reinstated. At the time of writing, the question of aid to private schools has still not been resolved in Manitoba.

The Hutterites have no objection to most of the school curriculum, and recognize that their economic survival depends to a great extent on an intelligent and properly trained labour force. Hence they want their youngsters to learn to read well, to learn numerous practical scientific principles, to be competent at arithmetic and accounting, and if possible to learn some basic business practices that might be applicable on their colonies. On the other hand, they view parts of the curriculum and most of higher education as being irrelevant for their purposes. Furthermore, any ideas that might cause their children to question their religious principles are naturally considered as a threat to their way of life. However, consistent with their doctrine of nonresistance, they have accepted the school system as it is, and are attempting to live with it. They try to counterbalance what they consider to be the negative effects of the public school by special religious instruction before and after the regular school hours.

3. The German School and Sunday School

Children of public school age attend the so-called German School before nine in the morning and after three thirty in the afternoon.

The purpose of this school is to give the children a working knowledge of German, some Hutterian history, and religious instruction. Much time is spent on the memorization of hymns, prayers, and Bible verses.

The German teachers do not have any formal pedagogical training, but they are men who are intellectually inclined and who have an interest in children. However, it seems that on many colonies the educational standards are not sufficiently high and that this is a cause of concern to the Hutterites.

Sunday school is attended by children over nine years of age and all young people until they join the Church. Instruction is provided by the German teacher and sometimes by the colony minister. The class is held Sunday afternoon at which time the morning's sermon is carefully explained. In addition, students get detailed instruction in church doctrine which prepares them for baptism.

4. The Apprenticeship Programme

When Hutterite children reach the age of fifteen they acquire a new role and henceforth begin to assume the responsibilities of adults. Prior to this time they take their meals in a separate dining room, but after this they eat with the adults and formally enter the work world of the colony.

Boys are apprenticed to the various colony enterprises. The procedure is usually quite informal and often a boy may be initially apprenticed under his father. After he becomes familiar with the work in that particular department, he is transferred to another. In the period of two years or more a boy will have familiarized himself with the work routine of several activities. There is no established period for a boy to work as an apprentice. The objective is to acquaint him with several farm activities to see if he has a special aptitude for any particular one. At the age of 17 or 18 a boy is usually given responsibility for a tractor during the summer—including both its maintenance and operation. Depending on the size of the colony and on the labour situation, but in any case usually within a few years, a young man will be asked to head one of the colony enterprises.

The training of girls during this period is even more informal. They take turns working as assistants in the kitchen, the laundry, the garden, the kindergarten, or they may simply help at home with the children. At about 17 the girls may begin to take their turn baking and cooking for the colony along with the other women.

The Colony Labour Force

In a sense the entire colony constitutes the labour force. Everyone is expected to work, including children. Although on the one hand, Hutterites consider work as a simple fact of life and therefore a necessity, on the other hand, they attach a value to work as such. They believe that the individual must contribute to the general welfare, and work is the physical manifestation of the individual's contribution to the group. Furthermore, all work is rated to be of equal value. The colony minister or any elder would not consider it beneath him to work at the most menial task. Obviously this attitude to work contributes immeasurably to the smooth functioning of their communal life.

Within the Hutterian communal way of life there is no direct remuneration for labour. Everyone is expected to work to the best of his ability at whatever task he is best able to perform, or at whatever the colony assigns to him. No records are kept of the time spent at work by anyone. Work is simply a basic human activity, and it is something that a Hutterite considers to be his personal contribution to the life of the colony. Although there is no remuneration in the form of money, every member of a Hutterite community has complete economic security. The colony provides him with food, shelter, clothing, and security in old age. Jokingly, Hutterites sometimes refer to their society as ''a big retirement scheme.''

The informal retirement age is approximately 55 for men and 45 for women. After this, the amount of work Hutterites do is entirely up to them. However, unless they suffer from some physical ailment practically all of them continue to work at some activity or other. The point is that there is no compulsion to work after these ages, and those who wish to continue working are usually employed at such jobs where their regular presence may not be required and they can come and go as they desire. There is no question that the greatest privileges in the colony are enjoyed by its senior members.

In order for the colony to function, labour must be expended not only on purely agricultural activities, but on construction, maintenance, the garden, the laundry, in the kitchen and all the work associated with food preparation, plus management responsibilities. The colony is of course an assembly of people of diverse ages, skills, and abilities, and consequently there is considerable specialization and division of labour.

Although to some degree the labour force includes practically all the members of the colony, in actual fact the labour force proper comes from the group between the ages of 15 and 55, and primarily from the male sector. The operation of all the agricultural enterprises and the work of construction and maintenance is done almost exclusively by the men within this age group. In essence, it is this group that is basically responsible for upholding the economy of the colony.

As shown by the tables at the beginning of this chapter, the group under the age of 15 may account for 45 percent to 60 percent of the total colony population. Women form one half of the remaining group, and when men over the age of 55 are excluded, the male labour force may range from about 12 to 30. In an average colony of about 100 members, this means that the core of the male labour force consists of about 15 to 18 men. The total number of full-time jobs in major enterprises on an average colony is about 15. Therefore, in a typical colony practically every eligible adult male is in charge and is basically responsible for a major sector of the colony's economy. This means that in smaller colonies there may be an actual shortage of labour, which may be reflected in a smaller scale of operations or a smaller number of enterprises. It follows that larger colonies are in a position to have a greater number of enterprises and to operate at a larger scale. However, even in the larger colonies there would never be more than two or three men to a major enterprise.

Those who are not in charge of departments are primarily the young men between the ages of 15 and 20. In the summer these men are either in charge of tractors or are assigned to other field duties. When field operations are concluded these labourers are assigned to work as assistants in the various enterprises.

While the farming operations are conducted by the men, women are responsible for gardening, clothes manufacture, laundry, painting, housekeeping, the preparation of food, and the operation of the kitchen. Although there is some division of labour, there are only about a half a dozen managerial jobs for women, for instance, the "Kuchenfrau" (the chief cook), the "Gartenfrau" (the woman in charge of gardens and canning), the seamstress, the kindergarten teacher, the midwife, and some full-time assistants. The rest of the women are divided into two groups: the young unmarrieds (girls 15 and over) and the married women. The married women take weekly turns primarily in the kitchen, and the younger married ones also work in the garden. In addition, however, the married women have their housework and children to look after, and they are responsible for sewing, knitting, and making clothes. The young unmarried women also help with clothing, but they do more of the garden work and jobs such as housepainting. Actually since the introduction of garden tractors and other implements plus various labour saving devices throughout the colony, there is a problem of finding enough worthwhile work for the unmarried women.

The work of children on a colony is not insignificant by any means. Their participation in various activities is intended to not only help the colony economically, but it is partly to help instill a proper work ethic. Actually work begins as "play" in early childhood. The Hutterites provide very few toys for their children, but instead allow them to play with tools and other farm devices. When a youngster gets to be about ten years old, he is given small regular work assignments with some degree of responsibility. The boys between 10 and 15 help with egg collecting and crating, livestock and poultry feeding, cattle herding, and sometimes even tractor operation. Often this frees the older men to do more important jobs. Girls of this age help with various household tasks and the care of smaller children. On some colonies these girls also help to collect and crate eggs.

As for the people who are ''retired'' after 55, the majority of them continue to work at various worthwhile jobs. Even men in their 70's may work at candling and crating eggs, or in the shoe repair shop, or at general maintenance work. The older women often help in the kitchen and of course they knit and sew and look after their grandchildren.

Future Hutterite Population Trends

The distinguishing characteristic of Hutterite population is probably the stability and permanence of their basic way of life. They are prepared to adopt almost any new technological advance if this helps to maintain or improve the operations of their colonies, but with the strict proviso that this new element must not threaten the cohesive character of their communal life style or in any way be contrary to their religious principles. The most notable rejections have been radio, television, and the passenger automobile. All colonies have panel trucks, but since there is a utilitarian need for such a vehicle it somehow does not have the ''worldly'' character of an automobile. Nevertheless the attractions of the outside world are still there, and an estimate has been made that on some colonies as many as 20 percent of the young people between 19 and 24 may leave the colony. The surprising thing is that apparently about 85 percent of these return—some almost immediately and others after a number of years.[20] In any case, up to the present, defection has not been a major problem for the Hutterites. They have survived the threat of defection for over four centuries and the majority have every confidence that their young people will not reject their way of life at this stage of history. It is indeed difficult to make any firm predictions for the future in this regard.

As far as Manitoba colonies are concerned, at present there are insufficient data for purposes of making an estimate of future population growth. However, as discussed in a previous section, some 20 years ago Eaton and Mayer made a remarkably accurate projection for the total Hutterite population for 1970. In the same publication, and also on the same basis of a 4.1 percent natural increase per year, these writers predicted that by the year 2,000 the total North American Hutterite population would be 64,500.[21] However, considering the greater time span, the current rapidity of change and the greater pressures of present-day life, their qualifying remarks are even more apropos today:[22]

. . . It cannot be over-emphasized that this is not a prediction of what will actually happen. The statistics are based on the assumption that there will be no change in the biological and social factors which have enabled the Hutterites to reproduce rapidly in the past.

It is hard to imagine that the "outside world" will continue to have relatively little effect on the Hutterites. Of course one of the main reasons why the Hutterites are so prolific is because they do not practice any type of birth control. It is contrary to their religion. The biblical admonition to Noah, "be fruitful and multiply," is followed to the letter. So long as they adhere to a literal interpretation of this biblical guidance, there is a strong likelihood that the Eaton and Mayer projection for the year 2000 may be almost as accurate as it was for 1970.

Notes and References

1. For source of 1970 data see footnote 4 in Chapter I.
2. Glenway's enterprises and landholdings were on a smaller scale than Milltown's (the founding colony), consequently the assets and population were divided on a 40:60 basis rather than the traditional 50:50.
3. The source of the 1968 population data is the Hutterian Brethren Church Genealogy Record, compiled by Reverend Jacob Kleinsasser of Crystal Spring Colony.
4. Dominion Bureau of Statistics, *1966 Census of Canada—Households and Families: Household Composition*, Vol. II (2-4), June 1968, p. 19-1.
5. Joseph W. Eaton and Albert J. Mayer, *Man's Capacity to Reproduce: The Demography of a Unique Population* (Glencoe: The Free Press, 1954), p. 20.
6. The basic information for this section was obtained mainly from discussions with Reverend Jacob Kleinsasser of Crystal Spring Colony.
7. Eaton and Mayer, *op. cit.*, p. 14.
8. Dominion Bureau of Statistics, *Canada Year Book 1970-71*, p. 286 for 1946-50 birth rate; Statistics Canada, *Vital Statistics, Preliminary Annual Report 1970*, May 1972, p. 9 for 1970 birth rate.
9. Eaton and Mayer, *op. cit.*, p. 32 for Hutterite death rate; *Canada Year Book 1970-71*, *op. cit.*, p. 286 for 1946-50 death rate, and *Vital Statistics, op. cit.*, p. 19 for 1970 death rate.

10. Eaton and Mayer, *op. cit.*, p. 38.

11. *Ibid.*, p. 8.

12. *Ibid.*, p. 44.

13. *Ibid.*, p. 45.

14. Ben J. Raber, *The 43rd Year of the New American Calendar, 1972* (Baltic, Ohio: Published by Ben J. Raber and printed by the Gordonville Printshop, Gordonville, Pennsylvania, 1972), pp. 4-5. See footnote 2 in Chapter I for additional information on this source.

15. Eaton and Mayer, *op. cit.*, p. 3. Eaton and Mayer compiled the data on the number of Hutterites that immigrated to the United States from field investigation and from photostatic copies of the 1880 United States Census records.

16. Victor Peters, *All Things Common: The Hutterian Way of Life* (Minneapolis: The University of Minnesota Press, 1965), p. 155.

17. Joseph W. Eaton and Robert J. Weil, *Culture and Mental Disorders: A Comparative Study of the Hutterites and Other Populations* (Glencoe: The Free Press, 1955), pp. 235-237.

18. The information for the sections on education and the colony labour force was obtained from discussions with Reverend Jacob Kleinsasser of Crystal Spring Colony, other colony ministers and managers, and colony German teachers. In addition, reference was made to chapters X and XI in Victor Peters' *All Things Common*.

19. Bertha W. Clark, "The Hutterite Communities," *Journal of Political Economy*, Vol. 32 (June 1924), p. 373.

20. This is an estimate made by Reverend Jacob Kleinsasser of Crystal Spring Colony.

21. Eaton and Mayer, *op. cit.*, p. 45.

22. *Ibid.*, p. 44.

CHAPTER 5

COLONY ORGANIZATION AND MANAGEMENT

The Colony Administrative System[1]

The administrative system of Hutterite colonies differs only in detail from the structure adopted by the Moravian colonies during the sixteenth century.[2] It is a complex organization that takes into account family autonomy and kinship groups, communal solidarity, and economic efficiency. The system is regulated partly by written codes and constitutions and partly by custom and tradition. The Hutterites have held to this system not merely because of reliance on dogma, but because the system has proved to be an extremely efficient way of operating a broad range of agricultural activities. To a large degree the durability and continued existence of the Hutterian social and agrarian way of life is the result of their time-tested organizational structure.

A colony is governed by a system which can perhaps be called a "managed democracy." This is a combination of egalitarian group decision and patriarchal authority. All the baptized married men and baptized single men (over the age of 25) have the right to vote, and all important decisions are made by them. Although Hutterites elect men to positions in the colony, they believe that such elections are the will of God, and on this basis once elected, a man has considerable authority. All important issues are openly discussed and debated at length, usually over a period of time, before being brought to a vote.

The administrative structure has a built-in system of subtle checks and balances designed to control factionalism and guarantee equal treatment for all. For example, kinship groups and colony economic activities have qualities which support solidarity and continuity, but they also have features which can be potentially divisive. In the case of kinship groups, loyalties of families and other kin groups have the power to injure colony unity. Colony unity can also be threatened if the various economic activities are allowed to compete for resources in an uncontrolled manner. However, the colony administrative structure is capable of coping with these and other problems, and thereby makes communal life possible.

A colony has two levels of administration: 1) Executive officers and an Executive Council direct the overall affairs of the colony, and 2) Agricultural Managers are in charge of the various agricultural enterprises. The colony church does not have a separate leadership structure. The Executive Council directs both colony and church affairs. Hence, this is an indication of how religion and daily life are blended.

The Colony Leadership

The Executive Council or the Board of Elders usually consists of six or seven men. These are the colony minister, a second colony minister during a number of years preceding a colony division, the colony manager or steward, the farm manager, sometimes the German teacher, and two or three farm enterprise managers who are elected on the basis of ability and seniority.

1. The Colony Minister

This person has the greatest authority in a colony and is the spiritual and temporal head of the community. In this dual role he is officially in charge of the colony church and conducts the services, and he is the president of the colony business operations. As part of his regular routine, in co-operation with the colony manager, he helps to plan the day to day colony activities as well as all matters of policy. In a general sense, he is considered as a *paterfamilias*. He is in charge of colony communications, colony discipline, and he is the arbitrator of intra-colony disputes and the guardian of morals and tradition.

He holds his position for life and his appointment is a combination of human selection and pure chance (or divine choice as the Hutterites interpret this). A few years before a colony subdivides, a second minister must be appointed who will eventually become the minister of either the parent or the daughter colony. The usual procedure is as follows: The colony informs the Senior Elder of the Hutterites in the province that a new minister is required. The Elder arranges a meeting at the colony on a certain date of all the ministers from other colonies together with one or two other members of each colony in Manitoba. Prior to this, the baptized married male members of the colony in question will already have nominated two or three candidates from among themselves. After an appropriate church service, all the baptized married male members of the colony and all the official Hutterite visitors file past the Elder and indicate to him by a verbal vote the candidate that they favour. The votes are counted and any candidate that receives less than five votes is eliminated. The Hutterites then pray for guidance in selecting the proper candidate on the basis of lot. Following this the names of the eligible candidates are placed in a hat and the Elder draws one name. This person becomes the new minister. He is placed on probation for several years and if he proves himself to be competent, he is ordained. He then holds the position of minister for life or until he wishes to retire. It should be pointed out that the method of selecting the minister in the final stage on the basis of lot has a practical consideration. This undoubtedly reduces the chances of partisanship within the colony before and after the election.[3] This is the only position in the colony to be selected by this particular method; all other officials are elected by simple majorities.

The minister receives his training for his position while acting as the second or assistant minister on a colony for a few years. At this time and even when he is a fully ordained minister he is not exempted from manual work. In addition to his various official duties he is expected to perform whatever tasks he is capable of doing or has time for. It should be borne in mind that prior to his election as minister, he may have been the colony manager or a manager of one of the colony enterprises, and therefore he usually has considerable experience in the colony's economic affairs. In his role as minister he occupies an exceptional place in the colony. For instance, he is required to eat his meals by himself in his own home. The food, however, is the same as that eaten by everyone else. Although the minister gets no special privileges, dresses the same as the other men, and takes part in the regular routine work of the colony, there is an undeniable air of respect for him on the part of all.

2. The Colony Manager or Steward

This is the person second in authority at a colony, but as the director of the colony's financial and economic operations there are occasions when he may be even more influential than the minister. In business transactions when the colony is regarded as a corporation, the colony manager acts as the secretary-treasurer and the minister acts as the president.

The colony manager is elected by a simple majority of the baptized married male members of the colony. Providing he is competent he may hold this office until he retires.

Together with the minister, the colony manager plans the daily routine and the overall colony programme. He keeps the colony's financial records and is thoroughly familiar with the colony's economic operations. He regularly checks the work in every farm enterprise to note the efficiency of the operation and to make certain that no one receives any special concessions or privileges. Since the numerous enterprises invariably compete for some of the colony's resources, primarily capital for expansion or alterations, the colony manager must be in a position to evaluate all such requests. He must be able to decide or to recommend which of the enterprises might be more deserving or the order of priority of the requests. Obviously for the good of the colony he must exercise diplomacy and good judgment in all his dealings with the colony personnel.

Depending on his ability, age, and personality the colony manager may sometimes be more influential than the minister. This is especially the case if the minister is old and primarily interested in the spiritual affairs of the colony.

3. The Farm Manager or Foreman

The farm manager is third in importance in the colony administration. He is directly in charge of agriculture proper and of the colony labour force. He is elected by the male congregation, the same as the colony manager. By being in charge of manpower, it is his responsibility, after consultation with the colony manager, to assign workers to various jobs. His greatest responsibility is the conduct of field operations during the summer. After consultation with the minister, the colony manager, and the enterprise managers, it is his responsibility to decide what crops to sow and where, and to make all decisions regarding plowing, seeding, harvesting, etc. In addition, he is in charge of all farm machinery and equipment. He is also the director of the apprenticeship programme for the older boys.

4. The German Teacher

The German teacher is not automatically a member of the Executive Council, but he is often elected to this position. His is a responsible position since he is in charge of the education of the children and sometimes he may also function as an assistant minister. Often he is called upon to settle disputes. On the managerial level, the German teacher is usually in charge of the colony garden.

5. The Farm Enterprise Managers

The number of enterprise managers varies from colony to colony depending on the size of the colony and the nature of its economic activities. Usually there are managers of cattle, hogs, chickens, turkeys, ducks and geese, plus technical management positions such as mechanic, electrician, carpenter, shoemaker. These men are elected or appointed by general concensus to their positions, but only two or three are elected to the Executive Council.

Each manager becomes a specialist in his area of work and usually there are assistants or apprentices in most departments. Each manager operates with a certain degree of autonomy, but nevertheless close contact is kept with the colony manager. The enterprise managers are expected to solve their own labour problems and to keep accounting records of their operations.

Colony Decisions and Management

On most colonies the day to day schedule is worked out jointly by the minister, the colony manager, and the farm manager. Usually the men meet at the minister's house either in the evening or after breakfast to discuss the programme for the day. Often it is only the minister and the colony manager who have these regular daily meetings. This consultation process is a basic part of the democratic fabric of the Hutterian community. A key feature of their way of life is the principle that no single person, regardless of his position, has the authority to make decisions affecting the whole colony.

Once a colony has been operating for some time the great majority of the colony work becomes a matter of routine. Each enterprise manager operates his department, often with the aid of assistants or apprentices, in a practically autonomous manner. The colony manager keeps in touch with all the operations and one of his prime functions is to allocate labour and capital to the enterprises in such a way that the entire colony economy is well balanced and properly coordinated. The day to day decisions made by the minister and colony manager usually deal with matters that are not routine or with special programmes or projects. During the summer of course, when the colony is extremely busy, field operations often require daily decisions and careful planning.

Decisions of major importance are made only after passing through an involved procedure. Examples of these would include colony subdivision, the purchase of additional land, the purchase of expensive equipment or machinery, the expansion or reduction of a farm enterprise, the construction of new buildings, proposals for significant technological change, and changes in management. If any of these proposals or requests come from a labourer or an enterprise manager, the first procedure is to present the case to the colony manager. The colony manager discusses it with the minister and if they feel that the proposal is unacceptable they reject it. However, if they concur with the request or if there is some uncertainty, they present the proposal to the Executive Council. The proposal may be rejected at this stage, but if the Council is undecided they present it for consideration at an assembly of all baptized male colony members. The decision is then made by a simple majority vote. On some colonies very important issues, such as the division of the colony, may require the unanimous approval of all the male congregation. In all instances before there is a meeting of the total assembly to consider an important proposal, the issue is fully discussed and debated by all concerned for a considerable period of time. A meeting is called only when it becomes apparent that further discussion would not be profitable or if a decision is urgent.

On the basis of their interpretation of some Old Testament ideas and their own chronicles the Hutterites believe that women lack the "right" to make decisions in colony affairs.[4] In fact, the Hutterite society has been described as "a society of men aided and assisted by women."[5] Nevertheless, while their formal status may be restricted, the informal status and influence of women is considerable. Hutterites have a close family relationship and within the family circle the husband and wife may often discuss colony affairs with frankness and equality. On matters of policy it is understood by all that women are privately asked their opinion, but they would never be openly or publicly consulted. Hutterite men acknowledge in a joking manner that women have considerable influence in persuading the male assembly to authorize funds for the purchase of kitchen equipment or items for use by women. It has been noted that Hutterite women have a calm assured air about them which indicates that although they are conscious of their official subordinate status, they are fully aware of their ability to overcome it in indirect ways.[6]

Hutterite executives and managers have some problems that are not encountered in a typical managerial position elsewhere in Canada. Because of their way of life and religious beliefs they are not allowed to exercise the full authority to which they are entitled. In performing a job a Hutterite must never make it appear that he is concerned about self-aggrandizement or prestige of any kind. He would then be guilty of the sin of pride, and could be subject to public rebuke. Consequently no one is ever given any credit for a job well done. Nevertheless, the Hutterites strongly emphasize the necessity for good leadership.

Another problem that colony leaders always encounter is the "progress" issue. On the basis of their religious beliefs a colony must avoid materialism, yet it must operate at a certain level of profit in order to maintain solvency. Hence the elements of progress and conservatism complicate the management of the farm enterprises. Some colony members are conservative and more hesitant about technical innovation, while others press for economic growth and advancement. It is always a problem for an executive to keep these factions in balance and to avoid open confrontation.

Incentive and Responsibility

When a managerial position opens up, or a full-time assistantship, every effort is made to appoint a person who appears to have a special aptitude for the job or at least indicates an interest in it. A person would never be assigned to an enterprise if he disliked it, because the operation would deteriorate through his lack of interest and it would be bad for the person's morale. It is highly unlikely, however, that this in itself would provide sufficient incentive and responsibility. The fundamental basis for this rests on the acceptance of the Hutterian value system in which a job is not a personal end but is viewed as a social means. The performance of the job is its own reward since it contributes to the welfare of the group. The Hutterites are inculcated with a strong sense of responsibility toward the welfare and preservation of their community. Their system functions and thrives even though there is no pay, no prestige, no status to speak of, and basically no competition between individuals. There seems to be no question that "the Hutterites exemplify the theory that strong incentive can exist in social systems that suppress individualistic competition and aspiration."[7]

Notes and References

1. The information for this chapter was compiled primarily from discussions and interviews with numerous colony ministers and managers, and particularly Reverend Jacob Kleinsasser of Crystal Spring Colony. Reference was also made to the relevant sections in Bennett (1967), Deets (1939), Hostetler (1967), and Peters (1965).

2. John W. Bennett, *Hutterian Brethren* (Stanford: Stanford University Press, 1967), p. 143.
3. Lee Emerson Deets, *The Hutterites: A Study in Social Cohesion* (Gettysburg: Time and News Publishing Company, 1939), p. 63.
4. Bennett, *op. cit.*, p. 111.
5. *Ibid.*
6. *Ibid.*, p. 113.
7. *Ibid.*, p. 160.

CHAPTER 6

FARMING PRACTICES AND GENERAL AGRICULTURAL POLICIES

Type of Farm Operation[1]

All Hutterite colonies are engaged in large-scale mixed farming operations. This means that their economy is based primarily on the production of crops and the raising of farm animals and poultry. Their highly diversified operations include crop production, mainly wheat, oats, and barley, and enterprises such as the raising of hogs, beef cattle, dairy cattle, laying hens for egg production, broilers, turkeys, geese, ducks, and apiculture. Emphasis on enterprises varies from colony to colony and some colonies may not be involved at all in some of the above listed activities. For example, although hog production is important in all colonies, the raising of broilers is done by only a few colonies, and ducks and geese are not of major importance on many colonies.

The rationale for the Hutterite mixed farm economy is based on tradition and practical considerations. Hutterite farm diversification was initially the result of attempts at communal self-sufficiency and dates back to the very first establishment of Hutterite communities in Moravia in the sixteenth century.[2] At that time the Hutterites tried to withdraw from the outside world as completely as possible, and the original ideal was one of total self-sufficiency. However, this was never fully realized in the past, and it is not even an objective at the present.

The original Hutterite attempts at self-sufficiency were not restricted to agricultural operations, but involved the practice of nearly every important sixteenth century craft. Their religious beliefs barred them from trade and commerce, and therefore their crafts were used primarily for colony needs, although some of their produce was sold during the Moravian period. Their craft industry declined during their period of settlement in the Ukraine and ceased almost entirely when they moved to North America. However, for a number of years they persisted in making most of their tools and household articles. Even now the Hutterites still produce a variety of homemade goods for the colony. For example, they construct all the colony buildings and produce their own furniture, in their machine shops they manufacture certain tools, farm implements, and some stainless steel kitchen utensils, they produce most of their own clothing and knitwear, and they do most of their machine repair work and maintenance.

Despite a certain amount of colony production, the Hutterites no longer strive for any form of self-sufficiency. Fundamentally this is an adjustment to a market economy. They realize that the cost of manufactured goods is low in comparison to the value of the labour that would be required to produce them on the colony. It has become obvious that labour yields higher returns when expended on the production of agricultural commodities which can be sold for relatively high prices. Moreover, in order to support a rapidly increasing population on a relatively limited land area, it was inevitable for the Hutterites to adopt mechanization and various labour saving devices. Mechanization has enabled the Hutterites to operate a wider range of enterprises on a large scale, thereby making their labour force more effective. The majority of the goods produced and the services conducted on the colonies at the present time are those which either do not divert excessive labour from agricultural production or those which clearly reduce colony operating expenses. These activities should nevertheless not be minimized, especially the value of home-produced food. Furthermore, construction work, machine maintenance, and general repair work leads to great savings on all colonies.

Although tradition is an important reason for maintaining a diversified farm operation, there are significant practical reasons for it. A diversified farm economy makes it possible to employ the sizeable Hutterite labour force effectively, both male and female. This in itself is an important consideration in both an economic and social sense. Economically, to maximize income all who are capable of work should be gainfully employed, and mixed farming allows for this. In a social sense, unemployment or even underemployment would tend to create various social problems and these are avoided by maintaining a diversified farm economy.

Mixed farming if operated on a large-scale basis with a sufficient labour force avoids the instability of traditional one-crop agriculture. The Hutterites have been eminently successful at this. During the depression of the 1930's the Hutterites were amongst the few farmers who managed to survive without severe economic deprivation. In more recent times, when grain farmers have suffered because of poor markets, the Hutterites were unaffected because they feed their grain to farm animals and poultry and sell the products. Hence operating a balanced mixed farm economy has been of great practical value.

Partly because of economic and labour considerations and partly because of tradition, many colonies up to now have put almost an equal emphasis on each enterprise, regardless of the income it yields. Some operations may require more labour and capital than others, but these colonies have felt that in the long run this helps to reduce economic risks and it helps to employ the labour force. Therefore, economic efficiency on many colonies is not the only factor that is considered in farming operations. However, a number of colonies are beginning to realize that their economic survival may depend on truly efficient operations, and on these colonies cost-accounting is being introduced with the viewpoint of placing emphasis on the most profitable activities.

One final consideration is the fact that by operating a mixed farm economy the Hutterites are able to make use of all kinds of land and to practice conservation techniques. Land that is unsuitable for grain crops can be used for hay purposes.

Capital-Intensive and Labour-Intensive Policies

The single most important consideration for the Hutterites is the survival and maintenance of their way of life. Throughout their history they have had to adapt to numerous changes of environment, both natural and social. On the one hand, their migrations confronted them with different physical conditions, while on the other hand, the passage of time brought about drastic social and economic changes in the world around them. To maintain their way of life the Hutterites had no alternative but to adapt to new conditions.

The adoption of mechanization and labour-saving equipment was a response of this kind. Faced with a rapidly growing population in a period of rising costs of production and high land prices, the Hutterites had no alternative but to adopt modern technology. However, this was a matter of conscious decision and only those technological changes were introduced which would enable the colony to be more productive without at the same time changing or threatening their basic values.

The first stage of mechanization took place in the 1930's when it became evident that horse-drawn equipment would have to be replaced by tractors and trucks. The second stage came in the 1940's when most of the old implements were replaced by powered and mechanical devices. It was at this time that capital requirements were increasingly emphasized over labour. The 1950's and 1960's brought in the final stage when highly specialized labour-saving devices were introduced. These included the latest agricultural field equipment, automatic milking apparatus for the dairy operation, elaborate automated equipment for egg production, sophisticated quarters and feeding apparatus for the hog enterprise, plus labour-saving devices such as hydraulic post-pounders and other equipment of this type.

Although the present-day colony is as highly mechanized as any of the most advanced private farms, the colony still benefits from an abundant labour supply. While the modern mixed farm, faced with labour limitations, can only specialize in two or three basic farm enterprises, the Hutterites are in a position to operate a broad range of enterprises mainly because of the relatively large labour supply. Since the colony operates on a large scale, capital is available for fully mechanizing any of the enterprises to make them as productive as possible. Consequently, Hutterite agriculture is characterized by both capital-intensive and labour-intensive features.

Source of Technical and Agricultural Information

Probably the single most important source of technical farm information for any colony is other Hutterite colonies. This is a comprehensive source since there are close to fifty colonies in Manitoba and in addition contact can be made with colonies in Saskatchewan, Alberta, and the United States. There is an extensive information network amongst the colonies which permits a rapid dissemination of any new ideas or technological developments. The closest contacts are between parent and daughter colonies or between colonies where several families are related by marriage. However, Hutterites are in the habit of making regular visits to other colonies, including those that may be at a considerable distance. In fact, the most common form of recreation for Hutterites is visiting. It is not uncommon for several families to go on extended trips that may last up to three weeks to colonies in South Dakota or Alberta. In addition, there are formal annual meetings of all Manitoba Hutterite ministers and farm managers for the express purpose of discussing mutual problems and exchanging information. This is particularly pertinent because it is based on experience in a Hutterite setting.

The Hutterites keep close contact with nearby farmers and are always ready to take note of new developments, especially those from success-ful large-scale operators.

Another important source of information is the provincial agricultural extension service and the Faculty of Agriculture at the University of Manitoba. The Hutterites fully realize that the University makes available research papers, reports, brochures, and pamphlets. Very often they write directly to the University for such publications. In addition, some enterprise managers may write to the Faculty of Agriculture for advice and information on specific problems. Another use made of University facilities is to have dead or diseased poultry examined by university laboratories. Moreover, Hutterites occasionally attend university agricultural conferences and special lectures. Perhaps of even greater significance is the fact that a number of them have enrolled in and completed university extension courses, for example, those in nutrition of poultry or hogs.

It is noteworthy that Hutterites are at times critical of some of the agricultural extension literature and of the advice and recommendations of local extension agents (or ''ag reps'' as they are known). It seems that the literature is often too general for their specialized purposes, and the recommendations of the ''ag rep'' are often only applicable to the needs of the small family farm and are not applicable to their large-scale commercial operations.

The Hutterites occasionally visit the Federal Experimental Farm at Morden. They speak very highly of the service provided there and often obtain valuable information from its staff of highly qualified experts.

Feed companies are an important source of information especially with regard to the care and feeding of cattle, hogs, and poultry. Competing feed representatives tour the colonies and give demonstrations of feeding routines and provide the Hutterites with various well-written technical manuals. Machine implement dealers provide a similar service by making available information on new machines and equipment.

Almost all colonies regularly subscribe to farm journals and magazines. Many of the enterprise managers purchase technical manuals and guidebooks. Together with the literature that they receive from extension officials and feed companies, the progressive managers have no difficulty in accumulating fairly impressive collections of technical material. It is a fairly safe assertion that the progressive enterprise managers possess a larger fund of technical knowledge than most farmers.[3]

Research, Experimentation, and Adoption of New Techniques

Only a farm operation with considerable capital reserves can afford serious research and experimentation. This excludes most of the average Manitoba farmers. In the case of the Hutterites, most colonies could afford a certain amount of experimentation, but this is sometimes hampered by ''conservative'' factions within the colonies who oppose new ideas for traditional reasons. However, colonies with progressive leadership often engage in a certain amount of experimentation. This is carefully observed by other colonies, and if a venture is successful the practice is often quickly adopted by the others. Areas of experimentation involve new varieties of seed, new animal and poultry breeds, different feeding formulas and techniques, different types of building construction, and new machines and equipment.

The fact that colonies differ in their agricultural operations is partly attributable to geographic location and resources, but it is partly a result of the differences in the skills and abilities of the colony executives and enterprise managers. Those colonies that place greater emphasis on literacy are invariably ahead of other colonies in innovation and management because they make a point of acquiring and reading technical material and are also prepared to experiment with new techniques. Sometimes a colony may wish to adopt new techniques but may be unable to do so because of a lack of funds or labour. Hence innovations that simply require the application of new methods without any additional expenditure are more readily transferred. Furthermore, the adoption of certain new practices may be impossible or simply impracticable if structures have to be drastically remodelled or if a new type of building may be required. In the same way in the case of machinery, even if the Hutterites are fully aware of the existence of better equipment they may have to use what they have until it becomes obsolete for simple economic reasons. Very often new ideas for building construction and interior equipment and new types of farm machinery can only be introduced when a new colony is being established. This makes it possible to introduce various new features without going to the expense of discarding old equipment or remodelling old buildings. Hence the new colonies are almost always far more technologically advanced than the old ones.

Source of Agricultural Equipment and Supplies

This study included the compilation of a detailed inventory of farm machinery for every colony.[4] This included the purchase price of the equipment, its present value, whether it was purchased new or used, and where it was purchased. Hutterites are often accused of not dealing with local businessmen but, instead, purchasing their equipment and supplies primarily from large centres and wholesale dealers. It is true that they do purchase certain goods primarily from Winnipeg dealers, but this is certainly not the case with regard to farm machinery.

The inventory shows that every colony purchases the bulk of its agricultural equipment from the local dealers. A certain amount of machinery and equipment is obtained from other colonies and other farmers and some is purchased in Winnipeg or other centres. This, however, is true of all farm operators who try to secure the best bargain. The point remains that this inventory shows conclusively that most colonies purchase as much as 80 percent of their equipment from local centres.

The prime reason for purchasing the bulk of the agricultural machinery from local dealers is convenience in servicing and repairs. Furthermore, agricultural machinery in Manitoba is almost the same price over large areas. It is of interest that in recent years many colonies have begun to show a preference for farm machines manufactured by the "Versatile" firm in Winnipeg. This machinery compares well with other models but on the average it is considerably cheaper, especially the tractors.[5] Furthermore, since it is manufactured in Winnipeg the Hutterites are assured of the immediate availability of spare parts. A breakdown and a subsequent repair delay because of lack of parts can be a very costly experience during harvest time.

Certain agricultural supplies are purchased primarily in Winnipeg, although some may be bought at Portage la Prairie or Brandon by the nearby colonies. Feed concentrate for poultry and hogs is the most important commodity purchased in the large centres. This is usually obtained on a contract basis from large feed companies. Although certain other supplies are sometimes purchased in the large centres, there is no set policy on this and decisions are largely determined by the prices charged by local dealers. Supplies such as oil, gasoline, diesel fuel, grease, lumber, cement, hardware, and groceries are purchased almost always in the nearby towns. Fertilizer and chemical sprays are usually purchased locally, but are sometimes purchased in Winnipeg.

With the exception of farm machinery, a detailed study was not made of the economic interrelationship of the colonies and their local regions. However, despite popular opinion to the contrary, there is strong evidence to indicate that the local economy benefits greatly from the Hutterite colonies.

Source of Capital

Fundamentally capital is self-generated by the colony economy, but there are times when a colony's savings are insufficient for certain expenditures. This is especially the case when a new colony is being established. Usually, by the time that a colony is ready to subdivide, the colony's savings are sufficient to finance a major part of the expansion.

However, the purchase of land, the construction of all the colony buildings, and the purchase of equipment and machinery is an immense financial undertaking. Consequently, most colonies have to borrow considerable sums at this time and for a number of years after until both the parent and the daughter colony are once again financially solvent. In addition, some colonies may have to borrow money to overcome sudden setbacks such as crop failure, flood, or fire damage.

The Hutterite colonies have a mutual aid system which makes it possible for some colonies, especially if struck by unforeseen disaster, to obtain interest-free repayable loans from other colonies. This of course is the best way for a colony to obtain needed capital. However, under normal circumstances most colonies obtain ordinary bank loans. Their credit rating is excellent because most creditors realize that the future of a colony is more assured than that of the average farmer. Furthermore, it is widely known that although each colony functions as a completely autonomous economic unit, the other colonies would always be ready to assist any colony that developed serious financial difficulties.

General Agricultural Policies and Practices

In general Hutterite agricultural operations are about as advanced as those of the most progressive farmers in the province. In fact, Hutterites have been in the forefront of certain developments. For example, they were among the first farmers in Manitoba to make large-scale use of fertilizer. At present some colonies are using liquid fertilizer which has only recently been shown to be more effective. So far only a few farmers in Manitoba have made this change.

Hutterites were among the first farmers in the province to abandon the traditional practice of summerfallow in those areas where seasonal moisture is sufficient to grow crops. In these areas soil fertility is now maintained by the addition of fertilizer, weeds are destroyed by chemical sprays, and the land is in continuous use for cropping. However, although some colonies pioneered this system, many other colonies still keep a considerable amount of land in summerfallow.

Along with other progressive farmers Hutterites have discovered that it is poor land use practice to graze cattle on high-grade pasture. It is far more profitable to plow up the good pasture land and produce grain crops on it. Cattle are now grazed only on land which is unsuitable for crop production.

Although the Hutterites have been very efficient in most of their farm practices, some of them realize that they still face certain operational problems. The chief difficulty is to devise a system for keeping an exact record of the home-grown grain that is used for feed by the various colony enterprises. Although on some colonies some enterprises do keep such a record, on no colony do all the enterprises keep such records. Without a total colony record it is impossible to determine the exact relative efficiency of each enterprise. On most colonies grain is stored in a central grain elevator and in a number of additional granaries, and each enterprise manager takes what he requires for his operations without recording the amount taken. Although most managers have a general idea of the amount of grain that they use, this is inadequate for a proper input-output analysis. In the past, an exact accounting system has not been necessary because the Hutterites have as a policy maintained all the enterprises regardless of their relative efficiency. This has been done primarily to maintain a long-range balanced operation and to provide employment for all the colony personnel. Today, competitive marketing and the ever-increasing costs of operation are making some colonies feel a need for more accurate accounting. For example, it would be very desirable to know which enterprise generates the greatest amount of revenue per dollar invested. With this knowledge, additional investment capital could be directed into the most profitable operations.

The problem of keeping an exact record of colony grown grain may appear to be simple, but it is in fact rather involved. On some colonies this could be solved by installing a scale to weigh the trucks before and after the loading of feed grain and a record could be kept for each enterprise. Such a scale would be very expensive, and a man would be needed to operate the scale and keep the records. This system would not work where, as in some colonies, an elaborate system of grain augers conveys the grain from the elevator or granary directly to the enterprise building where a grinder crushes the grain and automatically mixes it in the proper nutritional proportions. In such cases the amount of grain initially stored in the elevator can be determined, but there is no way of determining the exact amount remaining at any particular time. Although the total amount of concentrate that is used in the feed formulas is known, it would be a very complicated procedure to determine the total amount of grain used on this basis because there is a frequent change of formulas and several may even be used simultaneously to feed the livestock and poultry at different stages of growth. In any event, on many colonies there does not appear to be a practicable method of determining the exact amount of grain used by the various enterprises. These are some of the practical problems on the colonies, but if the need for proper cost-accounting becomes great enough, the Hutterites, who are very resourceful people, would undoubtedly find solutions.

Notes and References

1. The basic information for this chapter was obtained from discussions and interviews with many colony ministers and managers and from the writer's observation of Hutterite agricultural operations.
2. John W. Bennett, *Hutterian Brethren* (Stanford: Stanford University Press, 1967), p. 161.
3. This is the writer's impression after having compared the operations of many private farms with those of Hutterite colonies.
4. Farm machinery is discussed at greater length in the next chapter on crop production but see the machinery holdings of three representative colonies in Appendices D, E, and F.
5. Clarence L. Barber, ''Special Report on Prices of Tractors and Combines in Canada and Other Countries,'' *Royal Commission on Farm Machinery* (Ottawa: Queen's Printer for Canada, 1969), pp. 58, 148, 149.

CHAPTER 7

CROP PRODUCTION

Basis for Comparing Hutterite Farmland and Production with Other Manitoba Farms and Total Manitoba Farmland and Production

For census purposes Hutterite colonies are classified as "institutional farms" and each colony is considered a single farm unit. Although it is true that each colony does operate as a single economic unit, there are basic differences between a colony and the average Manitoba farm. In addition to differences in farm size and the number and scale of various farm enterprises, the most outstanding distinction is between the number of people on a colony and an ordinary farm. With very few exceptions, all farms in Manitoba are "family farms," that is, one family operates each farm. However, a Hutterite colony includes a number of families who operate their farmland on a cooperative basis. Therefore, although a colony operates as a single economic unit, as does an average farm, its population and management system are fundamentally different. The average number of families per colony in recent years has been approximately 15.[1] In other words, a typical Hutterite colony consists of 15 families operating the farm on a cooperative basis.

The operation and productivity of Hutterite colonies and other Manitoba farms can be compared in a number of ways. The writer has chosen, among others, productivity per acre, productivity per Hutterite family as compared to the average for Manitoba farms, and the Hutterite proportion of Manitoba production as related to their proportion of land owned and rented. In addition, in some instances a comparison has been made between the operation of the colony as a unit with that of an appropriate group of Manitoba farms. A comparison of productivity on the basis of labour force proved to be impracticable. Children, women, and older people provide a certain amount of labour for the colony but their contribution cannot be assessed accurately.

The scale of production on a Hutterite colony is so much greater than that of a typical Manitoba farm that a simple comparison of their

operations is almost meaningless. Therefore, for a realistic comparison, the Hutterite colony must be compared with either an equivalent
number of Manitoba farms or its output somehow must be subdivided
to place it on a comparable scale with the average for single Manitoba
farms. The consideration of the Hutterite family as a unit of production
makes it possible to make both of the above kinds of comparisons.
Productivity per Hutterite family is a suitable criterion for such comparison purposes for a number of reasons. Firstly, the typical Manitoba
"family farm" provides the basis of support for a single family, but a
typical Hutterite colony is the economic base for 15 families. Secondly,
as a result of communal living, each typical colony represents the
economic output of 15 families, but if the Hutterites ceased living on
colonies and wanted to continue farming in Manitoba, their only
alternative would be to establish individual family farms. In other
words, the present 48 colonies would become approximately 650
family farms (the approximate number of families in 1971). Therefore,
for comparison purposes, it is not inappropriate to consider the output
per Hutterite family with the average output of a Manitoba farm. This
concept also provides the basis for the corollary comparison, that is, the
output of a typical Hutterite colony should be the equivalent of the total
production of 15 Manitoba farms.[2] Since both comparisons are essentially a measure of the same thing, the per family comparison was used
almost exclusively in this study because it proved to be a simpler
procedure. A review of the literature indicates that neither of these
concepts have been used previously as the basis for comparison
purposes.[3]

This study has used the *1966 Census of Canada* definition for a
Manitoba farm, and production per Hutterite family or colony is compared with the average production per Manitoba farm.[4] Hence, the
"average Manitoba farm" is a statistical entity, unless otherwise
stated. Statistical data on Manitoba farms are available as overall
provincial totals and averages, and in addition the province is divided
into 14 crop districts and totals and averages are provided for each of
these.

Map 16 shows the 14 crop districts and the location of the Hutterite
colonies within these districts in 1968. Map 15 demonstrated that the
Hutterite colonies could be grouped into eight fairly distinct regions.
Unfortunately the official crop district boundaries cut through some of
these regions. For purposes of statistical comparison with district
farms, the crop districts of Map 16 are of greater consequence than the
Hutterite regions of Map 15. Although the crop districts do not coincide
with some of the Hutterite regional groupings, this does not create
serious difficulty except in the Brandon area where the four Hutterite

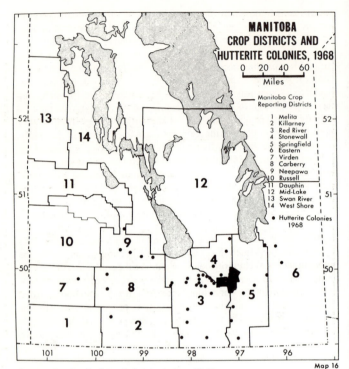

**MANITOBA
CROP DISTRICTS AND
HUTTERITE COLONIES, 1968**

0   20   40   60
Miles

—— Manitoba Crop
Reporting Districts

1 Melita
2 Killarney
3 Red River
4 Stonewall
5 Springfield
6 Eastern
7 Virden
8 Carberry
9 Neepawa
10 Russell
11 Dauphin
12 Mid-Lake
13 Swan River
14 West Shore

• Hutterite Colonies
1968

Map 16

Source: Yearbook of Manitoba Agriculture 1968

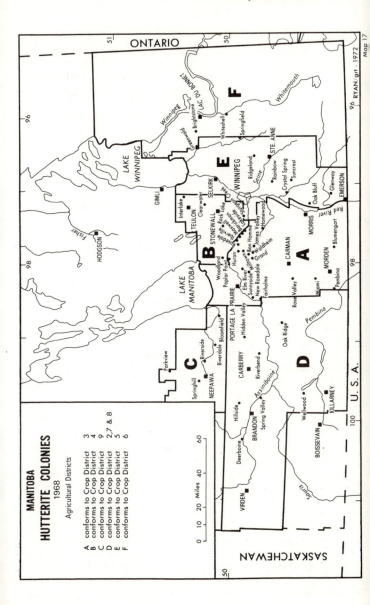

MANITOBA
HUTTERITE COLONIES
1968

Agricultural Districts

A conforms to Crop District 3
B conforms to Crop District 4
C conforms to Crop District 9
D conforms to Crop District 2, 7 & 8
E conforms to Crop District 5
F conforms to Crop District 6

RYAN. grt · 1972   Map 17

colonies are in three districts. To avoid singling out individual colonies within the crop districts and thereby unnecessarily revealing their production data, it was necessary to average out data for the three crop districts and thereby create a single composite crop district for the entire area. Map 17 shows this modification. The relevant crop districts so created have been designated as Agricultural Districts A to F.

Map 17 also shows the distribution of colonies in 1968 when there were only 43 of them.[5] It should be noted that Agricultural District A includes 21 colonies or almost one-half of the colonies at that time.

For the reasons outlined in the Introduction, 1968 is used as the base year for most of the statistical comparisons in this study.

Hutterite Farmland: Area and Land Use

In 1968 Manitoba Hutterites owned 158,930 acres of land or only .83 percent of the total farmland in the province (Table 7-1). They rented an additional 6,957 acres, and the total land owned and rented accounted for .87 percent of the provincial total. The amount rented is relatively insignificant since it was only 4.2 percent of total holdings of 165,887 acres. It should be noted that about half of the Hutterite farmland is in District A (Map 17), i.e., the area between Winnipeg and Portage la Prairie and extending from the Assiniboine River on the north to the U.S. border on the south.

Between 1968 and 1971 five more colonies were established and this raised the total amount of land owned by the Hutterites to 178,464 acres.[6] However, the average amount of land owned per colony remained almost the same.[7]

The average land area per colony in 1968 was 3,696 acres (Table 7-2). The size of colonies ranged from a high of 5,920 acres to a low of 1,979 acres.[8] It is noteworthy that only 7 colonies had over 4,500 acres and 10 had less than 3,000 acres. Hence, about 60 percent of the colonies had an acreage of between 3,000 and 4,500 acres.[9]

The size of Hutterite colonies needs to be looked at in relation to colony population. Tables 7-2 and 7-3 reveal several significant relationships of the Hutterite colonies. In 1968 there were 635 families in 43 colonies; the total population being 4,632. Hence the Hutterites had 36 acres per capita and 250 per family. However, the Manitoba farm population had 118 acres per capita and 500 per family farm. Therefore, the Hutterites had only 31 percent of the farmland per capita and 50 percent of the land of a typical Manitoba farm family (Tables 7-2 and 7-3). Another way of viewing this is to consider the size that a Hutterite colony would be if each Hutterite family had available to it the typical

TABLE 7-1

MANITOBA HUTTERITE COLONIES

AMOUNT OF FARMLAND OWNED AND RENTED, 1968[1]

Agric. district	No. of col's	Land owned (acres)	Land rented (acres)	Total owned & rented (acres)	Per cent owned	Per cent rented
A	21	80,689	3,815	84,504	95.5%	4.5%
B	4	14,427	560	14,987	96.3%	3.7%
C	5	21,087	1,372	22,459	93.9%	6.1%
D	4	16,170	760	16,930	95.5%	4.5%
E	6	18,712	200	18,912	98.9%	1.1%
F	3	7,845	250	8,095	96.9%	3.1%
TOTAL	43	158,930	6,957	165,887	95.8%	4.2%

Total Manitoba farmland 1966 (acres)[2]	Hutterite land owned as a % of total Manitoba farmland	Hutterite land owned and rented as a % of total Manitoba farmland
19,084,000	.83%	.87%

[1]Source: Data compiled from field work by J. Ryan.

[2]Source: *Yearbook of Manitoba Agriculture 1968*, p. 30. (Data are unavailable for total amount of farmland in 1968, but the difference for this comparison purpose would be insignificant.)

number of acres of an average farm. Table 7-3 shows that if this were the case the average size of colonies in the different districts of the province would range from 3,648 acres to 7,813 acres and that the average colony would have an acreage of 7,400. This of course is a hypothetical situation, nevertheless, it clearly dispels the popularly held view that Hutterite colonies are extremely large and that the Hutterites occupy more than their proportionate share of Manitoba farmland. It should be noted that if the Hutterites were to occupy their proportionate share, instead of the present .83 percent, they would own 1.7 percent of the Manitoba farmland.[10]

Table 7-4 shows the main types of agricultural land use in Manitoba and the Hutterite share of each. The percentage of land owned and rented by the Hutterites within each district should be examined in relation to the Hutterite proportion of each type of land use in the appropriate district. One of the most revealing facts in this table is that the Hutterites hold far more than their proportionate share of improved land within each district in the province. Conversely, their share of unimproved land is almost minimal. Of equally great significance is the fact that their amount of land in crops is considerably greater than their

TABLE 7-2

HUTTERITE POPULATION AND FARMLAND COMPARISONS 1968[1]

Agric. district	No. of col's	Total Hutt. pop.	Total no. of families	Average size of family	Average no. of families per colony	Average no. of acres per colony	Average no. of acres per capita [2]	Average no. of acres per family	Size of average district farm (acres) [3]
A	21	2,210	329	6.7	15.7	3,842	37	245	393
B	4	428	62	6.9	15.5	3,607	34	233	464
C	5	528	76	6.9	15.2	4,217	40	277	514
D	4	348	44	7.9	11	4,043	47	368	587
E	6	594	88	6.8	14.7	3,119	32	213	271
F	3	254	36	7.1	12	2,615	31	218	304
Total	43	4,362	635	6.9	14.8	3,696	36	250	480 (1966) 500 (1968)

[1]Source: Data compiled from field work by J. Ryan.

[2]Note that in 1966 the total farmland in Manitoba was 19,084,000 acres, the total farm population was 161,662, and the Manitoba per capita acreage was 118 (compiled from data in the Yearbook of Manitoba Agriculture 1968 pp. 30, 71). Hence the Hutterite per capita acreage is only 31% of the Manitoba average.

[3]Source: Yearbook of Manitoba Agriculture 1968, p. 31.
(data for average district farm is for 1966)

TABLE 7-3

NUMBER AND SIZE OF FARMS AND COLONIES

MANITOBA FARMS (1966)[1] AND HUTTERITE COLONIES (1968)[2]

Agric. dist-rict	Manitoba Farms		Hutterite Colonies					
	Number of farms	Acres per farm	No. of col's	Acres per col.	Av. no. of families per colony	Acres per family	3	4
A	5,795	393	21	3,842	15.7	245	62.3%	6,170
B	1,360	464	4	3,607	15.5	233	50.2%	7,192
C	2,221	514	5	4,217	15.2	277	53.9%	7,813
D	7,190	587	4	4,043	11	368	62.7%	6,457
E	6,209	271	6	3,119	14.7	213	78.6%	3,984
F	1,438	304	3	2,615	12	218	71.7%	3,648
Other districts	15,534	567	0	-	-	-	-	-
Total (Man.1966)	39,747	480	43	3,696	14.8	250	52.1%	7,104
Total (Man.1968)	38,200	500	43	3,696	14.8	250	50.0%	7,400

1Source: Yearbook of Manitoba Agriculture 1968, p. 31 (1968 data unavailable)

2Source: Data compiled from field work by J. Ryan (1966 data unavailable).

3Acres per Hutterite family as a per cent of average Manitoba farm acreage.

4... had the average number of acres of an average farm.

TABLE 7-4

LAND USE - SHOWING HUTTERITE SHARE OF EACH TYPE
MANITOBA FARMS (1966)[1] AND HUTTERITE COLONIES (1968)[2]

Agric. District	Crops			Fallow			Pasture			Other Improved Land		
	Man. total (000) acres	Hutt. (acres)	% Hutt.	Man. total (000) acres	Hutt. (acres)	% Hutt.	Man. total (000) acres	Hutt. (acres)	% Hutt.	Man. total (000) acres	Hutt.[3] (acres)	% Hutt.
A	1,677	65,568	3.9%	271	11,240	4.1%	69	4,843	7.0%	46	1,155	2.5%
B	295	11,292	3.8%	66	2,745	4.2%	32	495	1.5%	16	265	1.7%
C	518	15,545	3.0%	198	3,710	1.9%	54	1,655	3.1%	21	165	.8%
D	2,029	9,670	.5%	673	3,460	.5%	186	1,675	.9%	64	230	.4%
E	913	15,202	1.7%	219	1,585	.7%	70	660	.9%	36	240	.7%
F	136	5,210	3.8%	36	1,545	4.2%	30	690	2.3%	10	180	1.8%
Other districts	3,126	-	-	1,206		-	329	-	-	120	-	-
TOTAL	8,694	122,487	1.4%	2,669	24,285	.9%	770	10,018	1.3%	313	2,235	.7%

Agric. District	Total Improved Land			Unimproved Land			Total Manitoba farmland (000 acres)	Total Hutt. land owned & rented (acres)	% Hutt. land owned & rented	4
	Total Man. (000 acres)	Total Hutt. (acres)	% Hutt.	Man. total (000 acres)	Hutt. total (acres)	% Hutt.				
A	2,063	82,806	4.0%	215	1,698	.8%	2,278	84,504	3.7%	5.4%
B	409	14,797	3.6%	222	190	.09%	631	14,987	2.4%	4.4%
C	791	21,075	2.7%	351	1,384	.4%	1,142	22,459	2.0%	3.3%
D	2,952	15,035	.5%	1,228	1,895	.01%	4,180	16,930	.4%	.6%
E	1,238	17,687	1.4%	442	1,225	.3%	1,680	18,912	1.1%	1.4%
F	212	7,625	3.6%	225	470	.2%	437	8,095	1.9%	2.4%
Other districts	4,781	-	-	3,955	-	-	8,736	-	-	-
TOTAL	12,446	159,025	1.3%	6,638	6,862	.1%	19,084	165,887	.87%	1.6%

[1]Source: *Yearbook of Manitoba Agriculture 1968*, p. 30 (1968 data unavailable).

[2]Source: Data compiled from field work by J. Ryan (1966 data unavailable).

[3]The colony settlement area occupied by buildings, yards, roads, etc.

[4]The Hutterite proportionate share of land if each Hutterite family had the average number of acres of an average farm.

proportionate share in every district. Their share of cropland is especially high in Districts F and C. In District F the Hutterites own or rent 1.9 percent of the land, but they account for exactly twice this amount of cropland, i.e., 3.8 percent. In District C, on 2 percent of the land they account for 3 percent of the cropland.

Table 7-5 compares the proportion of each type of land use for Manitoba farms and for the Hutterite colonies. This table reveals several distinct differences between the land use patterns of the Hutterite colonies and Manitoba farms. It shows that Manitoba farms on the average have only 65 percent of their land improved, whereas Hutterite colonies have almost 96 percent of their land improved. Another striking difference is the fact that only 45.6 percent of Manitoba farms are in crops, whereas 73.8 percent of Hutterite land is in crops. Furthermore, the Hutterites have significantly more land in pasture— 6.0 percent as compared to 4.0 percent for Manitoba farms. However, the amount of land in summerfallow is almost the same for both the colonies and Manitoba farms—14.0 percent for Manitoba farms as compared to 14.6 percent for the Hutterite colonies.

Table 7-5 indicates that the differences in land use patterns are even greater within some of the Agricultural Districts than for the province as a whole. These differences are significant in all districts except in District A where there is a fairly close similarity in almost all types of land use. Most of the land in District A is highly suitable for crop production, and therefore it is not surprising that on the average close to three-quarters of the land is in crops in the case of both Manitoba farms and Hutterite colonies. All the other districts, however, include a considerable acreage which is unsuitable for crop production, as is indicated in the table. Note that District F, which borders on the Shield, has only 31.1 percent of its land in crops. Nevertheless, in each of these districts the Hutterites have a significantly high proportion of their land in crops. For example, in District F the Hutterites have 64.4 percent of their land in crops, as compared to 31.1 percent for all farms in the district. The high proportion of land in crops is probably one of the best indications that the Hutterites bought significantly better than average land in these districts. However, in the case of District F, although the colonies may now have better than average land, as pointed out in the chapter on physical environment, initially great efforts and expenditure were required to provide proper drainage and to clear the land of forest and peat.

Table 7-6 shows the detailed land use pattern for a typical Manitoba colony and the variations throughout the six provincial districts. It reveals that an average colony uses about 1,000 acres for oats, close to 800 acres for wheat, about 670 acres for barley, about 170 acres for hay, and only about 50 acres for other crops. This accounts for 2,728 acres of cropland. Of the remainder, an average colony has about 540 acres in summerfallow, 220 acres in pasture, 160 acres is non-agricultural land, and about 50 acres are occupied by the colony settlement. In 1968 this basic pattern was consistent in all the districts except District B where more barley was produced than oats. However, the overall land use pattern is remarkably uniform throughout the province. Even in districts where surrounding farmland is definitely marginal, such as District F, the basic Hutterite pattern remains unaltered.

Map 18 shows the land holdings of James Valley Colony in District A and the various types of land uses. This colony's land holdings and land uses are fairly representative of an average Manitoba colony. (See p. 202 for Map 18.)

Types of Crops Produced, Yields, and Total Production

The major types of crops produced by the Hutterite colonies are shown in Tables 7-6 and 7-7. Oats, wheat, and barley are the main grain crops; in 1968 these accounted for 38.3 percent, 29.0 percent, and 24.5 percent, respectively, of the crop acreage. Hay production accounted for 6.3 percent and all other crops accounted for only 1.9 percent of the crop acreage. Oats was the most important crop in terms of acreage in all districts except one. The percentage of cropland in oats ranged from 28.5 percent to 43.3 percent. Wheat was in second place in all districts except two, and its share of acreage ranged from 23.5 percent to 33.4 percent. Barley ranked third in four of the six districts with an acreage ranging from 17.4 percent to 31.5 percent.

In comparison with Manitoba farms in general, the Hutterites have a significantly smaller proportion of cropland in wheat, while the proportion in oats and barley is far greater than the provincial average (Table 7-7). Wheat accounts for 40.0 percent of all Manitoba cropland, but only 29.0 percent of Hutterite cropland. On the other hand, the Hutterite proportion of cropland in oats is more than twice the provincial average (38.3 percent) for the Hutterites as compared to 17.6 percent for Manitoba farms in general. Barley accounts for 9.5 percent of Manitoba cropland as compared to 24.5 percent of Hutterite cropland. The proportion of cropland in hay on Manitoba farms was more than twice the amount on Hutterite colonies, i.e., 13.4 percent as compared to 6.3 percent. An even more striking difference is in the comparison of the acreage in other crops. On Manitoba farms as a whole, other crops accounted for 19.5 percent of the acreage, but on Hutterite colonies

TABLE 7-5

LAND USE - SHOWING PROPORTION OF EACH TYPE

MANITOBA FARMS (1966)[1] AND HUTTERITE COLONIES (1968)[2]

Agric. districts	A				B				C				D			
	Man. farms		Hut. col's		Man. farms		Hut. col's		Man.		Hut. col's		Man. farms		Hut. col's	
Type of land use	acres (000)	%	acres	%	acres (000)	%	acres	%	acres (000)	%	acres	%	acres (000)	%	acres	%
Crops	1,677	73.6	65,568	77.6	295	46.8	11,292	75.3	518	45.4	15,545	69.2	2,029	48.5	9,670	57.1
Fallow	271	11.9	11,240	13.3	66	10.5	2,745	18.3	198	17.3	3,710	16.5	673	16.1	3,460	20.4
Pasture	69	3.0	4,843	5.7	32	5.1	495	3.3	54	4.7	1,655	7.4	186	4.5	1,675	9.9
Other improved land	46	2.0	1,155	1.4	16	2.5	265	1.8	21	1.8	165	.7	64	1.5	230	1.4
Total improved land	2,063	90.6	82,806	98.0	409	64.8	14,797	98.7	791	69.3	21,075	93.8	2,952	70.6	15,035	88.8
Unimproved land	215	9.4	1,698	2.0	222	35.2	190	1.3	351	30.7	1,384	6.2	1,228	29.4	1,895	11.2
Totals	2,278	100%	84,504	100%	631	100%	14,987	100%	1,142	100%	22,459	100%	4,180	100%	16,930	100%

Agric. districts / Type of land use	E Man. farms acres (000)	%	E Hut. col's acres	%	F Man. farms acres (000)	%	F Hut. col's acres	%	Other Districts Man. farms acres (000)	%	Other Districts Hut. col's acres	%	Total Manitoba farms acres (000)	%	Total Hutterite colonies acres	%
Crops	913	54.3	15,202	80.4	136	31.1	5,210	64.4	3,126	35.8	0	0	8,694	45.6%	122,487	73.8%
Fallow	219	13.0	1,585	8.4	36	8.2	1,545	19.1	1,206	13.8	0	0	2,669	14.0%	24,285	14.6%
Pasture	70	4.2	660	3.5	30	6.9	690	8.5	329	3.8	0	0	770	4.0%	10,018	6.0%
Other improved land	36	2.2	240	1.2	10	2.3	180	2.2	120	1.4	0	0	313	1.6%	2,235	1.4%
Total improved land	1,238	73.7	17,687	93.5	212	48.5	7,625	94.2	4,781	54.7	0	0	12,446	65.2%	159,025	95.8%
Unimproved land	442	26.3	1,225	6.5	225	51.5	470	5.8	3,955	45.3	0	0	6,638	34.8%	6,862	4.2%
Totals	1,680	100%	18,912	100%	437	100%	8,095	100%	8,736	100%	0	0	19,084	100%	165,887	100%

[1]Source: *Yearbook of Manitoba Agriculture 1968*, p. 30. (1968 data unavailable)

[2]Source: Data compiled from field work by J. Ryan. (1966 data unavailable.)

TABLE 7-6

LAND USE ON HUTTERITE COLONIES 1968[1]

Agric. districts	A			B			C			D		
Type of land use	% of colony area	% of crop-land	Average colony (acres)	% of colony area	% of crop-land	Average colony (acres)	% of colony area	% of crop-land	Average colony (acres)	% of colony area	% of crop-land	Average colony (acres)
Oats	29.7	38.3	1,142	21.4	28.5	774	27.9	40.4	1,179	21.6	38.1	860
Wheat	22.8	29.4	876	18.6	24.7	671	20.3	29.3	855	13.4	23.5	543
Barley	19.1	24.6	733	23.7	31.5	856	17.9	25.9	756	13.5	23.7	547
Hay	5.0	6.4	191	9.7	12.9	350	2.8	4.0	117	3.2	5.6	129
Other crops	1.0	1.3	39	1.8	2.4	65	.3	.4	11	5.2	9.1	210
TOTAL CROPS	77.6%	100%	2,981	75.3%	100%	2,716	69.2%	100%	2,918	57.1%	100%	2,309
Fallow	13.3		511	18.3		660	16.5		696	20.4		825
Pasture	5.7		219	3.3		119	7.4		312	9.9		400
Colony site[2]	1.4		54	1.8		65	.7		30	1.4		56
Unimproved land	2.0		77	1.3		47	6.2		261	11.2		453
TOTAL	100%		3,842	100%		3,607	100%		4,217	100%		4,043

Agric. districts	E			F			Average for Manitoba Colonies		
Type of land use	% of colony area	% of crop-land	Average colony (acres)	% of colony area	% of crop-land	Average colony (acres)	% of colony area	% of crop-land	Average colony (acres)
Oats	34.8	43.3	1,086	24.7	38.4	647	28.3%	38.3%	1,045
Wheat	26.9	33.4	636	19.1	29.7	500	21.4	29.0%	791
Barley	14.0	17.4	436	16.7	25.9	436	18.1	24.5%	668
Hay	3.3	4.2	105	3.5	5.4	91	4.6	6.3%	172
Other crops	1.4	1.7	43	.4	.6	10	1.4	1.9%	52
TOTAL CROPS	80.4	100%	2,508	64.4%	100%	1,684	73.8%	100%	2,728
Fallow	8.4		262	19.1		499	14.6%		539
Pasture	3.5		109	8.5		222	6.0%		222
Colony site[2]	1.2		37	2.2		58	1.4%		52
Unimproved land	6.5		203	5.8		152	4.2%		155
TOTAL	100%		3,119	100%		2,615	100%		3,696

[1] Source: Data compiled from field work by J. Ryan.

[2] The colony site constitutes the area occupied by colony buildings, yards, roads, etc. This category is listed as "other improved land" on other tables.

TABLE 7-7

PROPORTION OF CROPLAND IN VARIOUS TYPES OF CROPS

MANITOBA FARMS (1966)[1] AND HUTTERITE COLONIES (1968)[2]

Agric. district	Manitoba Farms										
	Total crop acres (000)	Wheat		Oats		Barley		Hay		Other crops	
		acres (000)	%	acres (000)	%	acres (000)	%	acres (000)	%	acres (000)	%
A	1,677	603	36.0	253	15.1	114	6.8	114	6.8	data	35.3
B	295	80	27.1	73	24.7	41	13.9	43	14.6	not	19.7
C	518	201	38.8	119	23.0	66	12.7	67	12.9	avail-	12.6
D	2,029	968	47.7	377	18.6	139	6.9	263	13.0	able	13.8
E	913	273	29.9	221	24.2	104	11.4	205	22.5		12.0
F	136	22	16.2	26	19.1	4	2.9	83	61.0		.8
Other districts	3,126	1,333	42.6	461	14.7	362	11.6	390	12.5		18.6
TOTAL	8,694	3,480	40.0	1,530	17.6	830	9.5	1,165	13.4	1,689	19.5

Hutterite Colonies

Agric. district	Total crop Acres	Wheat		Oats		Barley		Hay		Other crops	
		acres	%	acres	%	acres	%	acres	%	acres	%
A	65,568	19,305	29.4	25,130	38.3	16,095	24.6	4,165	6.4	873	1.3
B	11,292	2,790	24.7	3,223	28.5	3,557	31.5	1,453	12.9	269	2.4
C	15,545	4,555	29.3	6,280	40.4	4,035	25.9	620	4.0	55	.4
D	9,670	2,270	23.5	3,685	38.1	2,295	23.7	540	5.6	880	9.1
E	15,202	5,070	33.4	6,585	43.3	2,649	17.4	640	4.2	258	1.7
F	5,210	1,550	29.7	2,000	38.4	1,350	25.9	280	5.4	30	.6
Other districts	0	0		0		0		0		0	
TOTAL	122,487	35,540	29.0	46,903	38.3	29,981	24.5	7,698	6.3	2,365	1.9

[1]Source: <u>Yearbook of Manitoba Agriculture 1966 and 1968</u> (complete 1968 data unavailable).

[2]Source: Data compiled from field work by J. Ryan (1966 data not available).

only 1.9 percent is devoted to other crops. This difference is especially noticeable in Districts A and B.

Such differences between the production patterns of typical Manitoba farms and Hutterite colonies are evident in all districts of the province. In several districts the contrasts for some categories are even greater in some instances but less in others. In Agricultural District A the differences are less in the production patterns of wheat and hay, but they are more extreme in the case of oats, barley, and other crops. This is the district in Manitoba that produces most of the province's special crops such as flax, sugar beets, corn, sunflowers, and rapeseed. The Hutterite contribution to these crops is practically nil, and this accounts for the gross difference of this district's 35.3 percent acreage in other crops as compared to the Hutterite 1.3 percent. Other notable differences occur in Districts E and F where hay on typical Manitoba farms accounts for 22.5 percent of the cropland in District E and 61.0 percent in District F, in comparison with the Hutterite proportion of only 4.2 percent in District E and 5.4 percent in District F. Most of District F and the northern part of District E consists of marginal agricultural land which in most instances is suited for only hay production. However, the Hutterites by selecting some of the best agricultural land in these districts have been able to produce grain crops in the usual Hutterite proportions.

1. Oats

In 1968 the Hutterite colonies produced 2,532,785 bushels of oats which was 3.1 percent of Manitoba's total production of 81,000,000 bushels (Table 7-8). They managed to do this on 3.0 percent of Manitoba's acreage in oats, with a slightly higher than average yield of 54.0 bushels per acre as compared with the average for Manitoba of 51.3 bushels per acre. The Hutterite yields are close to the average yields in all districts, and where these are lower so are those of the Hutterites, e.g., in Districts E and F.

The total Hutterite production of oats is far greater than their proportionate share of farmland. In 1968 they owned and rented only .87 percent of the province's farmland, but they accounted for 3.1 percent of Manitoba's total production of oats. Their share of production in several districts is even more remarkable. In District D they produced 9.8 percent of the oats on only .4 percent of the district's land. In District A they accounted for 8.3 percent of the production on 3.7 percent of the land, in District C their production was 5.5 percent of the total on 2.0 percent of the land, and in District E they produced 5.8 percent of the oats on 1.9 percent of the land.

2. Wheat

The Hutterites produced 1,069,295 bushels of wheat in 1968 (Table 7-9). This accounted for 1.2 percent of Manitoba's total production. The Hutterite wheat yield was 30.1 bushels per acre, considerably higher than the provincial average of 26.8. With the exception of one district the Hutterites had higher than average wheat yields in all parts of the province.

Although they produced more than their proportionate share of wheat, i.e., 1.2 percent of the production on .87 percent of the land, their total wheat output is not as disproportionately large as in the case of oats. In fact, their wheat production is exceptionally large in only two districts—District D where they account for 2.8 percent of the production on .4 percent of the land and District F where their production is 4.9 percent on 1.9 percent of the land.

3. Barley

In 1968 the Hutterites produced 1,233,235 bushels of barley or 2.9 percent of the provincial total of 43,000,000 bushels (Table 7-10). As in the case of oats and wheat, the Hutterite barley yield was higher than the Manitoba average—41.1 bushels per acre as compared to 36.8 for the province as a whole. The Hutterite barley yield was higher than that of Manitoba farms in four out of the six districts, but there was a wide variation of yields—from a low of 23.7 to a high of 53.6.

The Hutterite share of barley production was notably large in four districts. In District F the Hutterites accounted for 17.3 percent of the barley production on 1.9 percent of that district's farmland. This becomes even more impressive when it is recalled that there are only three Hutterite colonies in District F, and that these are relatively small. Furthermore, these colonies actually experienced quite low yields in 1968, i.e., only 23.7 bushels per acre. In Districts A, C, and D the Hutterites also produced much more than their proportionate share of barley. In District A they produced 9.1 percent of the barley on 3.7 percent of the land, in District C they accounted for 7.4 percent of the production on 2.0 percent of the land, and in District D they produced 11.7 percent of the barley on .4 percent of the land.

4. Other Crops

As indicated in previous sections, the Hutterites produce small amounts of other crops (Table 7-11). Crops other than oats, wheat, and barley have been grown by only a few colonies and more or less on an

TABLE 7-8

PRODUCTION OF OATS 1968

MANITOBA FARMS[1] AND HUTTERITE COLONIES[2]

Agric. dist- rict	Manitoba			Hutterite Colonies				
	Acres (000)	Yield (bus. per acre)	Production (000 bus.)	Acres	Yield (bus. per acre)	Production (bus.)	Hutt. % of Man. acreage	Hutt. % of Man. production
A	320	55.1	17,627	25,130	58.4	1,468,475	7.9%	8.3%
B	74	56.2	4,156	3,223	54.8	176,620	4.4%	4.3%
C	113	54.8	6,191	6,280	54.1	339,500	5.6%	5.5%
D	377	55.6	20,954	3,685	55.6	205,025	9.8%	9.8%
E	234	40.7	9,526	6,585	42.2	278,165	2.8%	2.9%
F	28	39.5	1,106	2,000	32.5	65,000	7.1%	5.8%
Other districts	434	49.4	21,440	0	-	0	0	0
Total	1,580	51.3	81,000	46,903	54.0	2,532,785	3.0%	3.1%

[1]Source: *Yearbook of Manitoba Agriculture 1968*, p. 9.

[2]Source: Data compiled from field work by J. Ryan.

TABLE 7-9

PRODUCTION OF WHEAT, 1968

MANITOBA FARMS[1] AND HUTTERITE COLONIES[2]

Agric. district	Manitoba			Hutterite Colonies				
	Acres (000)	Yield (bus. per acre)	Production (000 bus.)	Acres	Yield (bus. per acre)	Production (bus.)	Hutt. % of Man. acreage	Hutt. % of Man. production
A	595	27.3	16,216	19,305	31.9	616,735	3.2%	3.8%
B	73	29.1	2,126	2,790	33.6	93,725	3.8%	4.4%
C	216	28.1	6,076	4,555	31.5	143,600	2.1%	2.4%
D	872	27.4	23,906	2,270	29.4	66,735	2.6%	2.8%
E	296	26.4	7,800	5,070	20.8	105,500	1.7%	1.4%
F	32	27.2	872	1,550	27.7	43,000	4.8%	4.9%
Other districts	1,316	25.8	34,004	0	-	0	0	0
Total	3,400	26.8	91,000	35,540	30.1	1,069,295	1.0%	1.2%

[1]Source: *Yearbook of Manitoba Agriculture 1968*, p. 7.

[2]Source: Data compiled from field work by J. Ryan.

TABLE 7-10

PRODUCTION OF BARLEY 1968

MANITOBA FARMS[1] AND HUTTERITE COLONIES[2]

Agric. district	Manitoba			Hutterite Colonies				
	Acres (000)	Yield (bus. per acre)	Production (000 bus.)	Acres	Yield (bus. per acre)	Production (bus.)	Hutt. % of acreage	Hutt. % of Man. production
A	211	35.7	7,542	16,095	42.8	688,985	7.6%	9.1%
B	72	38.7	2,788	3,557	28.8	102,440	4.9%	3.7%
C	65	37.1	2,414	4,035	44.1	178,000	6.2%	7.4%
D	262	40.0	10,485	2,295	53.6	123,050	8.8%	11.7%
E	124	33.1	4,100	2,649	41.1	108,760	2.1%	2.7%
F	5	37.0	185	1,350	23.7	32,000	27.0%	17.3%
Other districts	431	35.9	15,486	0	-	0	0	0
Total	1,170	36.8	43,000	29,981	41.1	1,233,235	2.6%	2.9%

[1]Source: Yearbook of Manitoba Agriculture 1968, p. 10.

[2]Source: Data compiled from field work by J. Ryan.

TABLE 7-11

PRODUCTION OF OTHER CROPS 1968

MANITOBA FARMS[1] AND HUTTERITE COLONIES[2]

Crops	Manitoba (acres)	Hutterite colonies (acres)	Hutt. % of Manitoba acreage
Corn - grain	2,500	0	0%
Corn - silage	29,500	225	.76%
Flax	820,000	410	.05%
Peas	33,000	90	.27%
Potatoes	26,500	300	1.13%
Rapeseed	91,000	255	.28%
Rye	120,000	790	.66%
Other Crops	415,779	295 (gardens)	.07%
Total	1,538,279	2,365	.15%

[1]Source: *Yearbook of Manitoba Agriculture 1968*, p. 6.

[2]Source: Data compiled from field work by J. Ryan.

TABLE 7-12

VALUE OF FARM MACHINERY 1968

MANITOBA FARMS[1] AND HUTTERITE COLONIES[2]

Agric. dist-rict	Manitoba Farms		Hutterite Colonies		
	Average value per farm	Average value per acre	Average value per colony	Average value per acre	Hutt. colony as a % of average farm per acre
A	$12,294	$ 31.28	$87,367	$ 21.96	70.2%
B	$10,758	23.19	79,506	21.22	91.5%
C	$ 9,851	19.17	80,446	17.91	93.4%
D	$12,738	21.70	80,994	19.14	88.2%
E	$ 7,967	29.40	60,275	19.12	65.0%
F	$ 5,173	17.02	53,408	19.79	116.3%
Other dist-ricts	$ 9,966	$ 17.58	0	0	-
Man. average	$10,268	$ 20.54	$77,623	$ 21.00	102.2%

[1]Source: - Yearbook of Manitoba Agriculture 1968, p. 34.
  - Farm Input Price Indexes, Statistics Canada, Dec. 1971.
  The Yearbook lists farm machinery prices for 1966, but a price index formula of 107.3% was applied to adjust the prices to 1968 values.

[2]Source: Data compiled from field work by J. Ryan.

experimental basis. However, it seems that unless the Hutterites increase their land holdings considerably, they will continue to concentrate on the production of oats, wheat, and barley. These grains are grown primarily for feed and serve as the basis for livestock and poultry enterprises. Most colonies simply do not have enough land to devote to other crops, if they are to maintain their present livestock and poultry undertakings.

In summary, the main crops produced by the Hutterites are oats, wheat and barley. Although other crops in addition to these are of significance on typical Manitoba farms, the Hutterites produce these three crops almost exclusively because they are used mainly for feed on the colonies. The Hutterites have higher yields in these three grain crops than the average yields for the province. The Hutterites also devote a significantly larger proportion of their farmland to these crops than do typical farmers. Consequently, because of these two reasons the Hutterite proportion of the province's production of oats, wheat, and barley is significantly greater than the proportion of Manitoba farmland that they own.

Farm Mechanization

On a typical mixed farm, next to the cost of the land the most costly investment is in farm machinery. This is also true of Hutterite colonies. In 1968 the average Hutterite colony had an estimated investment of $77,623 in farm machinery (Table 7-12).[11] The totals do not vary greatly from district to district, except in District F, where the three colonies involved are relatively small and this is reflected in the smaller amount of machinery that they own. However, there is a wide range from colony to colony in the amount invested in machinery. Although the average investment is $77,623, this ranges from a low of $30,150 to a high of $183,300. Most colonies with a relatively low investment in machinery are those that are smaller than average, or those with a lot of machinery that is rather old, or those with a lot of machinery that was purchased secondhand. The colonies with a high investment are usually those that make a practice of purchasing new machinery. Invariably these colonies are larger than average and financially better established.

Appendices D, E, and F show the type of machinery to be found on Hutterite colonies by listing all the farm machinery owned by three different colonies. This includes the colony with the highest investment in machinery, the colony with the lowest investment, and a colony that is representative of average investment. The average colony has 8

TABLE 7-13

INVESTMENT IN FARM MACHINERY 1968

PER MANITOBA FARM[1] AND PER HUTTERITE FAMILY[2]

Agric. dist- rict	Average invest- ment per Manitoba farm	Average no. of acres per farm	Average invest- ment per Hutterite colony	Average no. of families per colony	Average invest- ment per family	Average no. of acres per Hutt. family	Hutt. family invest- ment as a % of average farm	Hutt. family acreage as a % of average farm acreage
A	$12,294	393	$84,367	15.7	$5,374	245	43.7%	62.3%
B	10,758	464	79,506	15.5	5,129	233	47.7%	50.2%
C	9,851	514	80,446	15.2	5,293	277	53.7%	53.9%
D	12,738	587	80,994	11	7,363	368	57.8%	62.7%
E	7,967	271	60,275	14.7	4,100	213	51.5%	78.6%
F	5,173	304	53,408	12	4,451	218	86.0%	71.7%
Man. Total	$10,268	500	$77,623	14.8	5,245	250	51.1%	50.0%

[1]Source: Yearbook of Manitoba Agriculture 1968 (with amendments as listed in Table 7-12).

[2]Source: Data compiled from field work by J. Ryan.

tractors, 4 combines, 4 swathers, 3 discer-drills, 3 cultivators, 1 plow, and various other machines. A colony with a relatively low investment will have slightly fewer machines, and these will usually be older. On the other hand, a colony with a high machinery investment may have as many as 15 tractors and 6 or 8 combines; many of these will be new and valued at over $10,000 each. In addition, each colony usually has 6 or 8 trucks and almost invariably a ''Travelall'' station wagon. However, motor vehicles are not included in farm machinery investment.

On a per acre basis the Hutterite investment in farm machinery is only slightly more than the average for all Manitoba farms (Table 7-12). However, the difference is considerable in certain districts, in particular Districts A and E. In District A the Hutterites have an average investment of $21.96 an acre, but the average farm in this district has an investment of $31.28. District A produces most of Manitoba's special crops, and specialized machinery is needed for these crops. This is primarily the cause for the higher investment per acre. The Hutterites who do not produce special crops keep their investment very close to the overall Hutterite average of $21.00 an acre. District E contains many small farms around Winnipeg—the average farm is of only 271 acres (Table 7-3). Hence although the total value of the machinery is less than the provincial average, the small acreage of the farms results in a high per acre investment.

Comparing the investment in farm machinery of Hutterite colonies and average Manitoba farms on a per acre basis reveals only one aspect of the economic implications of machinery investment. Since practically all Manitoba farms are family farms, this means that usually a single farm family is responsible for each farm's machinery investment. However, in the case of a Hutterite colony, the machinery investment is shared by several families. Table 7-13 shows the investment in farm machinery on a family basis for the Hutterites and compares this with the average farm investment. Although the data do not make it possible to state that the average Manitoba farm is in fact a family farm, for all practical purposes, this is the case. The table also compares the acreage of the average ''family farm'' with the acreage per Hutterite family.

Table 7-13 shows that the average Manitoba farm (or average farm family) has an investment of $10,268 in farm machinery as compared with an investment of only $5,245 per Hutterite family. However, a Hutterite family has a much smaller acreage than the average farm. Although the Hutterite family has a machinery investment of only 51.1 percent of the average farm, it also has only 50.0 percent of the average farm's acreage. The comparison of machinery investment does not vary greatly from district to district, except in Districts A and F. In District A the Hutterite family's investment is only 43.7 percent of this district's average farm, but as pointed out in a previous section, many farmers in this district have an extra investment in machinery because of their emphasis on special crops. In the case of District F, the average farm is not as highly mechanized because of its large proportion of marginal land. However, the Hutterites have located on relatively better land and hence have almost an average investment in machinery.

Although the Hutterite family has only one-half the land and one-half the investment in machinery of the average farm on an overall provincial basis, these proportions vary considerably in several districts. In District E, on a family basis the Hutterites have 78.6 percent of the land of an average farm, but they have only 51.5 percent of the machinery investment. From the crop production records for this district (Tables 7-8, 7-9, and 7-10) it is evident that on the average the Hutterite colonies are more productive than the average farms. Hence it appears that the Hutterites can manage at this high level of efficiency with much less than their proportionate share of machinery investment. This is obviously a significant observation, and it holds true for all districts except District F.

One other method of comparing the farm machinery investment of Hutterite colonies and Manitoba farms is to compare the colony investment with the total investment of an equivalent number of individual farms (Table 7-14). This is essentially the same approach as that of conducting a per family comparison, but it places it in a somewhat different dimension. For statistical comparison purposes it has been possible to consider the Hutterite operation on a per family basis, but the reality of the situation is that the colony operates as a single economic unit. It should be useful to compare the colony as a single operational unit with an equivalent number of individual farms. Although this comparison can be done statistically, it is equally unrealistic since an aggregate of individual farms can in no way be considered the equivalent of a single economic unit. Obviously there are shortcomings to both approaches, but if the limitations are recognized, both approaches are valid.

Several conclusions can be drawn from these various comparisons of machinery investment. It is evident that on a per family basis the Hutterites have a much smaller investment in machinery than the average family farm. On the other hand, a Hutterite family's share of land is much less than that of the average farm. Hence if the Hutterites owned as much land as an equivalent number of average farms (based on the family farm concept), they would undoubtedly have to increase their amount of farm machinery. However, because of the rationalization that is possible through large-scale operations it is improbable that the Hutterites would have to purchase as much machinery as exists on an equivalent number of individual small farms. In other words, the single large economic unit would introduce an economy of scale making it possible for the Hutterite machinery to be used more efficiently than that of a series of small farms. In any event, on a comparable basis, the Hutterites, with less investment in machinery than the average farm, operate in general as efficiently as average Manitoba farms, and in most districts more efficiently.

The Operation of the Crop Production Enterprise

The crop production enterprise is under the direction of the farm manager. This is an extremely responsible position, and the farm manager is third in importance in the colony administration, being outranked only by the colony manager and the minister. The farm manager is elected by the male congregation of the colony, and he may hold the job for life providing he is competent. In addition to being responsible for the crop production enterprise, he is also in charge of the colony labour force and the apprenticeship programme of the older boys.

During the winter and early spring the farm manager plans the seeding programme and the overall land use of the colony fields for the next crop season. He does this in consultation with the colony manager and the minister. Such consultation and joint planning is essential because of the large number of factors to be considered. Although the farm manager knows the soil capability and the productivity of the various fields, it is the colony manager who knows the grain requirements for the various livestock and poultry enterprises.

Before the spring field operations commence the farm manager makes certain that all the farm machinery has been checked over, repaired if necessary, greased, and that it is fully operational. As mentioned previously, the farm manager assigns the colony's tractors to the unmarried men and to boys over the age of fifteen. They are then responsible for the operation, maintenance and care of these machines. School regulations permit the young boys to take up to six weeks off from classes to help with the spring work.

Hutterite field operations do not in any way differ from general farming practices. Perhaps the only difference that there might be is that the Hutterites usually operate larger machines and equipment than the average small farmer. However, the larger and more successful farmers operate the same type of machinery as do the Hutterites.

In spring the fields are first prepared for seeding in the usual manner,

TABLE 7-14

COMPARISON OF VALUE OF FARM MACHINERY ON A HUTTERITE
COLONY[1] AND AN EQUIVALENT NUMBER OF MANITOBA FARMS[2] 1968

Agric. district	Average no. of families per colony	Average value of machinery per colony	Equivalent no. of Manitoba farms[3]	Total value of machinery for an equivalent no. of Man. farms	Hutt. value of mach. as a % of value of mach. of equiv. no. of farms
A	15.7	$84,367	15.7	$193,016	43.7%
B	15.5	79,506	15.5	166,749	47.7%
C	15.2	80,446	15.2	149,735	53.7%
D	11	80,994	11	140,118	57.8%
E	14.7	60,275	14.7	117,115	51.5%
F	12	53,408	12	62,076	86.0%
Man. average	14.8	$77,623	14.8	$151,966	51.1%

[1]Source: Data compiled from field work by J. Ryan.

[2]Source: Data from column 2 of Table 7-12 multiplied by data from column 4 of this table, e.g. District A: $12,294. x 15.7 = $193,016.

[3]The equivalent number of Manitoba farms to a Hutterite colony is based on the family farm concept.

and then the seeding takes place. The colonies have different policies about the use of fertilizer, but typically they use as much fertilizer as other successful farmers. While a few colonies still do not use any fertilizer, most do, and some are in the forefront in the province in its use. In 1968 the average expenditure for the 43 colonies on fertilizer and chemical weed spray was $11,613 (Table 14-4). This ranged from no official declared expenditure on some colonies to over $40,000 on others. However, almost half of the colonies spent over $10,000 on these items, and primarily on fertilizer. Rather than do their own weed spraying, some colonies find it to their benefit to have their fields sprayed from an airplane. The contract is usually given to a local firm specializing in this type of work.[12]

Before grain harvesting begins the Hutterites try to complete their haying operations. Since there is a relatively small acreage in hay on most colonies, this can usually be accomplished in one or two weeks. In addition to cutting hay on their own land some colonies rent hayland or make arrangements to cut the hay on government road allowances.

As on other farms, the busiest time of the year on the colonies is during the grain harvest when each day of good weather is of crucial importance. Swathing and combining begin in early August and harvesting lasts for several weeks. In a year when rains occur frequently during the late summer and fall, the harvest may not be fully completed until late October and may extend into November. As sometimes happens in western Canada, in a year of bad weather some fields may not be harvested at all before the snow comes. Hence long hours and double shifts are the order of the day during good weather. With a large labour force and large machinery the Hutterites have a definite advantage at this time of year over the average farmer.

During the harvest period practically all the male members of the colony share in the various jobs connected with harvesting and field operations. This includes the managers of the various farm enterprises, the colony manager, and the minister. Admittedly, the first responsibility of the enterprise managers is the operation of their own enterprises, but sometimes some of the work can be delegated to the young boys and this may allow the managers to work a few hours in the fields. Hence at the beginning of each day the colony manager and the farm manager must coordinate the activities of the labour force. Since combining is such a responsible operation, the farm manager assigns this to the most experienced men, usually to those who can work full-time at it. However, swathing and hauling grain can be done by any of the colony men. As soon as a field is harvested it is disced or plowed. In addition, the land in summerfallow has to be cultivated regularly to preserve moisture and to kill the weeds.

It is important that all the harvested fields are disced, plowed, or cultivated and prepared for next year's seeding before winter sets in. All the machinery has to be checked over, and sometimes overhauled and repaired. Much of the maintenance and repair work can be done during the winter in the machine shop or the colony garage.

At the end of the summer's work the farm manager assesses the performance of the colony machinery. He must decide which machinery should be replaced and what new machinery is required. It is his responsibility to be familiar with the different types of new machinery on the market. Naturally he tries to observe how different machines operate and function on other colonies and on other farms. Once his machinery report is completed, he presents it to the colony manager and minister. The colony manager considers the proposed capital expenditure on machinery in the light of the needs and requests of all other colony enterprises. Since only a certain amount of capital is available, priorities have to be established on the basis of overall colony needs. Hence the farm manager may not get approval for the purchase of all the machinery that he would like. Furthermore, after the colony manager and minister review his requests, the proposals for major expenditures must be presented at a general meeting of the colony members. Since

TABLE 7-15

VALUE OF HUTTERITE

GRAIN PRODUCTION 1968

Type of Grain	No. of Bushels[1]	Price per bus.[2]	Value	%
Oats	2,532,785	$ .60	$1,519,671	37.4%
Wheat	1,069,295	$1.40	$1,497,013	36.8%
Barley	1,233,235	$ .85	$1,048,250	25.8%
Total value of grain produced			$4,064,934	100%

[1]Source: Data compiled from field work by J. Ryan.

[2]Source: *Yearbook of Manitoba Agriculture 1968*, p. 6.

TABLE 7-16

HUTTERITE GRAIN DISPOSAL 1968

	Value	% in each category
Total value of grain sold[1]	$ 966,765	23.8%
Total value of grain kept for feed[2]	3,098,169	76.2%
Total value of grain produced[3]	4,064,934	100%

[1]Source: Data compiled from the financial reports on each colony for 1968, as prepared by Meyers, Dickens, Norris, Penny & Company, the accounting firm employed by the Hutterite colonies.

[2]Source: Data obtained by subtracting value of grain sold from total value of grain produced.

[3]Source: Data obtained from Table 7-15.

TABLE 7-17

MANITOBA HUTTERITE COLONIES

GROSS SALES INCOME FROM THE CROP ENTERPRISE, 1968

Gross sales income from all enterprises	$11,598,282.40
Gross sales income from the crop enterprise	$ 966,765.06
Gross sales income from the crop enterprise as a % of total gross sales income	8.3%
No. of colonies reporting sales of grain	42
No. of families on these colonies	614
Average gross sales income per colony	$ 23,018.22
Average gross sales income per family	$ 1,554.28

Source: Data compiled by J. Ryan from the financial reports on each colony for 1968, as prepared by Meyers, Dickens, Norris, Penny & Company, the accounting firm employed by the Hutterite colonies.

the various enterprise managers may have requests for capital expenditures of their own, the farm manager must be able to justify all his requests and get the approval of the majority of the colony members. Following this, the selection and purchase of additional machinery is usually done jointly by the farm manager and the colony manager.

Significance of Crop Production to the Colony Economy

Crop production is of fundamental importance to the economy of every colony. Table 7-15 shows that the total value of the oats, wheat, and barley produced by the 43 colonies in 1968 was $4,064,934. Oats accounted for 37.4 percent of this, wheat accounted for 36.8 percent, and barley 25.8 percent. This is an average of $94,533 per colony. This of course is the total value of the grain produced and not the amount actually received from grain sales. In 1968 the colonies received only $966,765 from grain sales (Table 7-16 and 7-17). So in terms of value, the Hutterites sold only 23.8 percent of the grain produced and kept the remainder for feed purposes. On the basis of actual income received, grain sales ranked third in importance and accounted for only 8.3 percent of the total income of the colonies (Appendix G). However, if the total value of the crops produced is considered, i.e., $4,064,934, this would place grain almost in first place in terms of income. Of course all the grain produced would never in fact be sold. First, because of grain quota restrictions, and second, so long as the Hutterites are engaged in the production of livestock and poultry, the bulk of the grain produced is required for feed.

Since most of the grain produced is used for feed, government grain quotas are usually of little significance to the Hutterites.[13] However, many colonies produce more grain than they require for feed, and the surplus grain is sold. Many colonies manage to sell their full quota of wheat year after year. On the other hand, many need to purchase additional grain for feed, especially barley.

In 1968 the average gross income per colony from the sale of grain was $23,018.22, and per family it was $1,554.28 (Table 7-17). It should be noted that in that year one colony used all of its grain for feed purposes and did not make any sales. As shown by Appendix G, the gross income from the hog and chicken enterprises greatly out-classed the income from grain sales. However, since over three-quarters of the grain is usually kept for feed purposes, this is vital to the operation of the other colony enterprises. Hence in many ways crop production is at the very basis of the entire Hutterite economy.

Notes and References

1. This is based on data in the "Hutterian Brethren Church Genealogy Record," compiled by Reverend Jacob Kleinsasser and kept at the Crystal Spring Colony, Ste. Agathe, Manitoba.

2. The concept of the Hutterite family as a production unit and as the basis for both types of comparisons with Manitoba farms was discussed with the members of several Hutterite colonies. In their estimation this was a fair and realistic basis for comparison purposes. This approach was also discussed with Mr. M. Daciw, Agricultural Statistician for the Manitoba Department of Agriculture. Mr. Daciw stated that as far as he knew the method had never been used before, however, it seemed to be a logical and common sense approach. He pointed out that there are shortcomings to all statistical abstractions but there did not seem to be any unusual difficulties with this procedure. Moreover, he felt that this method would reveal some very interesting comparisons.

3. John W. Bennett in his *Hutterian Brethren* (1967) has a chapter entitled "Hutterian Enterprise and Individual Enterprise," pp. 227-241, but this compares individual colonies with selected nearby farms. The comparison is that of a single colony to a single farm, and no attempt is made to compare a colony with an equivalent number of farms or to compare the output per Hutterite family with that of a single farm. A review of the literature shows that other writers have not attempted such comparisons either.

4. The *1966 Census of Canada* definition of a farm is ". . . an agricultural holding of one acre or more with sales of agricultural products, during the 12-month period prior to the census, of $50 or more." This same definition is used by the *Yearbook of Manitoba Agriculture*, and most comparisons in this study are based on data from either the *Yearbook* or the *Canada Census*.

5. The colonies of Hidden Valley, Oak Ridge, Riverbend, and Suncrest were established in 1969 and Woodland Colony was established in 1970 (Map 12).

6. Data compiled from field work by the writer.

7. In 1968 the average amount of land owned by the 43 colonies was 3,696 acres per colony; in 1971 the average for the 48 colonies was 3,718 acres. This was a result of the new colonies being slightly larger plus the fact that some of the other colonies managed to purchase small amounts of additional land.

8. Spring Valley Colony located southeast of Brandon had the largest acreage, and Rainbow Colony located about 15 miles southeast of Winnipeg had the smallest acreage. Rainbow Colony's small size

is due to its proximity to the Winnipeg urban area which has caused high land prices. In 1968 the colony purchased an additional 371 acres at $150 an acre. However, in an interview with the writer on March 26, 1972, Sam Hofer, the colony manager, stated that the present policy of the colony is not to invest any more capital in land, but instead to enlarge the operations of some of the farm enterprises. Any additional grain required for feed purposes would then be purchased. An indication of good farm management is the fact that with the exception of 30 acres devoted to the colony settlement and another 30 acres of marginal land in pasture, all the land in the colony is cultivated and in agricultural use.

9. Data compiled from field work by the writer.

10. If the 43 colonies in 1968 had an average of 7,400 acres each, they would have owned 318,200 acres or 1.7 percent of the total Manitoba farmland of 19,084,000 acres.

11. As part of this study the writer compiled a list of all farm machinery for all 43 colonies in 1968. This included the model and year of the machine, the year it was purchased, whether purchased new or used, where it was purchased, its cost at the time of purchase, and its estimated value in 1968. This list is reproduced for three colonies in Appendices D, E, and F. These three colonies include the one with the greatest investment in farm machinery, the one with the smallest investment, and one that represents an average investment. The names of the colonies are not stated, so as to avoid revealing operation details about them.

12. Crystal Spring Colony has purchased a hovercraft, and in the spring of 1972 the colony mechanics were in the process of remodeling the craft with the intention of using it for crop spraying purposes. The adaption has still not been completed at the time of writing. If the craft functions successfully, in addition to spraying its own fields, the colony plans to use it for custom work.

13. Grain quotas are established by the Canadian Wheat Board to ensure all farmers the sale of a stipulated number of bushels per cultivated acre. At times of poor markets the quotas are low and the farmers may have to store the bulk of their grain until sales improve.

CHAPTER 8

THE CATTLE ENTERPRISE

Number of Cattle and Comparison with Manitoba Farms

The number of cattle on Hutterite colonies as compared with the number on all Manitoba farms in 1968 appears in Tables 8-1 and 8-2. The 43 Hutterite colonies had a total of 2,712 milk cows and heifers or 1.7 percent of the Manitoba total. This is slightly more than twice their proportionate share if related to the amount of land that they own, i.e., .83 percent of Manitoba farmland (.87 percent if rented land is included). Their proportion of milk cows and heifers varied from a low of .7 percent in District E to a high of 7.9 percent in District A. On the basis of land relationship they owned significantly more than their proportionate share in four out of the six districts. However, in regard to beef cattle, in 1968 the Hutterites owned only 1,176 head or .2 percent of the Manitoba total. Furthermore, they owned significantly less than their proportionate share in every district. In fact, there are appreciable numbers of beef cattle only in District A, and of the 1,006 head in this district, one colony, New Rosedale, accounted for 700 head.[1] Hence beef cattle are insignificant on all but a few colonies.

When calves and bulls are added to the totals of dairy and beef stock, the Hutterite holdings of cattle in 1968 numbered 5,005 head (Table 8-2). Although the Hutterites have more than their proportionate share of dairy cattle, their small holdings of beef cattle reduce their overall total to only .5 percent of the province's cattle. Moreover, in terms of the total number of cattle, the Hutterites have more than their proportionate share in only one district, i.e., District A.

Tables 8-1 and 8-2 compare the cattle holdings of Hutterite colonies and Manitoba farms in terms of absolute numbers, and this was related to the amount of farmland in only a general sense. Table 8-3 shows the average number of cattle per acre, and it thereby makes it possible to quantify the cattle-land relationship. Although the number of cattle per acre appears to be almost a meaningless fraction, it is nevertheless possible to use it to compare the Hutterite holdings with Manitoba

TABLE 8-1

NUMBER OF BEEF AND DAIRY CATTLE - JUNE 1, 1968

MANITOBA FARMS[1] AND HUTTERITE COLONIES[2]

Agric. district	Manitoba Farms						
	Milk cows over 2 yrs.	Milk heifers 1 - 2 years	Total milk cows & heifers	Beef cows over 2 yrs.	Beef heifers 1 - 2 years	Steers	Total beef cows, heifers, & steers
A	14,500	3,400	17,900	17,000	4,700	12,000	33,700
B	7,700	1,800	9,500	10,000	3,600	4,400	18,000
C	6,000	1,200	7,200	22,000	6,000	6,000	34,000
D	19,200	3,800	23,000	88,500	17,500	31,800	137,800
E	28,000	9,000	37,000	11,500	4,100	10,800	26,400
F	8,200	2,000	10,200	5,500	2,800	3,000	11,300
Other districts	49,400	8,800	58,200	173,500	40,300	57,000	270,800
Total	133,000	30,000	163,000	328,000	79,000	125,000	532,000

Hutterite Colonies

Agric. dist-rict	Milk cows over 2 yrs.	Milk heifers 1 - 2 years	Total milk cows & heifers	Hutt. % of Man. total	Beef cows over 2 yrs.	Beef heifers 1 - 2 years	Steers	Total beef cows, heifers, & steers	Hutt. % of Man. Total
A	982	438	1,420	7.9%	270	0	736	1,006	3.0%
B	284	69	353	3.7%	0	0	0	0	0%
C	224	83	307	4.3%	0	0	10	10	.03%
D	151	60	211	.9%	0	0	25	25	.02%
E	172	95	267	.7%	0	0	46	46	.2%
F	130	24	154	1.5%	64	10	15	89	.8%
Other dist-ricts	0	0	0	0	0	0	0	0	0%
Total	1,943	769	2,712	1.7%	334	10	832	1,176	.2%

1Source: <u>Yearbook of Manitoba Agriculture 1968</u>, p. 18.

2Source: Data compiled from field work by J. Ryan.

TABLE 8-2

TOTAL NUMBER OF CATTLE - JUNE 1, 1968

MANITOBA FARMS[1] AND HUTTERITE COLONIES[2]

Agric. district	Manitoba Farms					Hutterite Colonies						
	Total milk cows & heifers	Total beef cows, heifers & steers	Total calves under 1 yr.	Total bulls	Total beef & dairy cattle	Total milk cows & heifers	Total beef cows, heifers & steers	Total calves under 1 yr.	Total bulls	Total beef & dairy cattle	Hutt. % of Man. total	Hutt. % of Man. farm-land
A	17,900	33,700	20,500	1,200	73,300	1,420	1,006	659	36	3,121	4.3%	3.7%
B	9,500	18,000	9,500	500	37,500	353	0	62	5	420	1.1%	2.4%
C	7,200	34,000	19,700	1,000	61,900	307	10	101	6	424	.7%	2.0%
D	23,000	137,800	82,000	4,200	247,000	211	25	50	4	290	.1%	.4%
E	37,000	26,400	23,500	1,500	88,400	267	46	100	3	416	.5%	1.1%
F	10,200	11,300	8,500	800	30,800	154	89	88	3	334	1.1%	1.9%
Other districts	58,200	270,800	160,300	8,800	498,100	0	0	0	0	0	0%	0%
Total	163,000	532,000	324,000	18,000	1,037,000	2,712	1,176	1,060	57	5,005	.5%	.87%

[1] Source: *Yearbook of Manitoba Agriculture 1968*, p. 18.

[2] Source: Data compiled from field work by J. Ryan.

TABLE 8-3

NUMBER OF CATTLE PER ACRE OF FARMLAND - JUNE 1, 1968

MANITOBA FARMS[1] AND HUTTERITE COLONIES[2]

Agric. district	Manitoba Farms					Hutterite Colonies						
	No. of acres (000)	No. of dairy cattle	No. of dairy cattle per acre	No. of total cattle	No. of total cattle per acre	No. of acres	No. of dairy cattle	No. of dairy cattle per acre	No. of total cattle	No. of total cattle per acre	Hutt. dairy cattle as a % of Man. dairy cattle per acre	Hutt. total cattle as a % of Man. total cattle per acre
A	2,278	17,900	.0079	73,300	.032	84,504	1,420	.0168	3,121	.037	213%	116%
B	631	9,500	.0151	37,500	.059	14,987	353	.0236	420	.028	156%	47%
C	1,142	7,200	.0063	61,900	.054	22,459	307	.0137	424	.019	217%	35%
D	4,180	23,000	.0055	247,000	.059	16,930	211	.0125	290	.017	227%	29%
E	1,680	37,000	.0220	88,400	.053	18,912	267	.0141	416	.022	64%	42%
F	437	10,200	.0233	30,800	.070	8,095	154	.0190	334	.041	82%	59%
Other districts	8,736	58,200	.0067	498,100	.057	0	0	0	0	0	0%	0%
Man. totals	19,084	163,000	.0085	1,037,000	.054	165,887	2,712	.0163	5,005	.030	192%	55%

[1] Source: Data compiled from the Yearbook of Manitoba Agriculture 1968, pp. 18, 30. (Manitoba farm acreage available from 1966 only.)

[2] Source: Data compiled from field work by J. Ryan.

TABLE 8-4

AVERAGE NUMBER OF CATTLE - JUNE 1, 1968
PER MANITOBA FARM,[1] PER HUTTERITE COLONY,
AND PER HUTTERITE FAMILY[2]

	Manitoba Farms				
Column no.	1	2	3	4	5
Agric. district	Total no. of farms in district	No. of farms operating cattle enterprises	Total no. of cattle	Average no. of cattle per farm (based on column 1)	Average no. of cattle per farm (based on column 2)
A	5,795	3,394	73,300	12.6	21.6
B	1,360	907	37,500	27.6	41.3
C	2,221	1,717	61,900	27.9	36.1
D	7,190	5,637	247,000	34.4	43.8
E	6,209	3,492	88,400	14.2	25.3
F	1,438	1,111	30,800	21.4	27.7
Other districts	15,534	16,258	498,100	32.1	30.6
Total/Average	38,200	28,389	1,037,000	27.1	36.5

[1] Source:

Data on total number of farms and number of cattle
compiled from <u>Yearbook</u> <u>of</u> <u>Manitoba</u> <u>Agriculture</u> <u>1968</u>,
pp. 18, 31. (Number of Manitoba farms is based on 1966
data, except the total of 38,200 which is the 1968 figure.)

- Data on number of farms that operate a cattle enterprise
compiled from <u>1966</u> <u>Census</u> <u>of</u> <u>Canada</u>: <u>Agriculture</u> -
<u>Manitoba</u>, pp. 18-1, 18-2, 18-3. (Data on number of
farms available for 1966 only.)

[2] Source: Data on Hutterite production compiled from field
work by J. Ryan.

[3] All Hutterite colonies operated a cattle enterprise in 1968.

Hutterite Colonies						
6	7	8	9	10	11	12
Total no. of colonies in dist.[3]	Total no. of cattle	Average no. of cattle per colony	No. of Hutterite families	Average no. of cattle per family	Col. 5 as a % of Col. 8	Col. 10 as a % of Col. 5
21	3,121	149	329	9.5	14.5%	44.0%
4	420	105	62	6.8	39.3%	16.5%
5	424	85	76	5.6	42.5%	15.5%
4	290	73	44	6.6	60.0%	15.1%
6	416	69	88	4.7	36.7%	18.6%
3	334	111	36	9.3	25.0%	33.6%
0	0	0	0	0	0	0
43	5,005	116	635	7.9	31.5%	21.6%

farms and thereby obtain meaningful results. This table shows that although the Hutterite colonies have only 55 percent of the total cattle per acre of Manitoba farms, they have almost twice as many dairy cattle per acre (192 percent). In Districts E and F they have fewer dairy cattle per acre than the farm average, but they have significantly more in the remaining four districts. When it comes to the total number of cattle, only in District A do the Hutterites have more cattle per acre than the overall average for the farms. These conclusions are apparent from Tables 8-1 and 8-2, but not in the specific quantitative terms of Table 8-3.

Table 8-4 sets out to compare the average number of cattle per Manitoba farm, per Hutterite colony, and per Hutterite family. In addition to showing the total number of farms in each district, the table shows the number of Manitoba farms that actually operated cattle enterprises. Unfortunately, the data for the number of Manitoba farms (with the exception of the total number of farms for 1968) are available for 1966 only, whereas the Hutterite data are for 1968. The Manitoba data show that about three-quarters of the province's farms operated cattle enterprises in 1966, but it is unlikely that this proportion changed significantly in a matter of two years. Therefore, although the data in this table are not completely comparable, it is improbable that the differences would be sufficient to affect the overall pattern or the basic conclusions that could be drawn from these comparisons.

One of the most significant points revealed by Table 8-4 is that the average number of cattle per Hutterite family is only about 22 percent of the average number on a Manitoba farm that operates a cattle enterprise, i.e., an average of 7.9 head per Hutterite family as compared to 36.5 on a Manitoba farm. The table also shows that a Manitoba "cattle" farm with its average of 36.5 head has 31.5 percent of the cattle of a Hutterite colony which has an average of only 116 head. In Districts A and F the Hutterite proportions are higher than the overall average and this is a result of their holdings being larger than average while the Manitoba farm holdings were smaller than average. Although the previous tables showed that the Hutterites had a larger than average number of dairy cattle, their small holdings of beef cattle drastically reduce their overall proportion of total number of cattle.

The number of different types of cattle on an average Hutterite colony is shown in Table 8-5. In 1968 the average number of dairy cows and heifers per colony was 63. This ranged from a low of 45 in District E to a high of 88 in District B. Although the table is quite accurate in its portrayal of average numbers of dairy cattle, the statistical average for beef cattle is completely misleading. For the 43 colonies as a whole the table shows an average of 8 beef cows, .2 heifers, and 19 steers. However, in actual fact the majority of the colonies do not keep beef cattle at all, and those that do, keep much higher numbers than the indicated average. For example, in District A the table indicates an average of 13 beef cows per colony. However, only two colonies in the entire district kept beef cows, and one colony had 235 head or almost the entire holdings. This colony also kept 370 steers—more than ten times the indicated average for the district. Likewise in District F, although the table indicates an average of 21 beef cows per colony, one colony accounted for the entire district's beef cows—a total of 64. This colony also had 10 beef heifers, the only beef heifers kept by any of the 43 colonies. Although the table has serious shortcomings in the beef sector, it does reflect reality quite well in regard to dairy cattle, calves, and the overall average for total cattle per colony throughout the districts.

The Operation of the Cattle Enterprise

Every Hutterite colony has a cattle enterprise, and in 1968 this ranged from a low of 13 head at Glenway Colony to a high of 786 at New Rosedale. As indicated in Table 8-5, the average for the 43 colonies was 116 head. Of the total cattle over one year old, 70 percent was dairy stock and 30 percent beef stock. Thirty-one colonies had no beef cattle at all, and of the remaining 12, only 3 had larger beef herds than dairy herds. The main reason for the lack of emphasis on beef cattle is that the overriding majority of the colonies simply do not consider beef production to be a profitable venture, or at least not as profitable as other enterprises, primarily the hog enterprise.[2] Furthermore, many colonies have only moderate sized dairy herds and only a few colonies have in any way specialized in dairy production. In fact, the colonies that place any emphasis on cattle are primarily those that have some land that is unsuitable for anything else other than pasture. At one time some of the colonies had larger stocks of cattle, but it gradually became apparent that it was more profitable to plow up the good pasture land and to produce crops instead.[3] The colonies are unanimous in their opinion that with their relatively small land holdings, it would be uneconomical for them to place any reasonably good land into pasture. The alternative to pasture is a feedlot operation, but here again, the majority of the Hutterites believe that grain fed to hogs is more profitable than the production of cattle. While no colony appears to have conducted a careful input-output analysis of cattle production, this is the prevailing view.

TABLE 8-5

NUMBER OF CATTLE PER HUTTERITE COLONY - JUNE 1, 1968

Agric. district	Milk cows over 2 yrs	Milk heifers 1-2 yrs	Total milk cows & heifers	Beef cows over 2 yrs	Beef heifers 1 - 2 years	Steers	Total beef cows heifers & steers	Total calves under 1 yr	Total bulls	Total beef & dairy cattle
A	47	21	68	13	0	35	48	31	1.7	149
B	71	17	88	0	0	0	0	16	1.2	105
C	45	17	62	0	0	2	2	20	1.2	85
D	38	15	53	0	0	6	6	13	1.0	73
E	29	16	45	0	0	8	8	17	.5	69
F	43	8	51	21	3	5	29	29	1.0	111
Average	45	18	63	8	.2	19	27	27	1.3	116

Source: Data compiled from field work by J. Ryan.

1. Dairy Production

Most colonies have Holstein dairy herds, but a few have Brown Swiss and at least one colony has a small number of Jerseys. Some have mixed breeds, which although kept primarily for dairy purposes, allows them to raise the male calves as steers for beef purposes. In 1968 the smallest operation consisted of 7 milk cows while the largest had 70. Of course the actual dairy herds are larger because 20 percent to 40 percent of the cows are "dry cows," either those at the end of their annual milking period or those that are about to calve. In addition each colony has a certain number of heifers kept for either herd expansion or replacement purposes. Calves of course also form part of the herd. Most colonies keep a bull or two, but some rely on artificial insemination.

All the colonies have a standard type of dairy barn. The small operations use a stanchion milking system, while the large scale operations use the herringbone milking parlour. One man looks after a small enterprise, but the largest herd of over 200 requires only two men and one or two boys as helpers.

The large operators with at least 40 cows have milk contracts with dairy firms and supply fluid or market milk. The smaller operators sell their milk for manufacturing purposes, and some sell cream. In addition to income from the sale of milk or cream, the dairy operation also obtains income from the sale of bull calves, cull or surplus heifers, and old cows.

2. Beef Production

The beef cattle on most colonies are Herefords, but some have a Hereford and Shorthorn cross and at least two have some Charolais cattle. Of the 12 colonies that raised cattle for beef purposes in 1968 only 4 had over 100 head, and the average for the remainder was 30 head. Three colonies kept beef cows, while the operations of the other colonies were restricted to the raising of steers on a feedlot. These steers were usually bought as feeders in the fall and sold the following summer. The colonies that keep beef cows naturally raise their own steers, and some colonies with mixed dairy breeds raise their own steers as well.

The three colonies that keep beef cows—New Rosedale, Sunnyside, and Brightstone—all had land that was suitable for pasture. New Rosedale was by far the largest operation and had a total of 700 beef cattle, 235 head being Hereford and Charolais cows. New Rosedale had over 1,000 acres suitable only as hayland and pasture, and this is the main reason for their emphasis on beef cattle. The older steers on these colonies are nevertheless raised on a feedlot where they can be fed proper rations.

Most of the colonies involved in beef production have the standard pole-type loose housing barns for their stock. Beef cattle do not require the warm barns that are necessary for dairy cattle. All beef stock need is sufficient shelter to keep them dry and protected from wind in stormy or cold weather.

All the colonies raise their steers on feedlots. This allows them to feed a properly controlled ration which ensures a rapid gain in weight. In the fall the steers are fed hay plus only about 4 or 5 pounds of grain mixture per steer per day. Gradually the amount of hay is reduced and the amount of grain is increased. By spring the daily ration for each steer is only about 2 pounds of hay and about 20 pounds of grain. A feeder steer gains about 2 pounds a day and when it weighs about 1,100 pounds it is ready for sale.

On colonies that have a small number of steers, the entire cattle operation is handled by the dairy enterprise manager and his assistants. On the larger operations the beef enterprise is under separate management, but this requires only one man and one or two boys as helpers.

In summary, although every colony operates a cattle enterprise, the Hutterites are not highly specialized in this activity, especially in beef cattle. This is primarily because they lack sufficient and suitable land for pasture and hay purposes.

Significance of the Cattle Enterprise to the Colony Economy

Separate income data are not available for the dairy and beef enterprises, and only a single composite figure is available for the total sales of cattle, milk, and cream. In 1968 the 43 colonies received a gross sales income of $701,776.29 from the cattle enterprise (Table 8-6). This was an average of $16,320.38 per colony and $1,105.16 per family. In that year the gross sales income from the cattle enterprise accounted for 6.1 percent of the total gross sales income from all enterprises. On the basis of gross sales income the cattle enterprise ranked fifth in importance as a contributor to the overall Hutterite economy (Appendix G).

In addition to cash income from the sales of cattle, milk, and cream, this enterprise provides the colonies with meat and dairy products. In fact, every colony is almost self-sufficient in all beef and dairy produce. The value of colony consumption is unavailable, but considering the large population involved, the amount must be substantial. Furthermore, this is a considerable saving for the colonies because the food is available at the cost of production rather than the relatively high retail prices commanded by beef and dairy produce.

TABLE 8-6

MANITOBA HUTTERITE COLONIES

GROSS SALES INCOME FROM THE CATTLE ENTERPRISE, 1968

Gross sales income from all enterprises	$11,598,282.40
Gross sales income from the cattle enterprise	$ 701,776.29
Gross sales income from cattle enterprise as a % of total gross sales income	6.1%
No. of colonies reporting income from cattle enterprise	43
No. of families on these colonies	635
Average gross sales income per colony	$ 16,320.38
Average gross sales income per family	$ 1,105.16

Source: Data compiled by J. Ryan from the financial reports on each colony for 1968, as prepared by Meyers, Dickens, Norris, Penny & Company, the accounting firm employed by the Hutterite colonies.

Notes and References

1. Data compiled from field work by the writer.
2. In the course of his research work the writer made enquiries at almost every colony about the apparent lack of emphasis on beef cattle, and the answer was invariably that "it doesn't pay to keep steers." Furthermore, it was pointed out that it was more profitable to keep reasonably good agricultural land in crops, and that with little pasture land this limited their dairy herds as well.
3. Until about ten years ago a number of colonies had relatively large dairy and beef herds, especially Blumengart, Crystal Spring, and James Valley colonies. However, the herds were reduced and the former pasture is now in grain crops.

CHAPTER 9

THE HOG ENTERPRISE

Number of Hogs and Comparison with Manitoba Farms

The hog enterprise is of major importance on every Manitoba colony. In 1968 the sale of hogs formed the single largest source of income on 31 of the 43 colonies.[1] Furthermore, this same proportion, i.e., about 70 percent of the colonies, have received their largest source of income from hogs for at least a decade.[2]

Table 9-1 shows that on the census date June 1, 1968 the Hutterites had a total of 78,722 hogs on their colonies, or 15.0 percent of all hogs in Manitoba. This is obviously a major contribution to this sector of the province's economy. When considered that the Hutterites own and rent only .87 percent of the total Manitoba farmland, this contribution becomes all the more significant and indicates a very effective use of resources.

When examined on a district by district basis the proportion of hogs owned by Hutterites becomes more significant than when compared to the overall provincial total. This is mainly because there are no Hutterite colonies in about half of the province's crop districts and consequently this lowers their overall total. However, in the districts where there are Hutterite colonies, the Hutterite proportion of hogs varies from a low of 7.0 percent in District D to a high of 44.6 percent in District F (Table 9-1). Admittedly, District F, bordering on the Shield, is not particularly noted for its agricultural production, but it is remarkable nevertheless that three relatively small Hutterite colonies in this area account for almost 45 percent of the entire district's hogs. The significance of Hutterite hog production is perhaps best revealed in District A, the agricultural heartland of Manitoba. In this large district which stretches from Winnipeg to Portage la Prairie and extends southward to the American border, the 21 Hutterite colonies account for 31.4 percent of the district's hogs. Furthermore, in District C, the productive Neepawa area, five colonies on 2 percent of the land account for over one-third of that district's hogs.

TABLE 9-1

TOTAL NUMBER OF HOGS - JUNE 1, 1968

MANITOBA FARMS[1] AND HUTTERITE COLONIES[2]

Agric. ist-rict	Manitoba Farms				Hutterite Colonies				Hutt. % of total Man. hogs	Hutt. % of Man. farmland
	Boars	Sows	Market Hogs	Total Hogs	Boars	Sows	Market Hogs	Total Hogs		
A	Data			120,000	222	4,200	33,200	37,622	31.4%	3.7%
B	not			26,000	51	900	7,020	7,971	30.7%	2.4%
C	available			30,000	49	1,100	9,150	10,299	34.3%	2.0%
D	for			119,000	47	925	7,350	8,322	7.0%	.4%
E	districts			99,000	48	1,110	9,560	10,718	10.8%	1.1%
F				8,500	20	445	3,325	3,790	44.6%	1.9%
Other dist-ricts				123,500	0	0	0	0	0%	0%
Man. Total	D.N.A.	60,000	D.N.A.	526,000	437	8,680	69,605	78,722	15.0%	.87%

[1]Source: - *Yearbook of Manitoba Agriculture* 1968, p. 22. (source of data on total hogs)

- Dominion Bureau of Statistics. Cat. No. 23-005, "Report on Livestock Surveys - Hogs, June 1, 1968," p. 6. (source of data on total number of sows)

[2]Source: Data compiled from field work by J. Ryan.

Table 9-1 also shows that in 1968 there were 437 boars, 8,680 sows, and 69,605 market hogs on the Hutterite colonies. However, this more detailed information is not available for Manitoba farms, with the exception of the total number of sows—60,000. One index of the efficiency of hog production is the ratio of the total number of hogs to sows. In 1968 the average for Manitoba hog producers was 11.0 hogs per sow, but the average for the Hutterite colonies was 11.3 per sow.[3] Since the Hutterite sows produce larger litters, it appears that on this basis the Hutterites operate a more efficient hog enterprise than average Manitoba producers.

The hog-land relationship, as revealed in Table 9-2, is an indication of the intensity of land use in regard to hog production. This table shows that Manitoba farms on the average have only 5.9 percent of the hogs per acre that the Hutterites do. On a district basis this relationship ranges from 4.1 percent to 11.9 percent, but the high intensity of Hutterite land use is clearly evident in all areas. Although all Hutterite colonies produce hogs, not all Manitoba farms do, and consequently if only hog producing farms were considered, the average Manitoba hog production per acre would be considerably higher. Data are available on the total number of hog producing farms in Manitoba in 1966, but the acreage of these farms is not recorded, and therefore, it is impossible to make a per acre comparison of hog producers only.[4] These census data show that only 42 percent of Manitoba farms produce hogs, but it is evident that even if the Manitoba percentages were more than doubled in Table 9-2, the Hutterites would still have significantly more hogs per acre than the average hog producers.

Table 9-3 shows the average number of hogs in 1968 per Manitoba farm, per Hutterite colony, and per Hutterite family. The average number of hogs per colony was 1,831 as compared to an average of only 33 on Manitoba hog producing farms. Since the average farm is a single family operation, a more realistic basis of comparison with the Hutterites would be to consider the average number of hogs per Hutterite family. This table shows that the average number of hogs per Hutterite family is 124. Hence the average Manitoba hog producing farm has only 26.6 percent of the hogs of an average Hutterite family. The table indicates that this varies considerably from district to district, but the Hutterites are significantly larger producers in all areas.

Number of Hogs Sold

Although on June 1 of 1968 the Hutterites had 15 percent of the total Manitoba hogs, during that year they accounted for 15.9 percent of the

TABLE 9-2

NUMBER OF HOGS PER ACRE OF FARMLAND – JUNE 1, 1968
MANITOBA FARMS[1] AND HUTTERITE COLONIES[2]

Agric. district	Manitoba Farms			Hutterite Colonies			
	No. of acres (000)	Total no. of hogs	No. of hogs per acre	No. of acres	Total no. of hogs	No. of hogs per acre	Man. hogs as a % of Hutt. hogs per acre
A	2,278	120,000	.053	84,504	37,622	.445	11.9%
B	631	26,000	.041	14,987	7,971	.532	7.7%
C	1,142	30,000	.026	22,459	10,299	.459	5.7%
D	4,180	119,000	.028	16,930	8,322	.492	5.7%
E	1,680	99,000	.059	18,912	10,718	.567	10.4%
F	437	8,500	.019	8,095	3,790	.468	4.1%
Other districts	8,736	123,500	.014	0	0	0	0
Man. total	19,084	526,000	.028	165,887	78,722	.475	5.9%

[1]Source: Data compiled from *Yearbook of Manitoba Agriculture 1968*, pp. 22, 30.

[2]Source: Data compiled from field work by J. Ryan.

TABLE 9-3

AVERAGE NUMBER OF HOGS - JUNE 1, 1968
PER MANITOBA FARM,[1] PER HUTTERITE COLONY,
AND PER HUTTERITE FAMILY[2]

| Column No. | Manitoba Farms | | | | |
| | 1 | 2 | 3 | 4 | 5 |
Agric. dist-rict	Total no. of farms in district	No. of farms operating hog enterprises	Total no. of hogs	Average no. of hogs per farm (based on col. 1)	Average no. of hogs per farm (based on col. 2)
A	5,795	2,291	120,000	21	52
B	1,360	472	26,000	19	55
C	2,221	985	30,000	·14	30
D	7,190	2,784	119,000	17	43
E	6,209	2,165	99,000	16	48
F	1,438	645	8,500	6	13
Other dist-ricts	15,534	6,706	123,500	8	18
Total/ average	38,200	16,048	526,000	14	33

[1]Source:

- Data on total number of farms and number of hogs
  compiled from <u>Yearbook of Manitoba Agriculture 1968</u>
  (number of Manitoba farms is based on 1966 data,
  except the total of 38,200 which is the 1968 figure).
- Data on number of farms that keep hogs compiled from
  <u>1966 Census of Canada</u>: <u>Agriculture</u> - <u>Manitoba</u>, pp.
  18-1, 18-2, 18-3 (data on no. of farms is for 1966).

[2]Source: Data on Hutterite production compiled from field
             work by J. Ryan.

[3]All Hutterite colonies kept hogs in 1968.

	Hutterite Colonies					
6	7	8	9	10	11	12
Total no. of colonies in dist.[3]	Total no. of hogs	Average no. of hogs per colony	No. of Hutterite families	Average no. of hogs per family	Col. 4 as a % of Col. 10	Col. 5 as a % of Col. 10
21	37,622	1,792	329	114	18.4%	45.6%
4	7,971	1,993	62	129	14.7%	42.6%
5	10,299	2,060	76	136	10.3%	22.1%
4	8,322	2,081	44	189	9.0%	22.8%
6	10,718	1,786	88	122	13.1%	39.3%
3	3,790	1,263	36	105	5.7%	12.4%
0	0	0	0	0	0	0
43	78,722	1,831	635	124	11.3%	26.6%

total Manitoba hog sales (Tables 9-1 and 9-4). Their proportion of sales ranged from a low of 6.9 percent in District D to a high of 67.5 percent in District F. Their proportion of sales in District F is indeed remarkable because on June 1 of that year they accounted for only 44.6 percent of the hogs in that district. It means that in this district a great many farmers raised and sold only one litter per sow, whereas the Hutterites with their large scale operations on a full year-round basis managed to sell almost two litters per sow. This high productivity is evident in other districts as well, except for the notable exception of District B. Although on June 1 the Hutterites had 30.7 percent of the hogs in this district, they accounted for only 23.8 percent of the sales. This is explained mainly by the fact that Interlake Colony was remodelling and revamping its hog operation and consequently had fewer hog sales that year.

All Hutterite colonies transport their hogs to Winnipeg and all sales are made through the Manitoba Hog Commission. Almost every colony brings in a truckload of about 40 hogs to Winnipeg each week.

The Operation of the Hog Enterprise[5]

In 1968 the average Hutterite colony had 10 boars, 202 sows, and 1,619 market hogs, which made up a total of 1,837 hogs (Table 9-5). This varied from a low at Whiteshell Colony of 895—consisting of 5 boars, 65 sows, and 825 market hogs—to a high at Sturgeon Creek Colony of 3,500—consisting of 25 boars, 325 sows, and 3,150 market hogs.[6] However, even the smallest Hutterite operation is on a large scale as compared to average Manitoba producers.

In spite of the large size of these operations, on an average colony the hog enterprise manager has only one or two full-time assistants. Furthermore, during the summer these assistants may spend part of their time working on the fields.

TABLE 9-4

TOTAL NUMBER OF HOGS SOLD, 1968
MANITOBA FARMS[1] AND HUTTERITE COLONIES[2]

Agric. dist-rict	Manitoba farms	Hutterite colonies	Hutt. hogs as a % of Man. hogs	Hutt. % of Man. farmland
A	178,734	58,405	32.7%	3.7%
B	52,398	12,450	23.8%	2.4%
C	42,140	15,770	37.4%	2.0%
D	181,163	12,430	6.9%	.4%
E	142,250	15,455	10.9%	1.1%
F	6,946	4,690	67.5%	1.9%
Other dist-ricts	147,752	0	0%	0%
Man. total	751,383	119,200	15.9%	.87%

[1]Source: <u>Yearbook of Manitoba Agriculture 1968</u>, p. 21.

[2]Source: Data compiled from field work by J. Ryan.

At least five or six different types of quarters are required for a large scale hog operation, and these are usually housed in two or three barns on most Hutterite colonies. The following facilities are required:

1) a dry sow barn (where gilts and sows are bred and where they stay during the gestation period),
2) a farrowing barn (where the sows farrow and where they stay for about five weeks until the piglets are weaned),
3) a section for the 25 to 50 pound hogs,
4) a section for the 50 to 120 pound hogs,
5) a section for the 120 to 200 pound hogs or until they are marketed,
6) a feed preparation section and storage facilities for feed.

In addition, loading quarters are required for the hogs that are taken to market. Obviously, for purposes of efficiency and convenience, all these facilities have to be properly integrated. The modern hog complex at Crystal Spring Colony is shown on Map 3 and Plate 12.

TABLE 9-5

AVERAGE NUMBER OF HOGS PER HUTTERITE COLONY - JUNE 1, 1968

AND AVERAGE NUMBER OF HOGS SOLD PER COLONY IN 1968

Agric. dist- rict	Average no. of boars	Average no. of sows	Average no. of market hogs	Average no. of total hogs	Average no. of hogs sold
A	11	200	1,581	1,792	2,781
B	13	225	1,755	2,005	3,113
C	10	220	1,830	2,068	3,154
D	12	231	1,838	2,096	3,108
E	8	185	1,593	1,786	2,576
F	7	148	1,108	1,270	1,563
Average per colony	10	202	1,619	1,837	2,769

Source: Data compiled from field work by J. Ryan.

J. Ryan (1972)

PLATE 12. *The hog complex at Crystal Spring Colony* located 6 miles southeast of Ste. Agathe. Directly behind the grain storage tanks is the dry sow barn (230 sow capacity), the farrowing barn is in the middle (40 sow capacity), and the feeder or market hog barn is on the right (2,000 hog capacity). The hog sewage lagoon is behind the complex and is shown on Map 3. The buildings are interconnected, and their scale can be determined from Map 3. The complex has a liquid feed system and is one of the most modern in the province. It was constructed in 1970.

Not only must the physical plant be properly integrated but the whole hog operation has to be carefully programmed. In order to operate the hog enterprise efficiently and at full capacity, all facilities must be fully utilized, with no overcrowding or bottlenecks in some sections while other sections are only partially used. This means that at all times only a certain number of sows must be pregnant, a certain number must be in the farrowing stage, and all the other sections must have a proper quota of hogs at different stages of growth. When the operation is properly integrated, a certain number of hogs are marketed every week, and as these are moved out, other hogs move through the system to replace them. To be fully successful, this requires a great deal of planning and coordination.

There are three basic methods of feeding hogs: 1) hand-feeding, 2) self-feeding, and 3) automated feeding. Handfeeding, involving the shovelling of feed into the pens, is done on only a few colonies. The most common type of system employed by the Hutterites is self-feeding. The feeding units are filled by a network of augers, which greatly reduces manual labour. Automated feeding consists of two basic types—one is a dry feed system and the other is a liquid feed system. The dry feed system has been used for a number of years by several colonies, whereas the liquid feed system has been adopted by only four colonies since 1968.[7] In the dry feed system the feed is periodically dropped on the floor from an apparatus above each pen. Although feeding can be carefully controlled by this system, it is expensive to install. The liquid feed operation is the most advanced, but it requires complete remodelling of the old barns and preferably entirely new structures. The crushed feed is mixed with water and the mixture is piped throughout the barns and periodically pumped into special trough-feeders for the hogs. Because of the large capital investment for the proper type of equipment and the need for an integrated programmed operation, it seems that in Manitoba the automated liquid feed system has been successful only on these few Hutterite colonies.[8]

All large hog operations require some type of automated manure removal system. The most common type on the Hutterite colonies is the gutter system where the manure is scraped out daily by a chain-type gutter cleaner. The manure is then spread on the fields by a manure spreader. Some colonies have a pit system where the manure is mixed with water and periodically pumped into a special suction tank manure spreader and then sprayed on the fields. So far, only two colonies, Crystal Spring and Elm River, have special hog sewage lagoons into which the liquified manure is pumped directly.

The Hutterites have long been aware that genetically inferior hogs will consume as much feed as thoroughbred stock, but will nevertheless produce inferior carcasses. Hence almost all colonies have put a stress on obtaining superior quality breeding stock. This may be expensive in the initial stages, but on a long range basis this is by far the soundest economic policy. Most colonies have York sows which are bred by Durox, Temworth, or Hampshire boars. A few colonies have Tripway sows, a newly developed breed. In any event, practically all colonies have the most highly rated pedigreed hogs.[9]

As would be expected, certain specific formulas are followed in the preparation of hog feed. In an attempt to keep abreast of the latest developments in hog nutrition, most Hutterite hog enterprise managers subscribe to farm journals and are on the mailing list for various university and government farm bulletins. Some hog enterprise managers even attend university extension courses on livestock nutrition.[10]

Barley and wheat form the bulk of present-day hog feed, although oats was an important grain until a few years ago.[11] In addition to commercial hog feed concentrate, the recent and most commonly used formula for feeder hogs calls for a grain mixture of approximately one-third wheat and two thirds barley. For one ton of feed this works out as follows: 300 pounds of 40 percent protein-mineral-vitamin supplement (or concentrate), 570 pounds of wheat, and 1,130 pounds of barley.[12] This is the most commonly used formula on most colonies for feeder hogs between 50 to 200 pounds in weight. For little pigs from the time they are weaned until they weigh about 50 pounds, the common formula for a ton of feed is as follows: 400 pounds of 40 percent concentrate, 200 pounds of rolled oats, and 1,400 pounds of first-class wheat. Sows during gestation and lactation are fed the basic formula plus special vitamin enrichment. For those colonies that use the automated liquid feed system, each pound of feed is mixed with an additional three pounds of water. On all colonies the grain is brought in from the storage granaries by a system of augers and it is ground and mixed with the concentrate in the proper proportions by a large hammer-mill in the feed section of the hog complex. The mill is dial-controlled and the whole operation is completely automated.

A hog shortly after weaning requires about 1.8 pounds of feed per day and this should gradually be increased until the hog is fed about 7.8 pounds per day when it is ready for market at about 200 pounds.[13] Good quality hogs fed the proper recommended rations should start gaining about .7 pounds per day shortly after weaning, and from the time they reach 120 pounds the daily weight gain should be about 1.8 pounds per day until they reach the market stage.[14] This means that a well-bred hog properly fed should reach the market stage by the time it is about five to six months of age. However, these weight gains take place only under ideal conditions, and many hog producers, including Hutterites, have to keep some hogs longer than six months before they are ready for market. This of course reduces the number of hogs that can be sold in a year and correspondingly reduces the full potential profit of the hog enterprise.

The number of hogs sold should be about twice the capacity of the market hog complex so long as all the hogs can be sold within six months. Only a few colonies are doing this, and as Table 9-6 indicates, the average turnover of market hogs on Hutterite colonies is 171 percent, ranging from a low of 130 percent on one colony to a high of over 200 percent on others.[15] This is probably one of the best indices of hog production efficiency. Table 9-6 also indicates that the average for all Manitoba hog producers is only 161 percent. Hence on the basis of volume of hogs produced the Hutterite enterprises are more productive than average Manitoba producers.

TABLE 9-6

TOTAL HOGS SOLD IN 1968
AS A PER CENT OF MARKET HOGS ON HAND, JUNE 1, 1968
MANITOBA FARMS[1] AND HUTTERITE COLONIES[2]

Agric. dist- rict	Hutterite Colonies		
	No. of market hogs on colonies June 1	Total no. of hogs sold in 1968	Hogs sold in 1968 as a % of market hogs on colonies on June 1
A	33,200	58,405	176%
B	7,020	12,450	177%
C	9,150	15,770	172%
D	7,350	12,430	169%
E	9,560	15,455	162%
F	3,325	4,690	141%
Total for Hutterite Colonies	69,605 (70,142)[3]	119,200 (119,200)	171% (170%)

Manitoba Farms		
No. of market hogs (including boars) on farms June 1	Total no. of hogs sold in 1968	Hogs sold in 1968 as a % of market hogs (incl. boars) on farms on June 1
466,000	751,383	161%

[1]Source: - *Yearbook of Manitoba Agriculture 1968*, pp. 22-23.

- Dominion Bureau of Statistics, "Report on Livestock Surveys - Hogs, June 1, 1968," p. 6. (Manitoba farm data consists of total number of hogs minus sows. Data not available for individual districts.)

[2]Source: Data compiled from field work by J. Ryan.

[3]Boars are included in this classification for comparison purposes with Manitoba farms (Manitoba farm data consists of market hogs plus boars).

Significance of the Hog Enterprise to the Colony Economy

As already indicated, the hog enterprise is of major importance on every colony. In 1968 it brought in a gross sales income of $4,871,001.65 (Table 9-7). This was 42 percent of the total gross sales income from all sources. On the average, each of the 43 colonies received $113,279.11 or a proportion for each family of $7,670.87. Table 9-8 shows that the average gross sales income per colony was higher than the overall average in all districts except District F. All three colonies in this district have smaller than average hog operations and this brings down the overall gross sales income per colony. Among all the Hutterite colonies the income ranged from a low of $33,927 to a high of $256,732.[16]

Table 9-8 also shows that in 1968 the colonies received an average of $40.86 per hog. The price per hog was nearly uniform in all districts, except District C, where it was somewhat lower. Comparable data for the price per hog received by the average Manitoba hog producer are unavailable.[17] Probably the price received by the Hutterites was close to the Manitoba average. The number of hogs consumed on the col-

TABLE 9-7

MANITOBA HUTTERITE COLONIES

GROSS SALES INCOME FROM
THE HOG ENTERPRISE, 1968

Total gross sales income from all enterprises	$11,598,282.40
Gross sales income from the hog enterprise	$ 4,871,001.65
Gross sales income from hogs as a % of total gross sales income	42.0%
No. of colonies reporting sales of hogs	43
No. of families on these colonies	635
Average gross sales income per colony	$ 113,279.11
Average gross sales income per family	$ 7,670.87

Source: Data compiled by J. Ryan from the financial reports of each colony for 1968, as prepared by Meyers, Dickens, Norris, Penny & Company, the accounting firm employed by the Hutterite colonies.

onies is not known, but it must be substantial. It must make a considerable contribution to the economy of each colony.

The hog enterprise was consistently a very profitable economic activity for the Hutterite colonies until 1970, but serious problems have developed since. When the demand for Canadian grain exports declined seriously in about 1968, farmers were encouraged to diversify their operations. In particular they were urged to increase production of hogs and cattle. As a result, the number of hogs on Manitoba farms increased from 526,000 in 1968 to 612,000 in 1969, reached a record high of 884,000 in 1970, and levelled off to 850,000 in 1971.[18] This sudden rapid rise in production caused hog prices to fall considerably, particularly in 1970 and 1971.[19] All hog producers, including the Hutterites, were seriously affected by this drop in price, and there was a

TABLE 9-8

GROSS INCOME RECEIVED BY

HUTTERITE COLONIES FROM HOG SALES, 1968

Agric. dist- rict	No. of hogs sold	Gross Sales Income $	Average price per hog $	Average amt. rec'd per colony $
A	58,405	2,429,638.55	41.60	115,697.07
B	12,450	507,158.62	40.74	126,789.60
C	15,770	609,447.84	38.65	121,889.56
D	12,430	504,930.54	40.62	126,232.63
E	15,455	628,226.39	40.65	125,645.27
F	4,690	191,599.71	40.85	63,866.57
Total/ average	119,200	4,871,001.65	40.86	113,279.10

Source: - Data on number of hogs sold compiled from field work by J. Ryan.

- Data on gross sales income from the hog enterprise compiled by J. Ryan from the financial reports on each colony for 1968, as prepared by Meyers, Dickens, Norris, Penny and Company, the accounting firm employed by the Hutterite colonies.

consequent reduction in the number of hogs in 1971. The sudden decision of many Manitoba farmers to diversify their operations had serious repercussions on the long-established producers such as the Hutterites. Economic conditions in the colonies were extremely bad in 1971, mainly because of losses in both the hog and chicken enterprises. Of the 48 colonies, 4 reported nil income overall and 11 colonies experienced serious losses.[20] Fortunately, with the drop in hog production (mainly by farmers who, ill-advisedly, had initiated a hog operation), prices began to increase in 1972 and there was every hope of an improved overall situation by the end of that year. The serious economic reversal for many Manitoba farms that has been described illustrates one advantage of the Hutterite colonies. Because they are genuinely diversified, they can survive a serious temporary setback in one or two enterprises and can even carry them at a loss until economic conditions improve. This is very difficult for the highly specialized producer or the average farmer. Nevertheless the Hutterites remain anxious over future trends because hog production is the mainstay of many colonies.

Notes and References

1. Data compiled from the 1968 financial reports on each of the Manitoba Hutterite colonies as prepared by Meyers, Dickens, Norris, Penny & Company of Brandon, the accountants employed by the colonies.
2. Every colony authorized the release of its annual financial statements since 1961. The writer has copies of these records.
3. In determining the average litter size, gilts were excluded from the total number of sows. Data on gilts are not available for Manitoba hog producers, and they were compiled for only 18 Hutterite colonies. On these colonies gilts accounted for 20 percent of the total number of sows. This was considered to be an adequate sample, and on this basis the same proportion of gilts was excluded from both the Hutterite colonies and Manitoba producers. In other words, the size of litters was determined on the basis of 6,944 sows for the Hutterite colonies (80 percent of 8.680) and 48,000 sows for Manitoba producers (80 percent of 60,000).
4. *1966 Census of Canada: Agriculture—Manitoba*, pp. 18-1, 18-2, 18-3.
5. The basic information for this section was obtained by observing the operations of the hog enterprise on a number of colonies and by interviewing the enterprise and colony managers. In particular,

the writer made a detailed study of the operations at Crystal Spring, Fairholme, Grand, James Valley, Milltown, and Ridgeland colonies.

6. Data compiled from field work by the writer.

7. The automated liquid feed system has been adopted by Bloomfield, Clearwater, Crystal Spring, and Elm River colonies.

8. In an interview on March 17, 1972, Mr. D. S. Stevenson, the provincial swine specialist of the Manitoba Department of Agriculture, stated that the automated liquid feed system was not working out satisfactorily for Manitoba producers other than the Hutterites because of the complexity of the system.

9. The information on hog breeds was compiled from field work by the writer, and the quality of the pedigrees was checked with Mr. D. S. Stevenson, Provincial Swine Specialist.

10. Sam Kleinsasser, the hog enterprise manager at Crystal Spring Colony, completed a hog nutrition extension course offered by the Faculty of Agriculture at the University of Manitoba.

11. The Hutterites have been using much less oats in hog rations since 1968 and this is mainly as a result of recommendations by federal and provincial Departments of Agriculture, e.g., S. C. Stothers and J. C. Brown, *Guide to Practical Swine Rations in Manitoba*, Manitoba Department of Agriculture (Winnipeg: Queen's Printer for the Province of Manitoba, n.d.).

12. The formulas cited in this section are used at Crystal Spring Colony, but they are similar to those used on most colonies.

13. Stothers and Brown, *op. cit.*, p. 30.

14. *Ibid*.

15. Data compiled from field work by the writer.

16. Data compiled from colony financial reports.

17. Data on the value of hogs sold by Manitoba producers are available, but they are calculated from the gross amount paid by the packing plants. Handling, stockyard, and haulage costs are deducted from the gross amount before payment is made to the producers. The Hutterite sales income data are based on the amount that they actually receive, and so these data are not directly comparable with the packing plant data.

18. M. Daciw, ''The Livestock Situation in Manitoba'' (unpublished report by the Agricultural Statistician for the Manitoba Department of Agriculture, September 27, 1971).

19. *Ibid*.

20. Data compiled by the writer from the financial reports on each colony for 1971, as prepared by Meyers, Dickens, Norris, Penny & Company, the accountants employed by the Hutterite colonies.

CHAPTER 10

THE CHICKEN ENTERPRISE

Number of Chickens and Comparison with Manitoba Farms

The significance of the Hutterite chicken enterprise is graphically illustrated by Table 10-1. Hens for the purpose of egg production are their main area of specialty, while with the exception of a few colonies, the production of broilers is strictly secondary.

On the census date June 1, 1968 the Hutterites had a total of 506,000 laying hens or 17.9 percent of the Manitoba total. Their share of the province's laying hens ranged from 7.4 percent in District E to 63.5 percent in District C. In District A, the most productive agricultural region in Manitoba, the Hutterites accounted for 30.1 percent of the laying hens. When it is considered that the Hutterites own less than 1 percent of the Manitoba farmland, these production figures are nothing short of phenomenal.

Although the Hutterites in general do not specialize in the production of broilers (only 10 colonies produced broilers in 1968), they nevertheless accounted for 87,000 broilers or 2.5 percent of the provincial total. However, since the Hutterite colonies produce from two to five batches of broilers a year, Table 10-2 shows that the actual number of broilers sold in 1968 was 307,000 or 5.6 percent of the Manitoba total. This is considerably more than their proportionate share on the basis of land ownership.

With regard to the total number of hens and chickens, in 1968 the Hutterites had 593,500 or 9.3 percent of the Manitoba total. This is considerably less than their share of laying hens, but this is mainly because not too many Hutterite colonies have gone into broiler production. Nevertheless, in regard to total number of chickens, the Hutterite share ranged from 3.8 percent in District E to 29.9 percent in District C.

Table 10-3 shows the number of laying hens per Manitoba farm, per Hutterite colony, and per Hutterite family. The data in this table reveal that only 45 percent of the total Manitoba farms operate laying hen enterprises, as compared to 41 out of the 43 Hutterite colonies. For

TABLE 10-1

TOTAL NUMBER OF HENS AND CHICKENS - JUNE 1, 1968

MANITOBA FARMS[1] AND HUTTERITE COLONIES[2]

Agric. district	Laying Hens			Broilers & others			Total hens & chickens			
	Man. farms	Hutt. col's	% Hutt.	Man. farms	Hutt. col's	% Hutt.	Man. farms	Hutt. col's	% Hutt.	Hutt. % of Man. farmland
A	811,000	243,800	30.1%	686,000	43,500	6.3%	1,497,000	287,300	19.2%	3.7%
B	118,000	43,000	36.4%	120,000	24,500	20.4%	238,000	67,500	28.4%	2.4%
C	124,000	78,700	63.5%	149,000	3,000	2.0%	273,000	81,700	29.9%	2.0%
D	315,000	35,500	11.3%	460,000	0	0	775,000	35,500	4.6%	.4%
E	1,001,000	73,900	7.4%	1,390,000	16,000	1.2%	2,391,000	89,900	3.8%	1.1%
F	135,000	31,600	23.4%	172,000	0	0	307,000	31,600	10.3%	1.9%
Other districts	326,000	0	0	573,000	0	0	899,000	0	0	0%
Total	2,830,000	506,500	17.9%	3,550,000	87,000	2.5%	6,380,000	593,500	9.3%	.87%

[1]Source: *Yearbook of Manitoba Agriculture 1968*, p. 28.

[2]Source: Data compiled from field work by J. Ryan.

TABLE 10-2

NUMBER OF BROILERS SOLD 1968
MANITOBA FARMS[1] AND HUTTERITE COLONIES[2]

Agric. district	Manitoba farms	Hutterite colonies	% Hutterite
A		139,000	-
B	Data	115,500	-
C		3,000	-
D	Not	0	-
E		49,500	-
F	Available	0	-
Other districts		0	-
Total	5,471,000	307,000	5.6%

[1]Source: *Yearbook* *of* *Manitoba* *Agriculture* *1968*, p. 27.

[2]Source: Data compiled from field work by J. Ryan.

purposes of comparison with regard to the total potential resources, the table shows the average number of laying hens for the total number of farms and colonies as well as the average number for the farms and colonies that actually own laying hens.

As revealed by Table 10-3, the average number of hens for all farms in Manitoba is 74, while the average is 165 for just the farms that operate laying hen enterprises. The average for all 43 colonies is 11,779, while the average for the 41 colonies that own hens is 12,354. Since practically all Manitoba farms are single family operations, a more meaningful comparison with the Hutterites can be made if the average number of hens per Hutterite family is considered. On the basis of all colonies the average number of hens per family is 796, whereas for the colonies that operate laying hen enterprises the average is 825. This means that on the basis of the total number of farms and colonies in

Manitoba, the average farm has only 9.3 percent of the hens of a Hutterite family. When the farms and colonies that actually operate laying hen enterprises are considered, the average farm has 20 percent of the laying hens of a Hutterite family. With regard to the last category, the range varies from 9.5 percent in District C to 56.3 percent in District A. It becomes evident that in a large producing area such as District A, the average farm is not on a much smaller scale when Hutterite production is considered on a *per family* basis. This is significant because it is often claimed that the Hutterites operate on such a large scale that their activities cannot be fairly compared with those of other farmers.

The Operation of the Chicken Enterprise[1]

1. The Laying Hen Operation

In 1968 only 2 of the 43 colonies did not have a laying hen enterprise, and in the case of these two colonies (Glenway and Wellwood), this was probably a temporary situation because they were still newly established colonies. At that time the average number of laying hens per colony was 12,354 (Table 10-4). This ranged from a low of 3,800 at Iberville Colony to a high of 35,000 at Milltown.

On an average colony the chicken enterprise manager has only one full-time assistant during the winter plus two boys after school hours to help with egg collection. During the summer the manager is assisted by only three or four boys (or girls on some colonies). An operation with about 25,000 hens requires four full-time men during the winter plus about three boys to help with egg collection. However, Milltown with 35,000 hens manages to operate with a staff of only three full-time men and two boys during the winter. During the summer the manager operates the enterprise himself with the aid of only four boys. This is possible in the case of Milltown because this colony does not candle or grade its eggs—otherwise, it would have to double its staff. It is nevertheless amazing that these large scale operations can be handled with such a relatively small labour force. This is possible of course because of the highly automated nature of the enterprise.

The laying hen enterprise requires the following basic facilities: 1) a brooder barn (where chicks are raised until the pullets are 5-1/2 to 6 months of age and ready for laying), 2) a laying barn, 3) a feed preparation section in both the brooder and laying barns, and 4) a section adjacent to the laying barn consisting of a room for egg candling and grading, a cold storage room for eggs, and on some colonies a veterinary laboratory for the analysis of chicken diseases. The colonies

TABLE 10-3

AVERAGE NUMBER OF LAYING HENS, 1968
PER MANITOBA FARM[1], PER HUTTERITE COLONY,
AND PER HUTTERITE FAMILY[2]

Column no.		Manitoba Farms				Hutterite Colonies		
Agric. district	1	2	3	4	5	6	7	8
	Total no. of farms in district	No. of farms operating hen enterprises	Total no. of laying hens	Average no. of hens per farm (based on col. 1)	Average no. of hens per farm (based on col. 2)	Total no. of colonies in dist.	No. of colonies operating hen enterprises	Total no. of families in all colonies in dist.
A	5,795	1,947	811,000	140	417	21	21	329
B	1,360	506	118,000	87	233	4	4	62
C	2,221	961	124,000	56	129	5	5	76
D	7,190	2,748	315,000	44	114	4	3	44
E	6,209	2,445	1,001,000	161	409	6	5	88
F	1,438	818	135,000	94	165	3	3	36
Other districts	15,534	7,746	326,000	21	42	0	0	0
Total/Average	38,200	17,181	2,830,000	74	165	43	41	635

Hutterite Colonies

Column no. / Agric. district	9. No. of families in col's operating hen enterprises	10. Total no. of laying hens	11. Average no. of hens per colony (based on col. 6)	12. Average no. of hens per colony (based on col. 7)	13. Average no. of hens per family (based on col. 8)	14. Col. 4 as a % of col. 13	15. Average no. of hens per family (based on Col. 9)	16. Col. 5 as a % of col. 15
A	329	243,800	11,610	11,610	741	18.9%	741	56.3%
B	62	43,000	10,750	10,750	694	12.5%	694	33.6%
C	76	78,700	15,740	15,740	1,355	4.1%	1,355	9.5%
D	35	35,500	8,875	11,833	807	5.5%	1,014	11.2%
E	76	73,900	12,317	14,780	840	19.2%	972	42.1%
F	36	31,600	10,533	10,533	878	10.7%	878	16.8%
Other districts	0	0	0	0	0	-	0	-
Total/Average	614	506,500	11,779	12,354	796	9.3%	825	20.0%

[1] Source:
- Data on total number of farms and number of laying hens compiled from Yearbook of Manitoba Agriculture 1968, pp. 28, 31. (Number of Manitoba farms is based on 1966 data, except the total of 38,200 which is the 1968 figure.)
- Data on number of farms that operate a laying hen enterprise - compiled from 1966 Census of Canada: Agriculture - Manitoba, pp. 18-1, 18-2, 18-3. (Data on number of farms is for 1966).
[2] Source:
Data on Hutterite production compiled from field work by J. Ryan.

with very large operations usually have two brooder barns and two laying barns, and some colonies may have a large grain elevator located near the chicken barns and connected to them by a system of grain augers (Plates 13 and 14).

The laying hens are confined in wire cages (3 or 4 to a cage) and the cages form a back-to-back 2-tier structure (3 tiers on some colonies) extending the length of the barn (Plate 15). The cage structures are separated by an aisle wide enough to permit the passage of a feedcart or an egg collection cart. Most colonies use a battery-powered feedcart which dispenses a regulated amount of feed into troughs along both tiers as it is propelled along the aisle. On some colonies feed is distributed along the tiers by a chain system within the feed troughs and the operation is activated at set periods by an automatic timing device. Such sophisticated equipment is expensive but it reduces the amount of labour that would ordinarily be required.

The wire floor of each cage is slightly inclined so that as soon as an egg is laid it rolls out of the cage to an adjacent wire platform below the feed trough. This reduces the possibility of eggs getting dirty or cracked and it is convenient for egg collection.

Directly below each row of cages there is a deep pit extending the length of the barn where the chicken manure accumulates. This is cleaned out in the spring and in the fall by a tractor equipped with a front-end loader. In those barns where the pits are relatively shallow, the manure has to be cleaned out once a month. Afterwards the manure is spread on the fields as fertilizer. Surprisingly, even though there is a long interval between manure cleanings, the barns are so well ventilated that there is very little odour in the structures.

On every colony the breed of chicken that is kept for laying purposes is the White Leghorn. The hens are kept from 13 to 18 months, depending on the productivity of the flock and on the policy of the enterprise manager. The smaller enterprises replace one-half of the hens at a time, while those with 20,000 hens or more usually replace only one-third at a time.

The chicks are bought from hatcheries, usually in Winnipeg, and they are raised in the brooder barn. Ordinarily most White Leghorn pullets start laying at 20 weeks, but most managers try to delay the laying stage until the pullets are at least 22 weeks of age. If the pullets start laying too early, the first eggs are very small and uneconomical to sell. Furthermore, early laying causes the pullets to take longer to mature. It is possible to delay the onset of laying by feeding the pullets a slightly reduced protein diet and by limiting the hours of light.

Shortly before the pullets are transferred to the laying barn, the old hens are taken out and marketed. The laying barn is cleaned and disinfected, and the pullets are then placed in the laying cages. Within a few weeks the young hens are in full production.

The diet of the pullets and hens is very carefully controlled, and the productivity of the flock is very much the result of the enterprise manager's expertise in poultry nutrition. The managers acquire this knowledge through experience, observation of operations at other colonies, the advice and recommendations of feed companies, feed manuals, farm journals, and agricultural bulletins. In addition, some managers have taken university extension courses on poultry nutrition.[2]

Poultry nutrition is more involved and specific than the feeding system in any other enterprise. On most colonies about eight different types of rations are fed during the course of the operation. Since the poultry diet has a direct relationship to the type of grain used for feed on the colonies, the feeding system should be examined in some detail. The following feed programme is used on most colonies:[3] In the brooder barn during the first 5 weeks the chicks are fed a commercially produced complete feed (a 21 percent protein-mineral-vitamin supplement). After this stage, with the exception of a basic supplement, the feed is mixed on the colonies. However, about a half a dozen colonies purchase complete feed for the entire laying hen operation, but the ramifications of this will be discussed later. The rations change throughout the different stages of growth and development as follows: The pullets from 6 to 10 weeks are fed an 18 percent protein ration, from 11 to 14 weeks—16-1/2 percent, from 15 to 20 weeks—15-1/2 percent, and from 21 to 22 weeks—16 percent. Note that during the 15 to 20 week stage the protein content is cut down to delay the onset of laying. Once in production, the flock is fed as follows: for the first 6 months—an 18 percent protein ration, the next 3 or 4 months are at 17 percent, and the final 3 months or longer are at 16 percent.

An example of the content of some of the rations should be given to show the proportion and the different types of grain that are used. An 18 percent protein ration for pullets consists of the following proportions per ton of feed: 800 pounds of wheat, 500 pounds of barley, 200 pounds of oats, and 500 pounds of concentrate. A 15-1/2 percent ration for pullets consists of 800 pounds of barley, 550 pounds of oats, 300 pounds of wheat, and 350 pounds of concentrate. For laying hens an 18 percent protein ration consists of 1200 pounds of wheat, 250 pounds of barley, 400 pounds of concentrate, and 150 pounds of oyster shell. A 16 percent protein ration for hens consists of 600 pounds of wheat, 600 pounds of barley, 300 pounds of oats, 350 pounds of concentrate, and 150 pounds of oyster shell.

It should be noted that wheat and barley form the basis of the bulk of

J. Ryan (1972)

PLATE 13. *The chicken laying barn at James Valley Colony* located 5 miles south of Elie. The structure was built in 1971 and has a capacity for 16,000 laying hens. Large doors at the front and rear allow the entry of a tractor to clean the sunken manure pits. The candling, grading, and egg storage section is on the left. Note the grain auger pipe at the top of the feed storage tanks which leads from the grain elevator shown on Plate 14. The feed is prepared in the elevator and is conveyed by the auger system to the laying barn.

the rations and that oats plays a minor role. These are the rations that have been in use since about 1970, but prior to this period a greater proportion of oats was used in almost all enterprise feeds. Although the 1968 crop data still showed a predominance of oats on the colonies, with the change in nutrition policy, the proportion of oats now grown is considerably less.

In recent years a few colonies have been purchasing a commercially prepared complete feed for their entire chicken operation. The main reason for this has been that these colonies have not had enough land to produce sufficient grain for all their enterprises. In the past they simply purchased extra grain, and although many colonies still do this, other colonies have found it to their advantage to purchase the complex

J. Ryan (1972)

PLATE 14. *The chicken brooder barn and grain elevator* at James Valley Colony. The 25,000 bushel elevator was built in 1971. Note the grain auger pipe leading from the elevator to the feed storage tanks of the chicken laying barn, part of which is shown at the extreme left and all of it being shown on Plate 13.

chicken rations as a complete feed. Milltown, with a 35,000 laying hen operation, is one of the colonies that purchases complete feed, and this is one of the reasons for the small labour force in this enterprise.

The production of eggs is of course the main source of income in a laying hen operation and this phase must be dealt with as well. Eggs are collected by hand every day, usually in the afternoon. The eggs are placed in cartons and loaded on a special cart which is pushed along the aisles between the hen cages. This job can be handled just as efficiently by a young boy or girl as by an adult. To give an indication of the magnitude of this job, Milltown Colony produces between 23,000 and 28,000 eggs a day. As previously mentioned, Milltown does not candle or grade its eggs so in this phase of the operation the main labour is in

J. Ryan (1972)

PLATE 15. *Laying hens at Crystal Spring Colony*. The barn has a capacity for 9,600 hens and has four rows of 3-tier back-to-back cages. Note that as soon as the eggs are laid they roll out from the cages on the slightly inclined wire floor and accumulate directly under the feed troughs. The sunken manure pits are directly below each row of cages but this is not clearly shown in the picture.

egg collection. As a result the price that Milltown receives for its eggs is 2 to 3 cents less per dozen, but operating on this basis they can maintain a very large scale enterprise with a minimum of labour. All other colonies, however, do candle and grade their eggs. Although these procedures are highly automated, they are nevertheless time-consuming and require skilled labour (Plate 16).

A number of colonies have been entering national egg exhibition shows, and in 1971 Springhill Colony won the grand championship in the egg show at the Canadian National Exhibition in Toronto. Judging was based on the size and quality of the eggs, and the colony also won the sweepstake medal for scoring the most points of total entries submitted. This colony has an operation of 26,000 laying hens, and has been entering the exhibition egg show since 1954.[4]

TABLE 10-4

AVERAGE NUMBER OF HENS AND BROILERS

PER HUTTERITE COLONY - JUNE 1, 1968

AND AVERAGE NUMBER OF BROILERS SOLD PER COLONY IN 1968

Agric. district	No. of colonies operating hen enterprises	Average no. of hens per colony	No. of colonies operating broiler enterprises	Average No. of broilers per colony (June 1)	Average no. of broilers sold in 1968
A	21	11,610	5	8,700	27,800
B	4	10,750	3	8,167	38,500
C	5	15,740	1	3,000	3,000
D	3	11,833	0	0	0
E	5	14,780	1	16,000	49,500
F	3	10,533	0	0	0
Total/ Average	41	12,354	10	8,700	30,700

Source: Data compiled from field work by J. Ryan.

2. The Chicken Broiler Operation

In 1968 only ten colonies were in the broiler business, and of these only five were highly specialized. Table 10-4 shows that the average number of broilers per colony on June 1 was 8,700, and the average number of broilers sold per colony during 1968 was 30,700. The June holdings ranged from a low of 3,000 at Riverside Colony to a high of 13,000 at Interlake and Pembina colonies. Riverside sold only one flock in 1968, while Pembina and Interlake both sold five flocks during that year or a total of 65,000 broilers each.

If a colony specializes in broiler production and keeps broilers on a year-round basis, this becomes a separate enterprise with its own manager. However, on those colonies where only one or two sets of broilers are raised during the year, this comes under the directorship of the laying hen enterprise manager.

J. Ryan (1972)

PLATE 16. *Girls at Crystal Spring Colony packing eggs* in cartons from the egg grading machine. The machine grades the eggs according to weight and size and deposits them into the appropriate sections in front of the girls. Prior to grading, the eggs are candled in a section adjacent to the egg grading machine. A dark curtain surrounds the candling unit, part of which is shown at the extreme right. A man candles the eggs and they then proceed along a conveyor belt to the egg grading machine.

On a colony that specializes in broiler production, a special barn is constructed for this purpose, sometimes a two-deck structure. On several colonies, however, the same structure is used for both geese and broilers. Geese occupy the barn from the beginning of March to the end of June. During the rest of the year the barn is used for broiler production. One colony, Lakeside, uses the brooder barn for broilers when it is not being used for raising pullets for laying purposes. As the colony does not keep a large laying flock only one set of pullets is raised each year, but this occupies the barn for only six months. To make full use of the barn, two sets of broilers are produced during the rest of the year.

TABLE 10-5

MANITOBA HUTTERITE COLONIES

GROSS SALES INCOME FROM THE

CHICKEN ENTERPRISE, 1968

Total gross sales income from all enterprises	$11,598,282.40
Gross sales income from chicken enterprise	$ 3,241,275.67
Gross sales income from chicken enterprise as a % of total gross sales income	27.9%
No. of colonies reporting sales from chicken enterprise	41
No. of families on these colonies	614
Average gross sales income per colony	$ 79,055.50
Average gross sales income per family	$ 5,278.95

Source: Data compiled by J. Ryan from the financial
        reports on each colony for 1968, as prepared
        by Meyers, Dickens, Norris, Penny & Company,
        the accounting firm employed by the Hutterite
        colonies.

Broilers are ready for market 9 or 10 weeks after the chicks are purchased from the hatchery. As soon as the broilers are marketed, the barn is cleaned and disinfected, and another batch of chicks is brought in. Colonies specializing in broiler production can raise five sets of broilers each year.

Significance of the Chicken Enterprise to the Colony Economy

Separate income statements are not available for eggs, broilers, and fowl because colonies prepare a single combined income statement for the entire chicken enterprise. Consequently, it is impossible to compare the income with that of other Manitoba farms.

The chicken enterprise produces the largest gross sales income for the Hutterite colonies after hogs (Appendix G). In 1968 the colonies received a gross sales income of $3,241,275.67 from this operation and it accounted for 27.9 percent of the total gross sales (Table 10-5). The average sales income for each of the 41 colonies with chicken enterprises was $79,055.50, or $5,278.95 per family. Among the colonies gross sales income ranged from a low of $16,000 to a high of over $190,000.

The largest source of income is from the sale of eggs. Colonies that keep broilers also receive a substantial income from this. The sale of old laying hens produces little income. The price may be as low as 50 cents a bird, which is the cost of a replacement chick.

The price of eggs in Manitoba has been so low in recent years as to bring a crisis even to the Hutterites, despite their large-scale operations. Data on the actual operating expenses are unavailable, but the management personnel of the colonies are unanimous in stating that this activity has now become among the colonies' least profitable. Many colonies claim that they have been only breaking even since 1968, while several state that they have started to lose money. Meanwhile, so long as there is hope that prices will improve eventually, they feel they have no alternative but to carry on if only because of the large capital investment involved. In the meantime, the balanced structure of the colonies makes it possible for the other enterprises to cover the losses of any single enterprise, even for a number of years. Nevertheless, even the Hutterites cannot expect to continue losing enterprises for any considerable period. At the time of writing, the chicken enterprises on many colonies are in a very precarious position.

Notes and References

1. The information for this section was obtained by observing the operations of the chicken enterprise on many colonies and by interviews and discussions with the enterprise and colony managers. In particular, the writer made a detailed study of the operations at Crystal Spring, James Valley, Milltown, and Springhill colonies.
2. In 1965, Dan Kleinsasser, the chicken enterprise manager at Crystal Spring Colony, completed an extension course on poultry nutrition at the University of Manitoba. Since then he has taken two short courses on veterinary poultry science at the Salisbury Poultry Institute in Charles City, Iowa.
3. The ration specifications and the feeding programme for the chicken enterprise were provided by Andy Wurtz, the chicken enterprise manager at James Valley Colony.
4. This information was obtained from Springhill Colony and also from an article in the *Winnipeg Tribune* of August 25, 1971.

CHAPTER 11

THE TURKEY ENTERPRISE

Number of Turkeys and Comparison with Manitoba Farms

Although only 12 colonies were involved in the turkey enterprise in 1968, this operation was of major significance to both the colonies involved and overall Manitoba production. On 7 of the colonies involved, the turkey enterprise ranked first or second in importance in terms of total income received by these colonies.[1] In regard to overall Manitoba production, the Hutterites have long been acclaimed as major turkey producers.

On the census date June 1, 1968 the 12 Hutterite colonies had a total of 174,300 turkeys or 20 percent of the Manitoba total (Table 11-1). This table also shows that in 1968 the Hutterites sold a total of 223,300 turkeys or 23.7 percent of Manitoba production. Of the turkeys sold, 176,300 or 19.8 percent of Manitoba production were heavy weight mature turkeys. The remainder were the higher priced lighter weight broiler turkeys, which totalled 47,000 or 95.9 percent of overall Manitoba production. Obviously in regard to broiler turkeys, the Hutterites are almost the sole producers of this specialty product.

Table 11-1 shows that turkeys were produced by Hutterite colonies in only two agricultural districts—Districts A and E. The colonies in the other areas were not involved in turkey production for a variety of reasons. Some did not produce enough grain for an additional major enterprise, some did not have the extra labour force that would be required, and others did not consider that it would be a profitable or viable operation for a combination of reasons.

Table 11-2 shows the average number of turkeys on June 1, 1968 and the average number of turkeys sold in 1968 per Manitoba farm, per Hutterite colony, and per Hutterite family. Unfortunately, data on the number of farms that operated a turkey enterprise are available for 1966 only; however, it is highly unlikely that 1968 data would be significantly different. Furthermore, the differences between Hutterite operations and average farm operations are generally so great that there is

TABLE 11-1

NUMBER OF TURKEYS - JUNE 1, 1968

AND TOTAL NUMBER OF TURKEYS SOLD DURING 1968

MANITOBA FARMS[1] AND HUTTERITE COLONIES[2]

Agric. district	Hutterite Colonies			
	Total no. of turkeys June 1	No. of turkeys sold at mature stage	No. of turkeys sold at broiler stage	Total no. of turkeys sold in 1968
A	143,300	145,300	40,000	185,300
B	0	0	0	0
C	0	0	0	0
D	0	0	0	0
E	31,000	31,000	7,000	38,000
F	0	0	0	0
Total Hutt- erite	174,300	176,300	47,000	223,300
Total Manitoba	870,000	892,000	49,000	941,000
Hutt. turkeys as a % of Manitoba turkeys	20.0%	19.8%	95.9%	23.7%

[1] Source: <u>Yearbook of Manitoba Agriculture 1968</u>, p. 28. (data for individual districts unavailable)

[2] Source: Data compiled from field work by J. Ryan.

TABLE 11-2

AVERAGE NUMBER OF TURKEYS - JUNE 1, 1968
AND AVERAGE NUMBER OF TURKEYS SOLD DURING 1968
PER MANITOBA FARM,[1] PER HUTTERITE COLONY,
AND PER HUTTERITE FAMILY[2]

No. of Manitoba farms operating a turkey enterprise	2,864
Total number of turkeys, June 1	870,000
Average number of turkeys per farm, June 1	304
Total number of turkeys sold	941,000
Average number of turkeys sold per farm	329
No. of Hutterite colonies operating a turkey enterprise	12
Total number of turkeys, June 1	174,300
Average number of turkeys per colony, June 1	14,525
Average Man. farm as a % of average Hutterite colony	.02%
Total number of turkeys sold	223,300
Average number of turkeys sold per colony	18,608
Average Man. farm as a % of average Hutterite colony	.02%
No. of Hutterite families operating a turkey enterprise	191
Total number of turkeys, June 1	174,300
Average number of turkeys per family, June 1	913
Average Man. farm as a % of average Hutterite family	33.3%
Total number of turkeys sold	223,300
Average number of turkeys sold per family	1,169
Average Man. farm as a % of average Hutterite family	28.1%

[1]Source: -Data on turkeys compiled from Yearbook of Manitoba Agriculture 1968, p. 28.
- Data on number of farms operating a turkey enterprise compiled from 1966 Census of Canada: Agriculture - Manitoba, p. 18-1 (data on no. of farms available for 1966 only).

[2]Source: Data on Hutterite operations for 1968 compiled from field work by J. Ryan.

every assurance that the same basic conclusions could be drawn even if data on the number of farms in 1968 were available.

As indicated by Table 11-2 the average number of turkeys produced on the 2,864 Manitoba farms was 304 and the average number sold was 329. On the other hand, the average number of turkeys on a Hutterite colony was 14,525, while the average number sold was 18,608. Hence the average Manitoba producer had only .02 percent of the turkeys of a Hutterite colony and also accounted for only .02 percent of the sales. As discussed in previous chapters with regard to other enterprises, since the average Manitoba farm is a single family operation, a more meaningful comparison than the Hutterite colony as a unit would be the scale of operations per Hutterite family.

As shown in Table 11-2 there were 191 Hutterite families on the 12 turkey producing colonies, and on this basis the average number of turkeys per family was 913, while the average number of turkey sales was 1,169. A totally different picture now emerges because the average Manitoba producer has 33.3 percent of the turkeys of an average Hutterite family, and accounts for 28.1 percent of the turkey sales. On this basis, although the turkey operations per Hutterite family are significantly larger than those of the average Manitoba producer, they can now be considered as comparable. Hence, on a per family basis, the Hutterite turkey operations are not in a different category from average Manitoba producers. This observation is significant because Hutterite operations are very seldom considered from this point of view.

The Operation of the Turkey Enterprise[2]

In 1968 all 12 colonies involved in the turkey enterprise sold heavy weight mature turkeys, but only 4 of these colonies sold broiler turkeys (Table 11-3). The average number of turkeys sold per colony was 18,608, but this ranged from a low of 5,300 at Huron Colony to a high of 34,000 at Rosedale.[3]

The labour force for the turkey enterprise consists of the enterprise manager plus one assistant on the larger operations. Additional part-time help is provided whenever it is required, for example, when the turkeys are moved from the brooder barn to the range shelters.

The facilities required for the turkey enterprise are not elaborate, but on most colonies a considerable amount of yard space is utilized for the turkey range. A basic requirement is a large brooder barn for the turkey poults. In the past many of these used to be two-deck structures in an attempt to economize on building costs. However, these are unlikely to be built on any of the colonies in the future because of the inconveni-

TABLE 11-3

AVERAGE NUMBER OF TURKEYS

PER HUTTERITE COLONY - JUNE 1, 1968

AND AVERAGE NUMBER OF TURKEYS SOLD PER COLONY IN 1968

No. of colonies operating a turkey enterprise	12
Total number of turkeys June 1	174,300
Average no. of turkeys per colony June 1	14,525

No. of colonies selling turkeys at mature stage	12
Total no. of mature turkeys sold	176,300
Average no. of mature turkeys sold per colony	14,692

No. of colonies selling turkeys at broiler stage	4
Total no. of broiler turkeys sold	47,000
Average no. of broiler turkeys sold per colony	11,750

No. of colonies selling turkeys	12
Total no. of turkeys sold	223,300
Average no. of turkeys sold per colony	18,608

Source: Data compiled from field work by J. Ryan.

ence and the manual labour required in manure cleaning, and getting the turkeys in and out of the upper section. On those colonies that operate the turkey enterprise on a year-round basis, a second large barn is required for the older turkeys. In addition, large confinement barns or range shelters are required on the turkey range. These are for protection from heavy rainstorms and from cold weather in the early spring and late fall. Self-feeding units are installed in all the barns and special large units are located on the turkey range. The turkey range, consisting of several acres, must be partitioned by a high fence or two separate ranges are required for the purpose of segregating the male and female turkeys. This is an important economic consideration because if the turkeys are raised together, the turkey hens invariably peck at the backs of the turkey "toms" and the bruises and discoloration result in a substandard market grade for the "toms."

To raise turkeys to mature market standards takes about 21 weeks for turkey hens (average weight 15 pounds) and about 24 weeks for turkey "toms" (average weight 25 pounds). Turkeys raised for broiler purposes are usually sold at about 14 to 16 weeks when they weigh about 10 to 12 pounds. Broiler turkeys usually sell for about two or three cents a pound more than mature turkeys. Broiler turkeys are often raised on some colonies as a late fall or winter project. This is an attempt to make more efficient use of the turkey facilities, providing that the extra labour force and feed grain are available.

During the course of a year, a number of colonies raise two flocks of mature turkeys plus one flock of broiler turkeys. The first flock is usually purchased at the beginning of March and the hens are sold at the beginning of August and the "toms" at the beginning of September. The second flock would be purchased about mid-May (as soon as the first batch of turkey poults vacates the brooder barn) and these would be sold in October and November. A third flock may be purchased at the beginning of November and sold for broiler purposes near the end of February.

For rapid weight gain and proper carcass development, the turkeys have to be fed a carefully controlled diet. In recent years the nutritional programme has put an emphasis on wheat and minimized the amount of oats. As in rations for other enterprises, the key feature is the protein content of the feed. At the present time most colonies adhere to the following programme:[4] for the first three weeks—a feed content of 28 percent protein; the 4th and 5th week—25 percent protein; from 6 to 10 weeks—22 percent protein; from 11 to 14 weeks—18 percent protein; and from 15 to 24 weeks (or market time)—16 percent protein. To demonstrate the considerable amount of wheat and oats used and to show the complexity of the rations, the actual content of two formulas will be presented, as examples. The 25 percent protein formula for a ton of feed consists of the following: 1,150 pounds of wheat, 575 pounds soybeans, 100 pounds meatmeal, 50 pounds fishmeal, 50 pounds ground alfalfa, 50 pounds premix (minerals, vitamins, etc.), 15 pounds calcium carbonate, and 10 pounds tallow. The 16 percent protein formula (the one used for the longest period) consists of the following ingredients: 1,450 pounds wheat; 200 pounds oats; 200 pounds soybeans; 50 pounds meatmeal; 50 pounds premix; 25 pounds ground alfalfa; and 25 pounds calcium carbonate. In addition, several pounds of medicinal compounds are included in each ton of feed. Hence wheat forms the bulk of the turkey feed, while very little oats is used and no barley at all. Perhaps a surprising feature of these formulas is the fact

TABLE 11-4

MANITOBA HUTTERITE COLONIES

GROSS SALES INCOME FROM THE

TURKEY ENTERPRISE, 1968

Total gross sales income from all enterprises	$11,598,282.40
Gross sales income from the turkey enterprise	$ 908,694.94
Gross sales income from turkeys as a % of total gross sales income	7.8%
No. of colonies reporting income from the turkey enterprise	12
No. of families on these colonies	191
Average gross sales income per colony	$ 75,724.58
Average gross sales income per family	$ 4,757.57

Source: Data compiled by J. Ryan from the financial reports on each colony for 1968, as prepared by Meyers, Dickens, Norris, Penny & Company, the accounting firm employed by the Hutterite colonies.

that so much specialized feed has to be purchased.

Turkeys are not killed on the colonies but are transported live to the packing plants in Winnipeg. Each colony must therefore reserve in advance a specific day or days at the packing plants for delivery of the turkeys.

Significance of the Turkey Enterprise to the Colony Economy

The turkey enterprise was of major importance on all 12 colonies engaged in this operation in 1968. That year the total income from the sale of turkeys was $908,694.94 or an average of $75,724.58 per colony and $4,757.57 per family (Table 11-4). The turkey enterprise was the fourth largest producer of gross sales income and accounted for 7.8 percent of the gross sales income of all colonies (Appendix G). Although turkeys were produced on only 36 percent of the colonies, the total sales income from this operation was only slightly less than the amount received from the sales of grain (Appendix G). In fact, in 1967 the turkey enterprise was the third largest producer of gross sales income (displacing grain) and accounted for 9.7 percent of the total sales income.[5]

The total sales income includes the income from both broilers and mature turkeys so it is impossible to arrive at a realistic price per bird. Not very many turkeys are consumed on the colonies, but local use is nevertheless of some economic significance.

The turkey enterprise appears to be a profitable operation for all colonies and it is surprising that more colonies are not involved in it. The recent setbacks in the hog and chicken enterprises may encourage more colonies to go into turkey production in the future.

Notes and References

1. These data were compiled from the financial records of each Hutterite colony, prepared by Meyers, Dickens, Norris, Penny & Company of Brandon, the accountants employed by the colonies.
2. The basic information for this section was obtained by observing the operations on a number of Hutterite colonies and by interviewing some of the ministers and the enterprise and colony managers. In particular, the writer made a study of the operations at Crystal Spring and Fairholme colonies.
3. These data were compiled from field work by the writer.
4. The feed programme and the formulas for the turkey rations were provided by Dave Kleinsasser, the turkey enterprise manager at Crystal Spring Colony.
5. Data compiled from the financial records of the colonies.

CHAPTER 12

THE GOOSE AND DUCK ENTERPRISES

Although the goose and duck enterprises are not complex operations, their analysis is not simple because of the considerable number of variables. Most colonies operate either one or the other or both of these enterprises, but some have breeding flocks and others do not. The colonies with breeding flocks operate their own hatcheries, and they may either sell goslings or ducklings, or raise them to maturity, or do both. Hence the analysis of these enterprises is not as straightforward as their actual operation.

Number of Colonies Operating Goose and Duck Enterprises

In 1968 goose enterprises were conducted on 30 of the 43 colonies, and 23 colonies had goose breeding flocks (Table 12-1). Thirty-five colonies operated duck enterprises, but only 9 had breeding flocks (Table 12-2). Table 12-3 shows the various combinations of duck and goose enterprises. This table indicates that 26 colonies raised both ducks and geese, but only 8 colonies had breeding flocks of both ducks and geese. Thirteen colonies did not keep geese and 8 did not keep ducks, but only 4 colonies did not keep either geese or ducks.

Of the four colonies not involved in either of these enterprises, one of them, Wellwood, was a new colony and it now operates a goose enterprise. The remaining three, Glenway, Oak Bluff, and Whiteshell, have apparently been unable to persuade any of the colony personnel to operate these enterprises.

Nowadays the availability of a suitable river or stream for ducks and geese does not have a bearing on a colony's decision to operate these enterprises.[1] In the past, this was considered important and is undoubtedly one reason why so many colonies are located near rivers or streams.[2] The Hutterites have always had a tradition of raising ducks and geese, and it was thought that water was an essential element for

TABLE 12-1

NUMBER OF HUTTERITE COLONIES

INVOLVED IN DIFFERENT TYPES OF

GOOSE ENTERPRISES, 1968

Total number of Hutterite colonies in Manitoba in 1968	43	100%
No. of colonies that keep a breeding flock of geese	23	53.5%
No. of colonies with no goose breeding flock but who purchase goslings and raise geese	7	16.3%
Total number of colonies that operate goose enterprises	30	69.8%
No. of colonies that do not operate goose enterprises	13	30.2%

Source: Data compiled from field work by J. Ryan.

TABLE 12-2

NUMBER OF HUTTERITE COLONIES

INVOLVED IN DIFFERENT TYPES OF

DUCK ENTERPRISES, 1968

Total no. of Hutterite colonies in Manitoba in 1968	43	100%
No. of colonies that keep a breeding flock of ducks	9	20.9%
No. of colonies with no duck breeding flock but who purchase ducklings and raise ducks	26	60.5%
Total number of colonies that operate duck enterprises	35	81.4%
No. of colonies that do not operate duck enterprises	8	18.6%

Source: Data compiled from field work by J. Ryan.

TABLE 12-3

NUMBER OF HUTTERITE COLONIES

INVOLVED IN BOTH DUCK AND GOOSE ENTERPRISES, 1968

	No.	%
1. No. of colonies that keep breeding flocks of both ducks and geese	8	18.6%
2. No. of colonies that keep only a goose breeding flock	15	34.9%
3. No. of colonies that keep only a duck breeding flock	1	2.3%
4. No. of colonies with only a goose breeding flock but who purchase ducklings and raise ducks as well as geese	12	27.9%
5. No. of colonies with only a duck breeding flock but who purchase goslings and raise geese as well as ducks	0	0%
6. No. of colonies without goose or duck breeding flocks who purchase goslings and raise geese	7	16.3%
7. No. of colonies without goose or duck breeding flocks who purchase ducklings and raise ducks	14	32.6%
8. No. of colonies without goose or duck breeding flocks who purchase both goslings and ducklings	6	14.0%
9. Total number of colonies that raise both ducks and geese	26	60.5%
10. Total number of colonies that raise geese only	4	9.3%
11. Total number of colonies that raise ducks only	9	20.9%
12. Total number of colonies that do not raise either ducks or geese	4	9.3%
13. Total number of colonies in Manitoba in 1968	43	100%

Source: Data compiled from field work by J. Ryan.

TABLE 12-4

NUMBER OF GEESE - July 1, 1968

AND NUMBER OF GOSLINGS AND GEESE SOLD IN 1968

MANITOBA FARMS[1] AND HUTTERITE COLONIES[2]

Column No.	1		2	3	4	5	6	7
Agric. district	Breeding Flock		No. of goslings hatched	No. of goslings sold (plus 2% mortality bonus)	No. of goslings retained	No. of goslings bought by Man. Hut. col's with no br. flock (plus 2%)	Total no. of geese July 1[3]	No. of geese sold in 1968
	No. of ganders	No. of geese						
A	2,895	6,780	83,700	20,100	63,600	8,670	81,945	62,990
B	480	1,420	17,000	6,120	10,880	3,060	15,840	13,560
C	225	860	14,000	13,054	946	2,240	4,271	2,665
D	175	425	6,000	306	5,694	4,080	10,374	8,590
E	400	1,050	16,500	10,200	6,300	0	7,750	6,075
F	30	90	1,200	0	1,200	0	1,320	990
Total Hutterite	4,205	10,625	138,400	49,780	88,620	18,050	121,500	94,870
Total Manitoba								100,000
Hut. geese as a % of Man. geese								94.9%

[1] Source: Yearbook of Manitoba Agriculture 1968, p. 27. (The only data available are total Manitoba sales.)

[2] Source: Data compiled from field work by J. Ryan.

[3] The total number of geese on July 1 consists of the data in columns Nos. 1, 4 and 5.

their production. However, with present-day scientific feeding procedures, the Hutterites have discovered that a water supply is of little significance, and in fact it may even be a handicap. By being out on water the ducks and geese pick up large quantities of vegetative material which is low in protein content. This prevents them from eating a sufficient amount of properly balanced rations and retards their growth and development. However, since only one flock is raised a year, there is often no particular rush to get the ducks and geese off to market, and the Hutterites have allowed them to remain in their natural habitat.

A. The Goose Enterprise

Number of Geese and Comparison with Manitoba Farms

Census data are usually based on conditions as they exist on June 1 of any particular year, however, this date is inappropriate in the case of ducks and geese. The hatching season ends at the end of June, and consequently, July 1 is a far more appropriate date because it is then possible to list the full year's production of goslings and ducklings. As it turns out, no comparison problems are created by using July 1 as the census date for Hutterite geese and ducks because the only reliable information available for Manitoba production in 1968 is simply the total number of geese and ducks sold during the year.[3]

It is commonly known in Manitoba that the Hutterites are the main producers of geese, but it nevertheless is surprising that they account for 95 percent of the goose sales, at least they did in 1968 (Table 12-4). This refers to only mature geese that are sold in the fall. In addition, the Hutterites sell more than half of the mature geese as goslings in the spring (Table 12-4). However, this table also indicates that over one-third of the gosling sales are made to Manitoba Hutterite colonies which are without breeding flocks. The total number of geese owned by Hutterites on July 1, 1968 was 121,500. Manitoba data for 1968 are unavailable, but in 1966 the total number of geese in the province was 133,853.[4] The figure for Manitoba is based on the holdings on June 1, whereas the Hutterite data are based on July 1, at the end of the hatching season. However, the June hatch is generally small and it is estimated that this hatch accounts for only about 15 percent of the season's goslings.[5] Nevertheless, it is obvious that in Manitoba the Hutterites are almost in a complete monopoly position in regard to goose production.

TABLE 12-5

THE GOOSE ENTERPRISE, 1968

HUTTERITE COLONIES WITH A GOOSE BREEDING FLOCK

Number of colonies at the beginning of 1968 with a goose breeding flock = 23

	Totals for 23 colonies		Average no. per colony
	No.	%	No.
1. Size of breeding flock at the beginning of 1968: Ganders	4,205	28.4%	183
Geese	10,625	71.6%	462
Total flock	14,830	100%	645
2. Number of goslings hatched in 1968	138,400	100%	6,017
3. Average number of goslings per goose	13.0	-	13.0
4. Number of goslings sold	48,800	-	2,122
5. No. of goslings added as a bonus to the no. sold for anticipated mortality (2% of the number sold)	980	-	43
6. Goslings sold (plus 2% bonus) as a % of goslings hatched	-	36.0%	-
7. Number and % of goslings kept	88,620	64.0%	3,853
8. Total no. of geese July 1 (after hatching season and after sales of goslings, i.e. Items #1 and #7)	103,450	100%	4,498
9. Number of mature geese sold (by these 23 colonies)	79,670	-	3,464
10. Mature geese sold as a % of total geese July 1	-	77.0%	-

11. Number of geese consumed on the 23 colonies	1,410	-	61
12. Number of geese consumed as a % of total geese July 1	-	1.4%	-
13. Total gosling and goose mortality	6,220	-	270
14. Mortality as a % of total geese July 1	-	6.0%	-
15. Size of breeding flock at the end of 1968: Ganders	4,535	-	197
Geese	11,615	-	505
Total flock	16,150	-	702
16. Breeding flock as a % of total geese July 1	-	15.6%	-
17. Number of colonies with a goose breeding flock at the end of 1968 (out of the 23 colonies with breeding flocks at the beginning of 1968)	23		

Source: Data compiled from field work by J. Ryan.

TABLE 12-6

THE GOOSE ENTERPRISE, 1968

HUTTERITE COLONIES WITHOUT A GOOSE BREEDING FLOCK

Number of colonies without a goose breeding flock who purchase goslings and raise geese = 7

	Totals for 7 colonies		Average no. per colony
	No.	%	No.
1. Number of goslings bought (17,700 plus bonus of 2% or 350 for anticipated mortality)	18,050	100%	2,579
2. Number of mature geese sold (by these 7 colonies)	15,200	-	2,171
3. Mature geese sold as a % of goslings bought	-	84.2%	-
4. Number of geese consumed on the 7 colonies	420	-	60
5. Geese consumed as a % of goslings bought	-	2.3%	-
6. Total gosling and goose mortality	1,030	-	147
7. Mortality as a % of goslings bought	-	5.7%	-
8. Number of geese retained for breeding purposes: Ganders	400	-	-
Geese	1,000	-	-
Total flock	1,400	-	-
9. Geese retained for breeding purposes as a % of goslings bought	-	7.8%	-
10. Number of colonies at the end of 1968 with a newly established goose breeding flock (out of the 7 colonies without a breeding flock during 1968)	2	-	-

Source: Data compiled from field work by J. Ryan.

Comparison of Colonies with Goose Breeding Flocks and those without Breeding Flocks

Tables 12-5, 12-6, and 12-7 show the basic comparisons between the colonies with goose breeding flocks and those without. Probably the most significant difference is the scale of operations. At the peak of the season there is an average of 4,498 geese on a colony with a breeding flock as compared to only 2,579 on a colony without a breeding flock (Tables 12-5 and 12-6). Furthermore, a colony with a breeding flock has much more elaborate facilities—in addition to facilities being larger in size, there are quarters for the ganders and geese as well as an expensive goose hatchery. Hence the colonies with breeding flocks have a far greater investment in the operation.

It should be noted that 48,800 goslings or 36 percent of the total hatched were sold immediately (Table 12-5). It should be furthermore noted that over one-third of these are sold to the Hutterite colonies without breeding flocks (Tables 12-6 and 12-7). About one-half of the remainder are usually sold to commercial hatcheries in Winnipeg for further resale. Some of the final remainder are purchased by local farmers, but the greater part is exported to Saskatchewan, Alberta, and the U.S.A. (mainly to Hutterite colonies in these areas).[6] For example, in 1968 the number of goslings exported to the U.S.A. was 10,430.[7]

Of the total geese on hand on July 1, 94,870, or 78 percent, were sold as mature geese in the fall. The Hutterites consumed about 60 geese per colony or 1-1/2 percent, and there was a 6 percent overall mortality (Table 12-7). The remaining 14-1/2 percent consisted of the breeding flock. It should be noted that at the end of 1968 two more colonies had established a breeding flock, thus making a total of 25 colonies with breeding flocks at the end of the year.

The Operation of the Goose Enterprise[8]

Although the average size of a goose breeding flock in 1968 was 645 (Table 12-5), this ranged from a low of 120 at Greenwald Colony to a high of 1,500 at James Valley. The ratio of ganders to geese is usually about 1:3, but in recent years experiments are being made with a smaller number of ganders. Although a goose may lay up to 35 eggs, the maximum number of goslings that could usually be produced would be no more than 20. The average for all colonies in 1968 was 13 per goose, and this was considered to be satisfactory production. With a breeding stock of 1,500 at James Valley, the number of goslings produced in 1968 was 10,000. However, the number of goslings was relatively small because part of the flock was in its first year of

TABLE 12-7

THE GOOSE ENTERPRISE, 1968
ALL HUTTERITE COLONIES THAT RAISE GEESE

No. of colonies with breeding flocks at beginning of 1968 = 23
No. of colonies without breeding flocks but who purchase
goslings and raise geese   = 7
Total number of colonies that raised geese in 1968   = 30

		No.	%
1. Size of breeding flock at beginning of 1968: Ganders		4,205	28.4%
Geese		10,625	71.6%
Total flock		14,830	100%
2. Number of goslings hatched in 1968		138,400	100%
3. Total number of goslings sold (by 23 colonies)		48,800	-
4. No. of goslings added as a bonus to the no. sold for anticipated mortality (2% of the no. sold)		980	
5. Goslings sold (plus 2% bonus) as a % of goslings hatched		-	36.0%
6. No. of goslings sold to the 7 Hutt. colonies without br. flocks		17,700	
7. Goslings sold to Hutterites as a % of total goslings sold			36.3%
8. No. and % of goslings sold to other customers		31,100	63.7%

			No.	%
9. No. of goslings kept by the 23 colonies with breeding flocks	88,620	–		
10. Total no. of geese on all Hutterite colonies July 1 (after hatching season and after sales of goslings to customers other than Hutterite, i.e. Items #1 + #6 (inc. the 2% for mortality) + #9	–	–	121,500	100%
11. Total number of mature geese sold in 1968 by 30 colonies	–	–	94,870	–
12. Total mature geese sold as a % of total geese July 1	–	–	–	78.1%
13. No. and % of mature geese sold by 23 colonies with br. flocks	79,670	84.0%		
14. No. and % of mature geese sold by 7 col. without br. flocks	15,200	16.0%		
15. Total no. of geese consumed on 30 colonies	–	–	1,830	–
16. Total geese consumed as a % of total geese July 1	–	–	–	1.5%
17. Total gosling and goose mortality on 30 colonies	–	–	7,250	–
18. Total mortality as a % of total geese July 1	–	–	–	6.0%
19. Size of breeding flock at the end of 1968: Ganders Geese Total flock	4,935 12,615 17,550	28.1% 71.9% 100%	17,550	
20. Breeding flock as a % of total geese July 1	–	–	–	14.4%
21. Number of colonies with goose breeding flocks at end of 1968	25	–	–	–

Source: Data compiled from field work by J. Ryan.

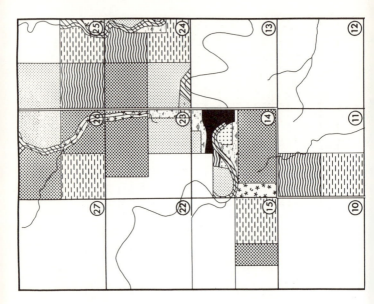

production. To follow this up, in 1971 this colony produced over 19,000 goslings with the same flock.[9]

Since goose and duck operations are so closely allied, unless both enterprises are on a large scale, they are often placed under the director-ship of one manager. In addition, there would be one full-time or part-time assistant, depending on the scale of operations.

On colonies with no breeding flock the facilities required are simply a brooder barn and a pasture area of several acres for the geese in the summer. As noted previously, access to a river or stream is not essential and may even be a hindrance. On colonies with a breeding flock, there must be a laying barn for the geese which is also used as shelter in the winter. Because the number of goslings kept is usually larger, the brooder barns are also more elaborate. These colonies also have a hatchery, and this constitutes a considerable investment.

The geese start laying at the beginning of March and end at the beginning of June. The hatchery goes into operation at about mid-March and the last hatch is usually completed at the end of June. A batch of eggs is set into the incubators every 7 to 10 days and after the initial 28-day hatching period, a flock of goslings is hatched at the appropriate 7 to 10 day interval until the end of the season. Usually

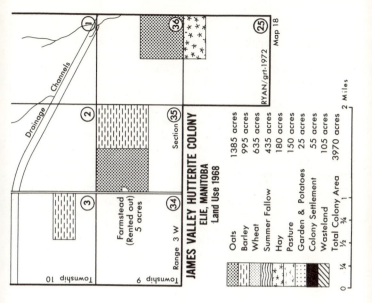

JAMES VALLEY HUTTERITE COLONY
ELIE, MANITOBA
Land Use 1968

Oats	1385 acres
Barley	995 acres
Wheat	635 acres
Summer Fallow	435 acres
Hay	180 acres
Pasture	150 acres
Garden & Potatoes	25 acres
Colony Settlement	55 acres
Wasteland	105 acres
Total Colony Area	3970 acres

RYAN/grt-1972

Map 18

about 10 or 11 hatches take place during the season.

The goslings that are to be sold are packed and shipped immediately after hatching. From the time that goslings are hatched, they can survive for about two days without food or water, and therefore with air transport, it is possible to ship them almost anywhere, including overseas.

The goslings that are to be raised are placed in the brooder barn and they stay there for 6 to 8 weeks. When they are adequately feathered, they are released and are free to roam on the goose pasture. The pasture is adjacent to the colony site and on some colonies may cover as much as 40 acres, e.g., James Valley (Map 18). The brooder barn and the pasture are appropriately equipped with self-feeders and watering units. The breeding flock is kept on a separate pasture and does not mingle with the market geese.

As with other enterprises, the geese are fed specific rations throughout their growing period. Although the bulk of their feed consists of wheat, it contains more oats than is fed in other enterprise rations. For the first 3 weeks the goslings are fed a 21 percent protein ration, from 4 to 6 weeks—19 percent protein, from 7 to 14 weeks—17 percent protein, and from the 15th week to market time—16 percent protein.[10]

It should be noted that from about the 7th week the geese are on pasture and that grazing supplements their feed considerably, especially if part of the pasture is sown in wheat or oats for their benefit. For an indication of the amount of wheat and oats that are fed, the content of two formulas will be presented. The 21 percent protein formula for a ton of feed consists of the following: 1,200 pounds of wheat, 450 pounds of soybeans, 155 pounds of oats, 55 pounds of premix (minerals, vitamins, etc.), 50 pounds of ground alfalfa, 50 pounds of calcium carbonate, and 40 pounds of fishmeal. The 16 percent formula and the one which is fed for the longest period consists of: 1,200 pounds of wheat, 400 pounds of oats, 250 pounds of soybeans, 55 pounds of premix, 50 pounds of ground alfalfa, and 50 pounds of calcium carbonate. The breeder flock are fed a standard 18 percent formula from the beginning of February to the end of June. Once they are through laying, they are fed only a minimal amount of grain and the bulk of their feed comes from grazing on pasture. In the winter they are also fed a minimal amount of grain until February; however, starting in January a mineral and vitamin concentrate is added to their feed to prepare them for laying. In other words, the breeder flock is fed a balanced and full diet only during the laying period.

Geese mature in 18 to 20 weeks and they are then marketed. There are apparently no facilities for the killing of ducks and geese in any of the packing plants in Manitoba, or for that matter in all of Canada.[11] Hence the ducks and geese have to be killed on the colonies, but they are eviscerated in the packing plants. The actual market time is determined by the packing plants because they assign certain dates to the colonies for the delivery of geese and ducks. Therefore, a few days before the scheduled time, the colony directs most of its labour force to the killing operation. Care is taken to not wet or soil the feathers during the plucking of the ducks and geese because these feathers are a highly marketable item. In fact immediately after the killing operation the feathers are dried in a special drier to keep them from spoiling and they are then crated for market. With the exception of a few hundred pounds of feathers that are purchased by Winnipeg bedding firms, all the feathers are exported to the U.S.A.

The Hutterites would prefer to have their geese and ducks killed at a properly equipped commercial packing plant. In fact, at the time of writing, negotiations are being conducted between the management of several colonies and the management of a poultry killing plant at Morden to remodel part of the plant and establish a large-scale goose killing section. Since the capital required would be considerable, the plan appears to include the Hutterites as producer-shareholders in a newly constituted company. This would be an economic innovation for Hutterites.[12]

B. The Duck Enterprise

Number of Ducks and Comparison with Manitoba Farms

With ducks the Hutterites are almost as outstanding as they are with geese. As there were apparently no other really large producers of ducks in Manitoba in 1968, it is somewhat surprising that the Hutterites accounted for only 62 percent of the duck sales in that year (Table 12-8).[13] However, as this table indicates, their duckling sales in the spring totalled more than three times the number of ducks sold in the fall. This is very different from the practice followed by the goose enterprise where the gosling sales were only about one-half the number of mature geese that were sold (Table 12-4). The total number of ducks owned by the Hutterites on July 1, 1968 was 46,200. Although Manitoba data for 1968 are unavailable, in 1966 the total number of ducks in the province 31,235.[14] The Manitoba data are based on the holdings on June 1, and therefore the figure would be somewhat higher for July 1, at the end of the hatching season. However, even taking this into consideration and the fact that the Hutterite data are for 1968, the Dominion Bureau of Statistics estimate for 1966 still seems to be low.[15] Details aside, the outstanding fact remains that the Hutterites account for the major part of duck production in Manitoba.

Comparison of Colonies with Duck Breeding Flocks and those without Breeding Flocks

The basic comparisons between the colonies with duck breeding flocks and those without are presented in Tables 12-9, 12-10, and 12-11. As in the case of the goose enterprise, the colonies with breeding flocks operate on a much larger scale. On July 1, 1968 the average number of ducks on a colony with a breeding flock was 2,923 as compared to an average of only 765 on a colony without a breeding flock (Tables 12-9 and 12-10). Contrasting with the goose enterprise where 23 colonies had breeding flocks, only 9 colonies had duck breeding flocks. On the other hand, there were 26 colonies that bought ducklings and raised ducks. However, these were mainly small scale operations and the ducks were raised primarily for domestic consumption (Table 12-10).

Another contrast with the goose enterprise is the fact that 75 percent of the ducklings are sold immediately after being hatched. However, 19,500 of these or 29 percent were bought by colonies without breeding flocks (Tables 12-10 and 12-11). As in the case of goslings, the majority of the ducklings are sold to Winnipeg hatcheries for further

TABLE 12-8

NUMBER OF DUCKS - JULY 1, 1968

AND NUMBER OF DUCKLINGS AND DUCKS SOLD IN 1968

MANITOBA FARMS[1] AND HUTTERITE COLONIES[2]

Column No.							
	1	2	3	4	5	6	7
	Breeding flock						
Agric. District	No. of drakes	No. of ducks	No. of ducklings hatched	No. of ducklings sold (plus 2% mortality bonus)	No. of ducklings retained	No. of ducklings bought by Man. Hut. col's with no br. flock (plus 2%)	Total no. of ducks July 1	No. of ducks sold in 1968
A	435	1,245	38,800	22,440	16,360	9,894	27,934	14,425
B	0	0	0	0	0	3,162	3,162	1,100
C	300	1,300	43,000	42,128	872	1,020	3,492	400
D	0	0	0	0	0	3,162	3,162	750
E	35	165	8,000	3,060	4,940	2,040	7,180	5,000
F	10	60	1,200	612	588	612	1,270	0

Total Hutterite	780	2,770	91,000	68,240	22,760	19,890	46,200	21,675
Total Manitoba								35,000
Hut. ducks as a % of Man. ducks								61.9%

[1] Source: *Yearbook of Manitoba Agriculture 1968*, p. 27. (The only data available are total Manitoba sales.)

[2] Source: Data compiled from field work by J. Ryan.

[3] The total number of ducks on July 1 consists of the data in column nos. 1, 4 and 5.

TABLE 12-9

THE DUCK ENTERPRISE, 1968

HUTTERITE COLONIES WITH A DUCK BREEDING FLOCK

Number of colonies at the beginning of 1968 with a duck breeding flock = 9

	Totals for 9 colonies		Average no. per colony
	No.	%	No.
1. Size of breeding flock at the beginning of 1968: Drakes	780	22.0%	87
Ducks	2,770	78.0%	308
Total flock	3,550	100%	395
2. Number of ducklings hatched in 1968	91,000	-	1,011
3. Average number of ducklings per duck	32.9	-	32.9
4. Number of ducklings sold	66,900	-	7,433
5. Number of ducklings added as a bonus to the number sold for anticipated mortality purposes (2% of the number sold)	1,340	-	149
6. Ducklings sold (plus 2% bonus) as a % of the ducklings hatched	-	75.0%	-
7. Number and % of ducklings kept	22,670	25.0%	2,529
8. Total number of ducks July 1 (after hatching season and after sales of ducklings, i.e., Item #1 + #7)	26,310	100%	2,923
9. Number of mature ducks sold (by these 9 colonies)	17,620	-	1,958
10. Mature ducks sold as a % of total ducks July 1	-	67.0%	-

11. Number of ducks consumed on the 9 colonies	4,155	-	462
12. Number of ducks consumed as a % of total ducks July 1		15.8%	
13. Total duckling and duck mortality	1,205	-	134
14. Mortality as a % of total ducks July 1		4.6%	
15. Size of breeding flock at the end of 1968: Drakes	685	-	86
Ducks	2,645	-	331
Total flock	3,330	-	417
16. Breeding flock as a % of total ducks July 1	-	12.6%	-
17. Number of colonies with a duck breeding flock at the end of 1968 (out of the 9 colonies with a breeding flock at the beginning of 1968)	8	-	-

Source: Data compiled from field work by J. Ryan.

TABLE 12-10

THE DUCK ENTERPRISE, 1968

HUTTERITE COLONIES WITHOUT A DUCK BREEDING FLOCK

Number of colonies without a duck breeding flock who purchase ducklings and raise ducks = 26

	Totals for 26 colonies		Average no. per colony
	No.	%	No.
1. Number of ducklings bought (19,500 plus bonus of 2% or 390 for anticipated mortality)	19,890	100%	765
2. Number of mature ducks sold (by these 26 colonies)	4,055	-	156
3. Mature ducks sold as a % of ducklings bought	-	20.4%	-
4. Number of ducks consumed on the 26 colonies	14,430	-	555
5. Ducks consumed as a % of ducklings bought	-	72.5%	-
6. Total duckling and duck mortality	1,095	-	42
7. Mortality as a % of ducklings bought	-	5.5%	-
8. Number of ducks retained for breeding purposes: Drakes	60	-	-
Ducks	250	-	-
Total flock	310	-	-
9. Ducks retained for breeding purposes as a % of ducklings bought	-	1.6%	-
10. Number of colonies at the end of 1968 with a newly established duck breeding flock (out of the 26 colonies without a breeding flock during 1968)	2	-	-

Source: Data compiled from field work by J. Ryan.

resale. In addition, large numbers are exported to Saskatchewan, Alberta, and British Columbia (mainly to hatcheries and Hutterite colonies), but there is no record of ducklings being exported to the U.S.A. in 1968.[16] Again as in the case of goslings, a considerable number of ducklings are sold to local farmers.

Of the total ducks on hand on July 1 of 1968, 21,675 or 47 percent were sold as mature ducks in the fall (Table 12-11). In a striking contrast with the goose enterprise where only 1-1/2 percent of the geese were consumed on the colonies, 18,585 ducks or 40 percent of the total were consumed. This works out to 462 per colony with breeding flocks and 555 per colony without breeding flocks. Considering that the average colony has a population of about 100, this does not make a large number of meals during the course of a year. One of the reasons why more ducks are consumed than geese is the fact that the selling price of a goose is almost twice that of a duck, and therefore it is much more economical to sell the geese.[17] Of the remaining ducks on hand on July 1, the breeding flock accounted for 8 percent and there was a 5 percent mortality (Table 12-11).

During 1968 one colony sold its breeding flock but two other colonies established new breeding flocks, so that at the end of the year there were 10 colonies with duck breeding flocks.

The Operation of the Duck Enterprise[18]

The average size of a duck breeding flock in 1968 was 395, but this ranged from a low of 30 at Poplar Point Colony to a high of 1,600 at Riverside Colony. Riverside Colony is highly specialized in its duck enterprise and it is by far the largest producer. In 1968 this colony hatched over 43,000 ducklings, but practically all of these were sold as ducklings (41,300 were sold). The ratio of drakes to ducks is usually 1:4 to 1:5. Unlike a goose, a duck may lay up to 75 eggs in a season and it is possible to hatch about 40 ducklings per duck. The Hutterites averaged 33 ducklings per duck in 1968, but this is still considered to be a high level of production.

As indicated in a previous section, there are separate managers for the duck and goose enterprises only on those colonies where both of the operations are conducted on a large scale basis. Otherwise, the duck and goose enterprises are under the direction of one man plus one full-time or part-time assistant.

The operations of the duck enterprise are almost identical with those of the goose enterprise. Except for Sunnyside Colony, all colonies with duck breeding flocks also have goose breeding flocks. Hence it is possible to make dual use of some of the facilities. The same hatchery is

TABLE 12-11

THE DUCK ENTERPRISE, 1968

ALL HUTTERITE COLONIES THAT RAISE DUCKS

- No. of colonies with breeding flocks at the beginning of 1968 = 9
- No. of colonies without breeding flocks but who purchase ducklings and raise ducks = 26
- Total number of colonies that raised ducks in 1968 = 35

		No.	%
1. Size of breeding flock at beginning of 1968:	Drakes	780	22.0%
	Ducks	2,770	78.0%
	Total flock	3,550	100%
2. Number of ducklings hatched in 1968		91,000	100%
3. Total number of ducklings sold (by 9 colonies)		66,900	-
4. No. of ducklings added as a bonus to the no. sold for anticipated mortality (2% of the number sold)		1,340	-
5. Ducklings sold (plus 2% bonus) as a % of ducklings hatched		-	75.0%
6. No. of ducklings sold to the 26 colonies without br. flocks		19,500	
7. Ducklings sold to Hutterites as a % of total ducklings sold			29.1%
8. No. and % of ducklings sold to other customers		47,400	70.9%

			No.	%
9. No. of ducklings kept by the 9 colonies with breeding flocks	22,760			
10. Total no. of ducks on all Hutterite colonies July 1 (after hatching season and after sales of ducklings to customers other than Hutterite, i.e., Items #1 + #6 (incl. the 2% for mortality) + #9	-	-	46,200	100%
11. Total number of mature ducks sold in 1968 by the 35 colonies	-	-	21,675	-
12. Total mature ducks sold as a % of total ducks July 1	-	-	-	46.9%
13. No. and % of mature ducks sold by 9 colonies with br. flocks	17,620	81.3%		
14. No. and % of mature ducks sold by 26 colonies without br. flocks	4,055	18.7%		
15. Total number of ducks consumed on 35 colonies	-	-	18,585	-
16. Total ducks consumed as a % of total ducks July 1	-	-	-	40.2%
17. Total duckling and duck mortality on 35 colonies	-	-	2,300	-
18. Total mortality as a % of total ducks July 1	-	-	-	5.0%
19. Size of breeding flock at the end of 1968: Drakes / Ducks / Total flock	745 / 2,895 / 3,640	20.5% / 79.5% / 100%	3,640	
20. Breeding flock as a % of total ducks July 1	-	-	-	7.9%
21. Number of colonies with duck breeding flocks at the end of 1968	10	-	-	-

Source: Data compiled from field work by J. Ryan.

used for both goose and duck eggs. However, on large-scale operations there is a separate brooder barn and laying barn for the ducks. There is also a separate pasture.

The hatching procedure is very similar for both ducks and geese. The operation of raising ducklings is almost identical with that of raising goslings. The feed rations are also basically the same. However, ducks mature much sooner than geese—within 10 to 13 weeks. Therefore, ducks are usually marketed before the geese, but this of course depends on when they were hatched.

TABLE 12-12

MANITOBA HUTTERITE COLONIES

GROSS SALES INCOME FROM THE GOOSE
AND DUCK ENTERPRISES, 1968

Total gross sales income from all enterprises	$11,598,282.40
Gross sales income from the goose and duck enterprise	$570,572.74
Gross sales income from geese and ducks as a % of total gross sales income	4.9%
No. of colonies reporting income from the goose and duck enterprise	32
No. of families on these colonies	486
Average gross sales income per colony	$17,830.40
Average gross sales income per family	$1,174.02

Source: Data compiled by J. Ryan from the financial reports
          on each colony for 1968, as prepared by Meyers,
          Dickens, Norris, Penny and Company, the accounting
          firm employed by the Hutterite colonies.

Significance of the Goose and Duck Enterprises to the Colony Economy

All colonies prepare combined income statements for the goose and duck enterprises. Hence separate income comparisons cannot be made for each. Nor is it possible to make income comparisons of the sale of goslings and ducklings as opposed to the sale of mature geese and ducks.

In 1968 the total sales income for the goose and duck enterprises was $570,572.74 or an average of $17,830.40 per colony and $1,174.02 per family (Table 12-12). The goose and duck enterprises accounted for 4.9 percent of the total gross sales of all colonies and ranked sixth in importance as producers of gross sales income (Appendix G). However, on the colonies where these enterprises are conducted on a large scale, these operations usually rank about fourth or fifth in importance in terms of sales income. On an individual colony basis, there is a very wide range in sales income from these enterprises. On some colonies sales income amounts to only a few hundred dollars, while on one colony it amounted to over $55,000.[19] Furthermore, seven colonies kept geese and ducks only for domestic consumption and did not make any sales.

Although the goose and duck enterprises are of considerable significance to the colonies in terms of sales income, the duck enterprise is particularly significant from the viewpoint of colony consumption. As indicated in a previous section, about 40 percent of the mature ducks are retained for this purpose.

Notes and References

1. The information on the present-day lack of significance of rivers and streams in the operation of goose and duck enterprises was obtained from a discussion with Reverend Jacob Kleinsasser of Crystal Spring Colony.
2. In 1968 only 6 of the 43 colonies did not have a river or creek near the colony site. However, 9 colonies had relatively insignificant creeks.
3. Full census data on ducks and geese are available for 1966, but for 1968 the *Yearbook of Manitoba Agriculture* lists only the number of ducks and geese sold.
4. *1966 Census of Canada: Agriculture—Manitoba*, p. 18-1.

5. This is an estimate made by Reverend Jacob Kleinsasser of Crystal Spring Colony, who throughout this study demonstrated an amazingly detailed knowledge of practically all Hutterite operations.

6. This information was supplied by Reverend Jacob Kleinsasser of Crystal Spring Colony.

7. Export licenses have to be issued for gosling and duckling exports to the U.S.A., and these are the official data released from the records at the Canada Department of Agriculture, Health of Animals Branch, 613 Federal Building, Winnipeg. This information was supplied by Dr. J. J. Andrich of that division on April 24, 1972.

8. The basic information on goose and duck enterprises was obtained from the observation of these operations on a number of colonies and from discussions with ministers and enterprise and colony managers. In particular, the operations were studied at Crystal Spring, Iberville, James Valley, and Riverside colonies.

9. Data on goose production at James Valley were obtained from Elie Wurtz, the goose enterprise manager.

10. The feed formulas for geese were provided by Dan Kleinsasser, the chicken enterprise manager at Crystal Spring Colony. Although he does not manage the goose enterprise, he prepares the feed formulas for it.

11. This was an assertion made by Reverend Jacob Kleinsasser of Crystal Spring Colony, but upon checking with the packing plants in Winnipeg this indeed seems to be the case.

12. Reverend Jacob Kleinsasser informed the writer of these negotiations during a discussion with him on April 28, 1972.

13. While filling out the questionnaires on the duck enterprise, the writer was often surprised by the large numbers of ducks that were claimed to be consumed on the colonies. This was almost always double-checked but the writer received assurances that most colonies do consume large numbers of ducks. For example, a colony with no breeding flock may purchase about 500 or 600 ducklings strictly for colony consumption during that year. Therefore, although the colonies produce most of the province's ducks, about 40 percent of them are consumed on the colonies (Table 12-11).

14. *1966 Census of Canada: Agriculture—Manitoba*, p. 18-1.

15. The writer compiled the 1968 data by visiting every colony at least two or three times, and the details of each enterprise were carefully recorded. Furthermore, after the interviews and the field work for this study were completed, the writer asked Reverend Jacob Kleinsasser of Crystal Spring Colony to check the raw data for each colony for possible errors. After hours of tedious work a few

minor errors or omissions were spotted and corrected. In any case the writer has every assurance that there is only a small margin of error in basic data such as the size of various enterprise operations. On the other hand, the Hutterites often posed the question how the Dominion Bureau of Statistics estimates are made (other than the detailed census every decade) because they claimed that few colonies are actually contacted about their operations.

16. This is according to a report from Dr. J. J. Andrich of the Canada Department of Agriculture (April 24, 1972).

17. In 1968 the average price of a duck was $2.10 while the price of a goose was $4.02 (*Yearbook of Manitoba Agriculture 1968* p. 27).

18. A number of duck enterprises were observed by the writer, in particular Riverside Colony.

19. Data compiled from the financial reports on the colonies.

CHAPTER 13

THE APIARY ENTERPRISE AND OTHER ECONOMIC ACTIVITIES

The apiary enterprise and various other economic activities are of minor significance on most Hutterite colonies. However, since these activities are a source of income and they do involve expenditure of labour, they should nevertheless be considered.

A. The Apiary Enterprise

Number of Honeybee Colonies and Comparison with Manitoba Beekeepers

Table 13-1 shows the number of honeybee colonies operated in 1968 by Manitoba beekeepers and by Hutterite colonies. More than three-quarters of the Hutterite colonies operated apiary enterprises, and there were some in operation in every district. The 33 colonies accounted for 4 percent of all Manitoba beekeepers. The Hutterites had a total of 2,925 honeybee colonies (or hives) and this accounted for 5.6 percent of the Manitoba total. The average number of hives per Manitoba beekeeper was 63, while the average per Hutterite colony was 89. Although the Hutterites operated on a somewhat larger scale than the average Manitoba beekeeper, the difference in scale is not as great as in most other enterprises.

The Operation of the Apiary Enterprise[1]

Although the average number of hives per Hutterite colony was 89 in 1968, this ranged from a low of 25 on several colonies to a high of 400 at Oak Bluff Colony.

The apiary enterprise is usually operated by one person, and on a number of colonies the minister takes charge of it.

The facilities for the average enterprise are relatively inexpensive, at least when compared with other enterprises. They consist of a building

TABLE 13-1

NUMBER OF HONEYBEE COLONIES, 1968

MANITOBA BEEKEEPERS[1] AND HUTTERITE COLONIES[2]

Agric. District	Manitoba Beekeepers			Hutterite Colonies					
Column No.	1 No. of Beekeepers	2 No. of honeybee colonies	3 No. of honeybee colonies per Man. beekeeper	4 No. of Hutterite colonies operating an apiary enterprise	5 No. of honeybee colonies	6 No. of honeybee colonies per Hutt. colony	7 Hutt. beekeepers as a % of Manitoba beekeepers (Col. 4 as a % of Col. 1)	8 Hutt. honeybee colonies as a % of Manitoba honeybee colonies	9 Average Manitoba beekeeper as a % of average Hutt. beekeeper (Col.3 as a % of Col. 6)
A				18	1,360	76	-	-	-
B		Data		3	250	83	-	-	-
C		Not		3	235	78	-	-	-
D		Available		2	85	43	-	-	-
E				5	835	167	-	-	-
F				2	160	80	-	-	-
Total/Average	830	52,000	63	33	2,925	89	4.0%	5.6%	70.8%

1 D.L. Smith, A.J. Kolach and D.G. McRory, "1968 Annual Report of the Entomology and Apiculture Division" (unpublished report, Manitoba Department of Agriculture Technical Services Branch, Entomology Section, 711 Norquay Building, Winnipeg), p. 2.

2 Data compiled from field work by J. Ryan and verified by data in the "1968 Apiary Inspection list" (unpublished report, Manitoba Department of Agriculture Technical Services Branch, Entomology Section, 711 Norquay Building, Winnipeg).

for honey extraction and for the storage of honey and equipment. The major equipment in the structure consists of a heating unit, honey extractors, straining equipment, honey tanks, storage tanks, packing jars, a honey scale, and other apparatus. In addition of course there are beehives for the bees, which are spaced out in a secluded area near the honey house.

Because of the severe winters in Manitoba it has been more economical to kill the bees in the fall and replace them with package bees in the spring. The Hutterites all follow this procedure, and the package bees arrive from the U.S.A. in the period from mid-April to early May. Once the bees are established, the next major procedure is the removal of honey from the hives during the summer. This is a highly specialized and skilled process which initially involves the removal of excess moisture before the honey is extracted. This is done in the honey house which is heated to approximately 100°F. The honey is then extracted, carefully strained, and immediately placed in storage tanks or packed in jars. If it is stored in bulk it has to be liquified later for repacking.

Every apiary operation in Manitoba must be registered with the appropriate division of the provincial Department of Agriculture. Apiary inspectors make periodic checks on each enterprise to examine the hives for possible disease. Each enterprise is also checked periodically by inspectors from the Federal Department of Agriculture to examine the sanitary standards.[2]

Significance of the Apiary Enterprise to the Colony Economy

Throughout the province the 1968 honey crop was seriously affected by the rainy weather experienced during the months of July and August.[3] This resulted in the lowest production and probably the lowest income of the previous 10-year average and it was less than half of the production of the following year.[5] Production data for the Hutterite colonies for 1968 are unavailable but in all likelihood the colonies were as badly affected as the average Manitoba beekeeper.[6]

The Hutterites had a total gross sales income of \$40,659.61 from the apiary enterprise in 1968 (Table 13-2). Although 33 colonies operated an apiary enterprise that year, only 29 colonies reported honey sales. This table shows that each colony received an average gross sales income of \$1,402.06 or \$91.17 per family. However, the gross sales income varied on the colonies from a low of \$25 to a high of almost \$11,000.[7]

In 1968 the gross sales income from the apiary enterprise accounted for only .4 percent of the total sales income of all the colonies (Table

TABLE 13-2

MANITOBA HUTTERITE COLONIES

GROSS SALES INCOME FROM THE APIARY ENTERPRISE, 1968

Total gross sales income from all enterprises	$11,598,282.40
Gross sales income from the apiary enterprise	40,659.61
Gross sales income from honey as a % of total gross sales income	.4%
No. of colonies reporting sales of honey	29
No. of families on these colonies	446
Average gross sales income per colony	$ 1,402.06
Average gross sales income per family	$ 91.17

Source: Data compiled by J. Ryan from the financial
reports on each colony for 1968, as prepared
by Meyers, Dickens, Norris, Penny & Co., the
accounting firm employed by the Hutterite
colonies.

13-2). As a producer of gross sales income the apiary enterprise ranked
ninth in importance (Appendix G). Although 1968 was a bad year for
honey production, a review of the financial reports on the colonies from
1961 to 1971 indicates that honey sales probably ranked eighth or ninth
in all these years.[8] In other words, the apiary enterprise is of such
relatively minor importance on the colonies that its income variations
are not sufficient to change its average rank in the economic structure of
the colonies (Appendix G).

B. Other Economic Activities

Every colony has several acres of land in garden and potatoes, and
although this is primarily for colony consumption, some sales are
made. The gross sales income totalled $45,248.65 in 1968 (Table
13-3). On the 35 colonies that reported income from vegetables and
potatoes, the average sales income was $1,292.82 per colony or $85.70
per family. This income is closely comparable to the amount produced
by the apiary enterprise, and is of minor consequence economically to

TABLE 13-3

MANITOBA HUTTERITE COLONIES

GROSS INCOME FROM CUSTOM WORK AND GROSS

SALES INCOME FROM VEGETABLES AND POTATOES, 1968

Total gross sales income from all enterprises	$11,598,282.40
Gross income from custom work	$126,957.82
Gross income from custom work as a % of total gross sales income	1.1%
No. of colonies reporting income from custom work	38
No. of families on these colonies	555
Average gross income per colony	3,341.00
Average gross income per family	228.75

Total gross sales income from all enterprises	$11,598,282.40
Gross income from sale of vegetables and potatoes	$44,248.65
Gross sales income from vegetables and potatoes as a % of total gross sales income	.4%
No. of colonies reporting income from sale of vegetables and potatoes	35
No. of families on these colonies	528
Average gross sales income per colony	1,292.82
Average gross sales income per family	85.70

Source: Data compiled by J. Ryan from the financial reports
on each colony for 1968, as prepared by Meyers,
Dickens, Norris, Penny and Company, the accounting
firm employed by the Hutterites.

the colonies. However, the significance of the garden and potato
operations must not be minimized because they provide the colonies
with a large amount of food which would otherwise have to be purchased. Furthermore, they provide work for the women.

Almost every colony does a certain amount of custom work for
neighboring farmers. Such farmers may not have sufficient machinery

or may need help with various operations. If the colonies can spare the labour force and the equipment, they provide this neighbourly assistance. Such work is usually in connection with harvesting.

In 1968 the gross income from such custom work was \$126,957.82 (Table 13-3). On the 38 colonies reporting such income, this came to an average of \$3,341.00 per colony and \$228.75 per family. However, it ranged from a few hundred dollars on some colonies to as high as \$17,000 on one colony. Obviously in this case the income was significant.

The colonies receive very little income from any other economic activities. Some do machinery repair work or other types of maintenance work for local farmers, but this does not add significantly to income.

Notes and References

1. The apiary enterprise was observed by the writer on a number of colonies, in particular at Iberville, Poplar Point, and Sturgeon Creek colonies. The operation was discussed at length with Reverend Andrew Gross of Iverville Colony.
2. The source of this information is R. G. Barker, Apiarist, Manitoba Department of Agriculture (telephone interview, May 24, 1972).
3. D. L. Smith, A. J. Kolach and D. G. McRory, "1968 Annual Report of the Entomology and Apiculture Division" (unpublished report, Manitoba Department of Agriculture, Technical Services Branch, Entomology Section), p. 2.
4. *Ibid.*, p. 1.
5. Dominion Bureau of Statistics, "Estimated Value of Honey Production, 1969" Cat. No. 23-007, May 25, 1970, p. 2.
6. Although the writer did not collect data on honey production, his field notes contain comments from three colony managers that 1968 was the worst year for honey production on record for those colonies.
7. These data are from the financial reports of the colonies as prepared by their accountant.
8. The gross sales income for each enterprise for each of these eleven years was not actually tabulated, however, the income from honey sales is so small that it is not difficult to determine its approximate rank. On most colonies the income from the sale of vegetables and potatoes is the only other item that is in the same league as honey sales.

CHAPTER 14

ECONOMIC SIGNIFICANCE OF HUTTERITE AGRICULTURAL OPERATIONS

The Order of Importance of Hutterite Enterprises in Terms of Gross Sales Income

Certain enterprises produce the largest sales income on practically all colonies. Table 14-1 lists the major Hutterite enterprises and indicates their order of importance as producers of gross sales income. On this basis, the three most important enterprises on most colonies are hogs, chickens, and grain, in that order. The table shows that in 1968 the hog enterprise produced the largest sales income on 31 of the 43 colonies, or on 72 percent of the colonies. On the remaining 12 colonies, the hog enterprise ranked second. The chicken enterprise, consisting of the sale of eggs, broilers, and periodically old laying hens, was the second largest producer of gross sales income on 56 percent of the colonies. This enterprise ranked first on 7 colonies, second on 23 colonies, third on 7 colonies, and fourth on 4 colonies. The sale of grain placed this enterprise in third place on 40 percent of the colonies. However, this enterprise ranged from first to sixth place, and it actually ranked fifth on almost one-third of the colonies.

The turkey enterprise is in a rather special position because although in 1968 it was the fourth largest producer of gross sales income for the Hutterite colonies, it was conducted on only 12 colonies. This enterprise was the largest producer of sales income on 3 of these colonies and it was the second largest producer on 4 of them. Hence, on the majority of the colonies that operate a turkey enterprise, this activity is of major significance and it displaces the usual position of hogs, chickens, and grain.

The cattle enterprise is conducted on all colonies, but the operations on most colonies are not as significant in terms of income as the enterprises already discussed. In 1968 the enterprise ranked fourth in terms of gross sales income on 16 of the 43 colonies or on 37 percent of the colonies. Furthermore, it ranked fifth on 12 percent of the colonies and sixth on 25 percent of the colonies. Although the actual operations vary from colony to colony, the cattle enterprise as such consists of the sales of milk, cream, and beef and dairy cattle.

Although the goose and duck enterprise was conducted on 39 colonies in 1968, there were 7 colonies that kept geese and ducks for domestic consumption only and made no sales that year. As a producer of gross sales income, this enterprise was usually fourth and fifth in importance on most colonies, accounting for 34-1/2 percent and 28 percent of the colonies in these categories, respectively.

Custom work is not an ''enterprise'' as such because this consists of work done by the Hutterites for other farmers. This is work such as seeding, swathing, combining, etc., but it is an important source of income for some colonies and it should be recognized as a separate category. On the majority of the colonies, this source of income was sixth and seventh in importance.

Vegetables and potatoes are grown on every colony primarily for domestic consumption, but some colonies manage to sell a considerable amount of produce. This source of income was seventh and eighth in importance on most colonies.

The apiary enterprise was conducted on 33 of the 43 colonies in 1968, but sales of honey were made by only 29 colonies. Although its importance as a source of income ranged from fifth to ninth place, it ranked in eighth place on over one-third of the colonies.

Gross Sales Income from Hutterite Enterprises[1]

In 1968 two enterprises, hogs and chickens, accounted for almost 70 percent of the total gross sales income of all Hutterite colonies (Table 14-2). Although the previous section indicated the relative importance of these enterprises, the economic significance of these operations is not fully appreciated until the actual income data are examined. The gross sales income from hogs totalled $4,871,001.65 or 42 percent of the total Hutterite sales income. This worked out to $113,279.11 per colony and $7,670.87 per family. The chicken enterprise was in a strong second position and totalled $3,241,275.67 or 27.9 percent of the total sales income. This resulted in a gross sales income of $75,378.50 per colony and $5,104.37 per family. The importance of these two enterprises is not an isolated phenomenon for 1968. In the case of hogs, the financial statements of the Hutterite colonies from 1961 to 1971 indicate that the hog enterprise has been of major significance on every colony throughout this entire period. Although the chicken enterprise is not conducted on every colony, it nevertheless has also been of major importance throughout this period.

TABLE 14-1

HUTTERITE ENTERPRISES RANKED ACCORDING TO
THEIR PRODUCTION OF
GROSS SALES INCOME PER COLONY, 1968[1]

Enterprise	Rank of enterprise based on production of gross sales income[2]									
	1st		2nd		3rd		4th		5th	
	No. of colonies	%	No. of colonies	%	No. of colonies	%	No. of colonies	%	No. of colonies	%
Hogs	31/43	72%	12/43	28%	-	-	-	-	-	
Chickens & eggs	7/41	17%	23/41	56%	7/41	17%	4/41	10%	-	
Grain	2/42	5%	2/42	5%	17/42	40%	5/42	12%	13/42	31%
Turkeys	3/12	25%	4/12	33%	2/12	17%	2/12	17%	1/12	8%
Cattle	-		2/43	5%	9/43	21%	16/43	37%	5/43	12%
Geese & Ducks	-				6/32	19%	11/32	34½%	9/32	28%
Custom work	-				1/38	2½%	5/38	13%	6/38	16%
Vegetables & potatoes	-		-		-		-		2/35	6%
Honey	-		-		-		-		6/29	21%

Enterprise	6th No. of colonies	6th %	7th No. of colonies	7th %	8th No. of colonies	8th %	9th No. of colonies	9th %	No. of colonies involved in enterprise but not reporting any income	No. of colonies not involved in enterprise
Hogs	-		-		-		-		0	0
Chickens & eggs	-		-		-		-		0	2
Grain	3/42	7%	-		-		-		1	0
Turkeys	-		-		-		-		0	31
Cattle	11/43	25%	-		-		-		0	0
Geese & Ducks	3/32	9½%	1/32	3%	2/32	6%	-		7	4
Custom work	11/38	29%	11/38	29%	3/38	8%	1/38	2½%	0	5
Vegetables & potatoes	8/35	23%	12/35	34%	9/35	26%	4/35	11%	8	0
Honey	4/29	14%	7/29	24%	10/29	34%	2/29	7%	4	10

[1] Data compiled by J. Ryan from the financial reports on each colony for 1968, as prepared by Meyers, Dickens, Norris, Penny & Company, the accounting firm employed by the Hutterite colonies.

[2] Key to interpretation of table: As an example, the entry "Hogs: 31/43 - 72%" should be interpreted as follows: "As a producer of gross sales income, the hog enterprise ranked 1st on 31 out of the 43 colonies involved in this enterprise, or on 72% of the colonies involved in hog production."

TABLE 14-2

GROSS SALES INCOME OF HUTTERITE COLONIES, 1968
PER ENTERPRISE, PER COLONY, AND PER FAMILY[1]

Column no.	1	2	3	4
Enterprise	Total Gross Sales Income	% of total	Average Gross Sales Income per colony[2]	Average Gross Sales Income per family[3]
Hogs	$ 4,871,001.65	42.0%	$113,279.11	$ 7,670.87
Chickens	3,241,275.67	27.9%	75,378.50	5,104.37
Grain	966,765.06	8.3%	22,482.91	1,522.46
Turkeys	908,694.94	7.8%	21,132.44	1,431.02
Cattle	701,776.29	6.1%	16,320.38	1,105.16
Geese & Ducks	570,572.74	4.9%	13,269.13	898.54
Custom work	126,957.82	1.1%	2,952.51	199.93
Vegetables & Potatoes	45,248.65	.4%	1,052.29	71.26
Honey	40,659.61	.4%	945.57	64.03
Misc.	125,329.97	1.1%	2,914.65	197.37
Total/ Average	11,598,282.40	100%	269,727.40	18,265.01

[1] Data compiled by J. Ryan from the financial reports on each colony for 1968, as prepared by Meyers, Dickens, Norris, Penny & Company, the accounting firm employed by the Hutterite colonies.

[2] Determined on the basis of the total 43 colonies in 1968.

[3] Determined on the basis of the total 635 families in 1968.

[4] More colonies may actually be engaged in some of the enterprises than this column indicates, e.g., all 43 colonies in 1968 were involved in grain production, but one colony did not make any grain sales in that year.

5	6	7	8
No. of colonies reporting income from enterprise[4]	No. of families on colonies reporting income from enterprise	Average Gross Sales Income per colony (based on Col. 5)	Average Gross Sales Income per family (based on col. 6)
43	635	$113,279.11	$ 7,670.87
41	614	79,055.50	5,278.95
42	622	23,018.22	1,554.28
12	191	75,724.58	4,757.57
43	635	16,320.38	1,015.16
32	486	17,830.40	1,174.02
38	555	3,341.00	228.75
35	528	1,292.82	85.70
29	446	1,402.06	91.17
43	635	2,914.65	197.37
-	-	-	-

Grain sales in 1968 accounted for $966,765.67 or 8.3 percent of the total gross sales income of the Hutterite colonies. However, this is not a true indication of the full significance of the crop enterprise. As indicated in Table 7-16 in the chapter on crop production, only 23.8 percent of the grain produced was sold. This table also shows that at 1968 grain prices the full value of Hutterite grain production was $4,064,934. Therefore, the major part of the grain produced was used as feed on the colonies and in this way this enterprise served as the basis for the other enterprises.

The turkey enterprise brought in a gross sales income of $908,694.94 and accounted for 7.8 percent of the total Hutterite gross sales income in 1968 (Table 14-2). As mentioned in the previous section, this enterprise was conducted on only 12 colonies so this is a major contribution by these colonies. The gross income for the colonies involved averaged $75,724.58 per colony and $4,757.57 per family. On a per colony basis for the colonies involved, this was only slightly less than the income from the chicken enterprise.

The gross sales income from the cattle enterprise in 1968 totalled $701,776.29 and accounted for 6.1 percent of the total gross sales income. The goose and duck enterprise brought in a total of $570,572.74 or 4.9 percent of the year's sales income. However, since the sale of geese and ducks took place on only 32 colonies as compared to the 43 colonies operating a cattle enterprise, for the colonies involved the per colony income from geese and ducks was higher than the income from cattle (Table 14-2).

The income from custom work, vegetables and potatoes, honey, and miscellaneous sources amounted to only 3 percent of the 1968 total gross sales income. On some colonies one or more of these activities were of some importance, but on the average they are usually of little significance. The income from miscellaneous sources includes monies received from interest, investment income, rentals, rebates, grain drying, hay sales, and other such sources. Custom work was primarily income from work done for other farmers, e.g., seeding, swathing, combining, baling hay, etc.

Table 14-3 compares the gross sales income of the Hutterite colonies with the gross sales income of all Manitoba farms in 1968. The Hutterite sales income was 3.2 percent of the province's farm total, and considering that the Hutterites owned only .83 percent of the farmland, this was considerably more than their proportionate share on this basis. Furthermore, this table shows that the gross sales income per farm in Manitoba in 1968 was $9,550, while the sales income per Hutterite family was $18,265 or 191 percent of the amount received by the average farm.

TABLE 14-3

GROSS SALES INCOME, 1968

PER MANITOBA FARM[1], PER HUTTERITE

COLONY AND PER FAMILY[2]

Gross Sales Income of total Manitoba farms	$364,816,000.00
No. of farms in Manitoba (1968)	38,200
Gross Sales Income per farm	$ 9,550.00

Gross Sales Income of Hutterite colonies	$ 11,598,282.40
Gross Sales Income of Hutterite colonies as a % of Gross Sales Income of Manitoba farms	3.2%
Total number of Hutterite colonies (1968)	43
Gross Sales Income per Hutterite colony	$ 269,727.40
Total number of Hutterite families (1968)	635
Gross Sales Income per Hutterite family	$ 18,265.01
Gross Sales Income per Hutterite family as a % of Gross Sales Income of average Manitoba farm	191.3%

[1]Source: Yearbook of Manitoba Agriculture 1971, p. 78.

[2]Source: Data on Hutterite colonies compiled from field work by J. Ryan and from the financial reports on each colony for 1968, as prepared by Meyers, Dickens, Norris, Penny & Company of Brandon, the accounting firm employed by the Hutterite colonies.

Operating Expenses of Hutterite Colonies

Data are not available on the operating expenses for each separate enterprise on the Hutterite colonies. Consequently, it is impossible to analyze the relative profitability of each enterprise. As it turns out, although most colonies have an adequate accounting system for one or more of their enterprises, no colony has reliable records on all of them. Even though the Hutterites do have a general idea of the profitability of each enterprise, it was beyond the scope of this study to attempt a compilation of such data.[2]

Although specific data on the operating expenses of each enterprise are unavailable, the total operating expenses in a more generalized form are available for each colony. Table 14-4 lists the various expense items, the total operating expenses for all 43 colonies in 1968, and the average operating expenses per colony and per item. Although the items in this table may appear to be listed in sufficient detail to be made applicable to individual enterprises, this is really not the case. For example, most colonies list their total purchases of feed and concentrate for all enterprises as one single entry entitled "feed and concentrate." Although the table includes expense categories for cattle, hogs, and poultry, various colonies include different costs under these headings, e.g., some colonies may include feed and concentrate while others do not. In any case, the colonies compile these expense records primarily for tax purposes and they are not directly comparable with those of individual enterprises.

Table 14-4 does reveal the major gross expenses of the Hutterite colonies. On all colonies the major expenses include feed and concentrate, maintenance and repairs, gasoline and oil, fertilizer and weed spray, plus expenses directly attributable to specific enterprises. It should be noted that only the expenses directly related to farm production are listed. Personal expenses, costs of school operation, maintenance and care of retired people, etc., are not included. Hence the items considered as operating expenses appear to be comparable with those of average Manitoba farms.

Unfortunately, because the major items cannot be attributed to individual enterprises, it is impossible to make a complete analysis of Hutterite operating expenses.

Net Sales Income of Hutterite Colonies[3]

Unlike the gross sales income which is known for individual enterprises, e.g., Table 14-2, the net sales income can be learned only for the

TABLE 14-4

MANITOBA HUTTERITE COLONIES
EXPENSES AND DEPRECIATION, 1968
TOTAL, PER ITEM, PER COLONY, AND PER FAMILY[1]

Expense Item	Total amount	Amount per colony[2]	Amount per family[3]
Feed and concentrate	$3,784,119.69	$88,002.78	$ 5,959.24
Maintenance and repairs	1,355,042.00	31,512.60	2,133.92
Poultry	621,183.31	14,446.12	978.24
Gasoline and oil	613,767.94	14,273.67	966.56
Fertilizer and spray	499,361.30	11,613.05	786.40
Interest and exchange	271,605.71	6,316.41	427.73
Taxes and licenses	260,045.14	6,047.56	409.52
Telephone and hydro	244,293.09	5,681.23	384.71
Cattle	212,384.17	4,939.17	334.46
Hogs	209,868.46	4,880.66	330.50
Insurance	108,266.43	2,517.82	170.50
Travel	86,617.28	2,014.36	136.40
Legal and accounting	67,533.45	1,570.55	106.35
Veterinary supplies	56,987.01	1,325.28	89.74
Heat	40,320.31	937.68	63.50
Rent	21,275.00	494.77	33.50
Custom work	15,818.96	367.88	24.91
Bees	14,898.32	346.47	23.46
Freight and duty	4,715.37	109.66	7.43
Miscellaneous	61,997.54	1,441.80	97.63
Depreciation	1,674,019.52	38,930.68	2,636.25
Total/Average	10,224,120.37	237,770.20	16,100.97

[1]Data compiled by J. Ryan from the financial reports on the
Hutterite colonies prepared by Meyers, Dickens, Norris, Penny & C

[2]Determined on the basis of the total 43 colonies in 1968.

[3]Determined on the basis of the total 635 families in 1968.

colony as a whole. The net sales income is directly related to expenses, since it is the amount left after expenses are deducted from the gross sales income. As discussed in the preceding section, expenses cannot be related to individual enterprises, and therefore neither can the net sales income.

Table 14-5 shows that the net sales income of all Hutterite colonies in 1968 was $1,374,162.03 or 1.8 percent of the total net sales income for all Manitoba farms. This table also shows that the net sales income was $31,957.25 per colony and $2,164.03 per Hutterite family. Since the Hutterites own only .83 percent of the Manitoba farmland, on this basis their net sales income is more than twice their proportionate share. However, their net sales income is almost half of their proportion of gross sales income, i.e., 1.8 percent as compared with 3.2 percent (Table 14-3). Therefore, this indicates that to reduce the net sales income to this amount their operating expenses must be significantly greater than those of average Manitoba farms. In other words, if their operating expenses had been proportionately the same as that of Manitoba farms, their net sales income should have been 3.2 percent of the net sales income of Manitoba farms, i.e., the same proportion as their gross sales income. Therefore, although it has been impossible to examine their operating expenses in relation to the individual enterprises, it is evident that in 1968 the overall operating expenses of Hutterite colonies were significantly greater than the average for Manitoba farms. Nevertheless, because the gross sales per Hutterite family were so much greater than those of the average Manitoba farm, in spite of the greater operating expenses, the net sales income per family was greater than the amount per Manitoba farm, i.e., $2,164.03 per Hutterite family as compared to $1,990 per Manitoba farm (Table 14-5).

Income and Expenses of Hutterite Colonies, 1961-1971

Up to this point the analysis of gross sales income, expenses, and net sales income has been based on data for 1968, but to arrive at any valid conclusions in this regard, it is essential to examine the data over a period of several years. Tables 14-6 and 14-7 portray these data over an eleven-year period, i.e., 1961 to 1971.

Table 14-6 shows that the average Hutterite expenses based on the eleven-year period are 81.7 percent of the gross sales income and that the corresponding net sales income is 18.3 percent. Of immediate note is the fact that 1968 was not an average year in this regard. The

TABLE 14-5

NET SALES INCOME, 1968, PER MANITOBA

FARM[1], PER HUTTERITE COLONY AND PER HUTTERITE FAMILY[2]

Gross Sales Income of total Manitoba Farms	$364,816,000.00
Total cash expenses and depreciation	$288,814,000.00
Net Sales Income of Manitoba farms	$ 76,002,000.00
Number of farms in Manitoba (1968)	38,200
Net Sales Income per farm	$ 1,990.00

Gross Sales Income of Hutterite colonies	$ 11,598,282.40
Total cash expenses and depreciation	$ 10,224,120.37
Net Sales Income of Hutterite colonies	$ 1,374,162.03
Net Sales Income of Hutterite colonies as a % of Net Sales Income of Manitoba farms	1.8%
Number of colonies in Manitoba (1968)	43
Net Sales Income per colony	$ 31,957.25
Number of Hutterite families (1968)	635
Net Sales Income per family	$ 2,164.03
Net Sales Income per Hutterite family as a % of Net Sales Income of average Manitoba farm	108.7%

[1]Source: Data compiled from <u>Yearbook</u> <u>of</u> <u>Manitoba</u>
<u>Agriculture</u> <u>1971</u>, pp. 72, 78.

[2]Source: Data on Hutterite colonies compiled from field
work by J. Ryan and from the financial reports
on each colony for 1968, as prepared by Meyers,
Dickens, Norris, Penny & Company of Brandon,
the accounting firm employed by the Hutterite
colonies.

TABLE 14-6

MANITOBA HUTTERITE COLONIES, 1961-1971

GROSS SALES INCOME, EXPENSES
AND NET SALES INCOME

Year	No. of colonies	Gross Sales Income $	Cash Expenses & Depreciation $	Net Sales Income $	Expenses as % of Gross Sales Income	Net Sales Income as % of Gross Sales Income	Average Gross Sales Income per colony	Average expenses per colony	Average Net Sales Income per colony
1961	32	5,423,926	3,884,528	1,539,398	71.6%	28.4%	169,498	121,392	48,106
1962	36	6,214,609	4,438,607	1,776,002	71.4%	28.6%	172,628	123,295	49,333
1963	36	6,663,444	4,914,156	1,749,288	73.7%	26.3%	185,096	136,504	48,592
1964	38	7,217,184	5,666,533	1,550,651	78.5%	21.5%	189,926	149,119	40,807
1965	39	9,311,545	6,852,856	2,458,689	73.6%	26.4%	238,757	175,714	63,043
1966	41	10,703,295	8,709,579	1,993,716	81.4%	18.6%	261,056	212,429	48,627
1967	42	10,496,639	9,200,856	1,295,783	87.7%	12.3%	249,920	219,068	30,852
1968	43	11,598,282	10,224,120	1,374,162	88.2%	11.8%	269,727	237,770	31,957
1969	44	14,925,893	11,915,929	3,009,964	79.8%	20.2%	339,225	270,817	68,408
1970	47	13,374,114	11,077,005	2,297,109	82.8%	17.2%	284,556	235,681	48,875
1971	48	12,323,740	11,575,241	748,499	93.9%	6.1%	256,745	241,151	15,594
Average	40.5	9,841,152	8,041,765	1,799,387	81.7%	18.3%	242,719	198,339	44,380

Source: Data compiled by J. Ryan from the financial reports on each
colony, as prepared by Meyers, Dickens, Norris, Penny &
Company of Brandon, the accounting firm employed by the
Hutterite colonies.

expenses in 1968 were 88.3 percent of the gross sales income and the corresponding net sales income was 11.7 percent. Next to 1971, 1968 had the highest operating expenses during this entire eleven-year period. It is obvious that 1971 was a disastrous year for the Hutterite colonies. For example, the net sales income per colony was almost one-third of the average for the eleven-year period. Another significant observation is the fact that throughout these years there has been a definite trend towards higher operating expenses and a lower net sales income.

The full significance of Hutterite income and expense data is not apparent until a comparison is made with comparable data for Manitoba farms. The most striking fact presented by Table 14-7 is that Manitoba farms during this eleven-year period had operating expenses of 72 percent of their gross sales income and a corresponding net sales income of 28 percent, as compared to Hutterite expenses of 82 percent and a net sales income of 18 percent. A difference of this magnitude is extremely difficult to explain. Throughout this study evidence was presented that the Hutterite colonies appeared to be more productive in terms of volume of output than the average for Manitoba farms. However, with the presentation of the data in Table 14-7, it appears that the superior Hutterite productivity may have been achieved by an excessive amount of capital input. On the other hand, this may be an indication that a truly diversified farm operation has higher operating costs than less diversified farms. Although these and other related questions are of fundamental importance, it is beyond the scope of this study to pursue the matter at length. It would require a full cost-accounting analysis of each Hutterite enterprise, but this was not one of the objectives of the present study. In any event, although a number of other observations will be made regarding the data in Table 14-7, these will be presented more as questions than as explanations.[4]

Although there is an average difference of 10 percent between Manitoba farms and Hutterite colonies in expenses and net sales income, there are interesting variations during the eleven-year period. In one of them, 1970, the expenses on Hutterite colonies were slightly less than on Manitoba farms. This was the year the federal government placed restrictions on wheat production and the Manitoba wheat crop was only about one-third of that in the immediately preceding years. This was as a consequence one of the worst years on record for net sales income on Manitoba farms. However, the Hutterite colonies were hardly affected by the restrictions on wheat production mainly because normally only a small part of their income is from wheat sales. Furthermore, hog prices were only beginning to decline in 1970, so this was a better than average year for the Hutterites, while mainly because of the

TABLE 14-7

GROSS SALES INCOME, EXPENSES, AND NET SALES INCOME, 1961-1971

MANITOBA FARMS[1] AND HUTTERITE COLONIES[2]

Manitoba Farms

Year	Gross Income from sales $	Cash Expenses and Depreciation $	Net Income from sales $	Expenses as a % of Gross Sales Income	Net Sales Income as a % of Gross Sales Income
1961	243,060,000	155,707,000	87,353,000	64.1%	35.9%
1962	261,529,000	177,371,000	84,158,000	67.8%	32.2%
1963	270,213,000	185,542,000	84,671,000	68.7%	31.3%
1964	299,734,000	199,136,000	100,598,000	66.4%	33.6%
1965	342,163,000	215,747,000	126,416,000	63.1%	36.9%
1966	377,186,000	243,946,000	133,240,000	64.7%	35.3%
1967	372,933,000	271,395,000	101,538,000	72.8%	27.2%
1968	364,816,000	288,814,000	76,002,000	79.2%	20.8%
1969	351,941,000	279,979,000	71,962,000	79.6%	20.4%
1970	339,674,000	283,263,000	56,411,000	83.4%	16.6%
1971	372,560,000	300,845,000	71,715,000	80.8%	19.2%
Average	326,891,720	236,522,270	90,369,450	72.4%	27.6%

			Hutterite Colonies					
Year	Gross Income From Sales $	Cash Expenses and Depreciation $	Net Income from Sales $	Expenses as a % of Gross Income	Net Sales Income as a % of Gross Income	Hutt. Gross Income as a % of Gross Sales Income	Hutt. Expenses as a % of Man. farm expenses	Hutt. Net Sales Income as a % of Man. Net Sales Income
1961	5,423,926	3,884,528	1,539,398	71.6%	28.4%	2.2%	2.5%	1.8%
1962	6,214,609	4,438,607	1,776,002	71.4%	28.6%	2.4%	2.5%	2.1%
1963	6,663,444	4,914,156	1,749,288	73.7%	26.3%	2.5%	2.6%	2.1%
1964	7,217,184	5,666,533	1,550,651	78.5%	21.5%	2.4%	2.8%	1.9%
1965	9,311,545	6,852,856	2,458,689	73.6%	26.4%	2.7%	3.2%	1.9%
1966	10,703,295	8,709,579	1,993,716	81.4%	18.6%	2.8%	3.6%	1.3%
1967	10,496,639	9,200,856	1,295,783	87.7%	12.3%	2.8%	3.4%	1.3%
1968	11,598,282	10,224,120	1,374,162	88.2%	11.8%	3.2%	3.5%	1.8%
1969	14,925,893	11,915,929	3,009,964	79.8%	20.2%	4.2%	4.3%	4.2%
1970	13,374,114	11,077,005	2,297,109	82.8%	17.2%	3.9%	3.9%	4.1%
1971	12,323,740	11,575,241	748,499	93.9%	6.1%	3.3%	3.8%	1.0%
Average	9,841,152	8,041,765	1,799,387	81.7%	18.3%	2.7%	3.1%	1.8%

1Source: Data compiled by J. Ryan from the *Yearbook of Manitoba Agriculture 1971*, pp. 72, 78.

2Source: Data compiled by J. Ryan from the financial reports on each colony, as prepared by Meyers, Dickens, Norris, Penny & Company, the accounting firm employed by the Hutterite colonies.

wheat situation, 1970 was a very abnormal year for Manitoba farms in general. An interesting comparison can also be made of 1969. Hutterite expenses were then only slightly more than the Manitoba average. The market for Canadian wheat was very poor in 1969 and this had a serious effect on average Manitoba farms. However, 1969 proved to be a record year for the Hutterites, mainly because hog prices were near an all-time high. Consequently, their net sales income that year was 4.2 percent of the Manitoba net sales income, as compared to the eleven-year average of 1.8 percent.

Probably the most disastrous year the Hutterites have ever experienced was 1971. This is especially interesting because the two preceding years had been better than average, especially as compared with Manitoba farms. Furthermore, in 1971 conditions began to improve for Manitoba farms. As discussed in the chapter on hogs, the economic setback in 1971 for the Hutterites was largely due to the sudden attempt by many farmers to diversify during the two preceding years. Manitoba farmers had been urged by the federal and provincial governments to expend their livestock operations. A large number of hogs were suddenly placed on the market, so hog prices collapsed in 1971. For a similar reason egg prices also dropped. Since these two enterprises are responsible for the bulk of Hutterite income, it is not surprising that the Hutterite colonies were suddenly faced with economic disaster. As mentioned in a previous section, in 1971 there were 4 Hutterite colonies that registered an overall nil income and 11 colonies had serious losses. At the time of writing in 1972, egg prices are still abnormally low, but hog prices have risen, and in all likelihood this should be a better year for the Hutterite colonies than 1971.

Until data based on a proper cost-accounting for each Hutterite enterprise are available it will be impossible to calculate accurately the profitability and economic efficiency of the Hutterite colonies. Without the benefit of such data, it can be said that, although the colonies are productive in terms of volume of output in relation to land employed, they are engaged in high-cost enterprises which bring relatively low returns because of low market prices. Of equal significance is the fact that the average Hutterite family has available only one-half the land area of an average Manitoba farm. Hence their farming units may be too small to meet present-day requirements. If this is the case, it suggests that were the Hutterite colonies each about twice their present size, it would increase their grain production and this would reduce the amount of feed that they now have to purchase. Perhaps only then would the Hutterite colonies be on equal terms with average Manitoba farms in regard to expenses and net sales income.

TABLE 14-8

MANITOBA HUTTERITE COLONIES, 1971

ASSETS, LIABILITIES, AND EQUITY

	Value of land $	Buildings, equipment & inventory $	Total assets $	Total liabilities $	Equity $
No. of col's 48	18,558,864.30	20,928,085.81	39,486,950.11	10,298,320.26	29,188,629.85
Average per colony	386,643.00	436,001.70	822,644.70	214,548.30	608,096.40
% of total assets	47.0%	53.0%	100%	26.1%	73.9%

Source: Data compiled by J. Ryan from the 1971 financial reports on each of the 48 colonies, as prepared by Meyers, Dickens, Norris, Penny & Company, the accountants employed by the Hutterite colonies.

Assets, Liabilities, and Equity of Hutterite Colonies, 1971

Table 14-8 shows the assets, liabilities, and equity of Manitoba Hutterite colonies in 1971. Comparable data for Manitoba farms are unavailable so it is not possible to make comparisons. Furthermore, these data are unavailable for previous years for Hutterite colonies, so comparisons cannot be made in this regard either.

The table shows that in 1971 the 48 colonies had total assets, consisting of land, buildings, equipment and inventory, of $39,486,950.11. Buildings, equipment, and inventory accounted for $20,928,085.81 or 53 percent of the total assets. Land was valued at $18,558,864.30 or an average of $386,643.00 per colony. Land value per colony ranged from a low of $89,900 to a high of $675,377, but the average value was representative of most colonies. In 1971 the colonies owned 178,464 acres, and this meant that the average price per acre was $104. It is certain that there was a wide range in the price per acre from district to district, but data on this are not available.

Liabilities, consisting mainly of bank loans, mortgages, and inter-colony loans, accounted for $10,298,320.26 or 26.1 percent of the total assets. The average liabilities per colony were $214,548.30, but this ranged from a low of $1,500 to a high of $829,000. However, the liabilities for most colonies were near the overall average.

The total Hutterite equity amounted to $29,188,629.85 or an average of $608,096.40 per colony. Although the equity on most colonies was near the overall average, it ranged from a low of $126,414 to a high of $1,243,436. In fact, several colonies had an equity of over $1,000,000.

Notes and References

1. The Hutterite financial reports are prepared on the basis of gross sales income and do not contain data on total gross income. Total gross income would have to include annual inventory change as well as farm sales, but the colony reports do not include inventory change and are based on sales income only. This does not present any comparison problems with Manitoba farms because the *Yearbook of Manitoba Agriculture* contains both "gross income" and the equivalent of "gross sales income." The *Yearbook* uses the term "cash income" rather than "gross sales income," but Mr. Daciw, Manitoba Agricultural Statistician, states that the terms are equivalent.

2. The difficulties of obtaining data on Hutterite operating expenses for each enterprise are discussed at length in the concluding chapter of this study.

3. As already pointed out, the Hutterite financial reports are based on "gross sales income" and not on "total gross income." For tax purposes, a separate section of the financial reports consists of operating expenses plus annual depreciation on buildings and machinery. When this amount is deducted from the "gross sales income," the remainder is referred to as "personal benefits." For the purposes of this study, the writer has taken the liberty of referring to "personal benefits" as "net sales income." Since depreciation was included with the expenses, the assumption was made that cash outlay for new buildings and equipment would be equal to the annual depreciation, and therefore "net sales income" would be an appropriate term. Mr. Daciw, Manitoba Agricultural Statistician, approved of this terminology.

4. The question of the economic efficiency of Hutterite colonies is discussed further in the concluding chapter.

CHAPTER 15

SUMMARY AND CONCLUSIONS

Productivity of Hutterite Colonies in Comparison with Manitoba Farms

On the basis of total agricultural operations, Hutterite colonies make more intensive use of their resources than average Manitoba farms. In fact, with the exception of part of one enterprise, the Hutterite colonies are more productive in terms of physical volume of output than Manitoba farms in every major agricultural enterprise. These conclusions are valid for comparisons on a per acre basis or on a comparison of the output per Manitoba farm with the output per Hutterite family.

A basic indication of the intensity of use of farmland is the amount of land in crops and the amount of total improved farmland. In 1968 the Hutterites had 73.8 percent of their farmland in crops as compared to an average of only 45.6 percent for Manitoba farms (Table 7-5). This table also shows that the Hutterites had a far greater proportion of total improved farmland—95.8 percent as compared to 65.2 percent for Manitoba farms.

In the case of grain production, in 1968 the Hutterites had substantially higher yields in the three major grain crops produced in this province. The yields for wheat, oats, and barley were as follows: wheat—Hutterites 30.1 bushels per acre, Manitoba farms 26.8 bushels per acre (Table 7-9); oats—Hutterites 54.0 bushels per acre, Manitoba farms 51.3 bushels per acre (Table 7-8); barley—Hutterites 41.1 bushels per acre, Manitoba farms 36.8 bushels per acre (Table 7-10).

The cattle enterprise is the only agricultural operation in which the Hutterites are not highly specialized. This is basically because of shortage of suitable land for pasture and for hay purposes. However, although their total number of dairy and beef cattle per acre is only 55 percent of the Manitoba average, they have almost twice the number of dairy cattle per acre—192 percent of the average Manitoba farm (Table 8-3). Therefore, although they have substantially smaller numbers of beef cattle, their dairy operation compares very favourably with the Manitoba average.

Several factors indicate that the Hutterites are more productive in terms of volume of output in the hog enterprise than average Manitoba hog producers. When related to intensity of use of farmland, the Hutterites on a per acre basis have 17 times the number of hogs of the Manitoba average (based on data in Table 9-2). Furthermore, the average Manitoba hog producer has only 26.6 percent of the hogs per Hutterite family (Table 9-3). Another indication of productivity is the size of sow litters—the Manitoba average is 11.0 piglets per sow while the Hutterite average is 11.3 per sow (Table 9-1 and footnote 3 in Chapter 9). And finally, the Hutterites have a larger turn-over of market hogs per year than average Manitoba hog producers. Table 9-6 shows that in 1968 the Hutterites marketed 170 percent of the hogs on hand on June 1 of that year, while the average for Manitoba producers was only 161 percent.

The Hutterites have a particularly large volume of output in the poultry enterprises. In 1968 the average Manitoba laying hen enterprise had only 20 percent of the laying hens per Hutterite family (Table 10-3). In the case of turkeys, the average Manitoba turkey producer had only 33.3 percent of the turkeys per Hutterite family, and sold only 28.1 percent of the turkeys per Hutterite family (Table 11-2). A particularly good index of productivity in the turkey enterprise is the fact that the Hutterites sold a considerably greater proportion of turkeys than their average holdings during the year. As for the goose and duck enterprises, the Hutterites operate these on such a large scale that it is futile to make any comparisons with the occasional Manitoba farm that keeps a small number of ducks and geese.

Although the apiary enterprise is of minor significance on most Hutterite colonies, the Hutterites nevertheless have a larger number of honeybee colonies than the average Manitoba beekeeper. In 1968 the average Manitoba beekeeper had only 71 percent of the honeybee colonies of a Hutterite enterprise (Table 13-1). However, data are unavailable on the amount of honey produced on the Hutterite colonies, and therefore, a production comparison cannot be made.

Significance of the Hutterite Contribution to the Manitoba Agricultural Economy

The contribution of the Hutterite colonies to the agricultural economy of Manitoba is of a magnitude far greater than the proportion of land owned by these people. The Hutterites own less than 1 percent of the Manitoba farmland (Table 7-1), but their economic contribution in every major enterprise, with the exception of part of one, is significantly greater than would normally be expected from the operation of this amount of land.

In the crop enterprise, the Hutterites produce significantly larger amounts of oats, barley, and wheat than their proportionate share on the basis of land ownership. In 1968, on .87 percent of the Manitoba farmland that they owned and rented, the Hutterites produced 3 percent of Manitoba oats, 2.6 percent of Manitoba barley, and 1 percent of Manitoba wheat (Tables 7-8, 7-9, 7-10). It should be pointed out, however, that these are the main crops produced by the Hutterites and that very few other crops are of importance on the colonies. Therefore, this should be taken into consideration because other crops such as flax, rye, field peas, rapeseed, and sugar beets, are of significance on average Manitoba farms. On the other hand though, since Hutterite production of oats, barley, and wheat is so much greater than their proportionate share, this in all likelihood more than makes up for their lack of other crops. In any case, there is no question about the basic fact that Hutterite crop production makes a substantial contribution to the Manitoba agricultural economy.

As mentioned in a previous section, the Hutterites are not highly specialized in the cattle enterprise. According to them, the basic reason for this is a lack of sufficient and suitable land for pasture and hay purposes. This is not surprising, however, since on a per family basis the Hutterites have only one-half the land of an average family farm (Table 7-2). Most Hutterite land is highly productive and too valuable to be placed in pasture; therefore, only relatively small numbers of cattle are kept. Hence, the beef enterprise is conducted on very few colonies, and Hutterite beef cattle account for only .2 percent of the Manitoba total (Table 8-1). However, all colonies operate dairy enterprises, and although these operations are not large on some colonies, the total Hutterite dairy cattle account for 1.7 percent of all Manitoba dairy cattle (Table 8-1). Therefore, on the basis of land ownership, as far as the dairy enterprise is concerned, the Hutterites have more than twice their proportionate share of dairy cattle. Hence even in an enterprise in which the Hutterites are not highly specialized, their contribution to the provincial economy is nevertheless considerable.

An operation in which the Hutterites are highly specialized is the rearing of hogs. This enterprise is of major significance on every colony. In 1968 the Hutterites accounted for 15 percent of the hogs in Manitoba and for 15.9 percent of the total hog sales (Tables 9-1 and 9-4). Furthermore, these tables show that in some districts the Hutterites account for 45 percent of the hogs and for 68 percent of the hog sales. This is a major contribution to the province's agricultural economy and is completely out of proportion on the basis of land ownership.

The Hutterite scale of operations in the laying hen enterprise is comparable to their high specialization in hogs. Almost every colony has a significant chicken enterprise. In 1968 the Hutterites accounted for almost 18 percent of the Manitoba laying hens and 2.5 percent of the broilers and 5.6 percent of broiler sales (Tables 10-1 and 10-2). Similar to the situation in hogs, in the districts where the Hutterite colonies are located, their share of production is far greater than their provincial average, e.g., in one district they account for almost 64 percent of the laying hens. Obviously, the Hutterite share of Manitoba egg production is of major consequence.

The Hutterites are even larger producers of turkeys than they are of hogs or chickens. In 1968 the Hutterites accounted for 20 percent of Manitoba turkeys, 20 percent of mature turkey sales, 96 percent of turkey broiler sales, and an average of 24 percent of all Manitoba turkey sales (Table 11-1). The significance of this is even more striking when it is considered that only 12 colonies produced turkeys in 1968.

It has already been indicated that in the goose and duck enterprise, the Hutterites are almost in a monopoly position. Because of the relative insignificance of this operation on other Manitoba farms, reliable province-wide data on geese and ducks are available for only the main census years, i.e., 1961 and 1966. Data are available on total sales in 1968, however, and in that year the Hutterites accounted for 95 percent of the goose sales and 62 percent of the duck sales (Tables 12-14 and 12-8). In addition to this, these tables show that the Hutterites sold almost 50,000 goslings (almost one-half of their sales of mature geese) and over 68,000 ducklings (more than three times their sales of mature ducks). The Hutterites, in other words, are the major suppliers of goslings and ducklings for the commercial hatcheries in Manitoba, and in addition they make substantial exports to hatcheries and other Hutterite colonies out of the province.

The Hutterites make a substantial economic contribution in other activities as well. In the apiary enterprise, the Hutterites account for 5.6 percent of the total Manitoba honeybee colonies (Table 13-1). In terms of gross sales, their income from vegetables and potatoes is even higher than their income from the sale of honey (Table 14-2). The Hutterites do a considerable amount of custom work for local farmers, and this brings in an annual income of over $3,000 for most colonies (Table 14-2). The custom work that the Hutterites are able to provide, such as seeding, swathing, and combining, is of considerable significance to a number of neighboring farmers who lack sufficient farm machinery.

As a conclusion to this section, there is ample evidence that the

Hutterites, on less than 1 percent of Manitoba farmland, are responsible for a prodigious amount of total agricultural produce. Their agricultural operations in this province would be sorely missed, especially in the production of hogs, chickens and eggs, turkeys, ducks and geese.

The Hutterite Contribution to Local Communities

Largely because the Hutterites have different cultural standards, do not participate in local recreation, and do not send their children to local schools, various myths have been perpetrated about their overall contribution to local communities. The charge usually levelled against them is that they make few local purchases and are therefore of little help to the community economically. Although this study did not investigate this issue fully, certain facts were revealed which appear to be sufficient to dispel the charge of lack of economic participation in local communities.

The average Hutterite colony has an investment of almost $80,000 in farm machinery, apart from a substantial investment in motor vehicles (Table 7-12). Hutterite purchase records indicate that about 80 percent of the farm machinery is purchased within approximately a 25-mile radius, and largely in the immediate local communities (Appendices D, E, and F). In addition, most of the Hutterite purchases of gasoline, oil, diesel fuel, grease, fertilizer, weed spray, lumber, cement, and hardware are apparently made in local regions. Some of these are purchased in the larger centres mainly because they are unavailable in the immediate local hamlets. Admittedly, the Hutterites purchase commercial feed and concentrate in Winnipeg, but these commodities are unavailable in local areas, at least in the quantities the colonies require. They also purchase dry goods and various other supplies in Winnipeg, but so do many other farmers. In any event, although such data were not systematically collected for this study, there appears to be sufficient evidence to indicate that the Hutterites make a substantial economic contribution to local communities.

The Economic Efficiency of Hutterite Colonies

The study has shown that on the basis of all significant criteria, the Hutterite colonies appear to operate their farmlands more intensively and achieve a greater per unit volume of production than average Manitoba farms. This appears to be true in crop production as well as all other enterprises. With this evidence on the one hand and the generally accepted view of the efficiency of large scale production on the other, the logical conclusion should be that the Hutterite colonies are profitable business operations and are economically efficient. Yet, the most surprising aspect of this study is the revelation of apparently equally sound evidence that, contrary to this seemingly obvious conclusion, the Hutterites may not be efficient after all. Data based on financial reports over an eleven-year period indicate that the operating expenses on Hutterite colonies are substantially higher and the corresponding net income significantly lower than the average for Manitoba farms (Tables 14-6 and 14-7). This is one of the major findings of this study, but with the information available it remains almost inexplicable. To account fully for this apparent lack of economic efficiency would require detailed cost-accounting of each Hutterite enterprise. This was beyond the scope of the present study.

Without the aid of cost-accounting of each enterprise, it is possible to offer only partial explanations for this state of affairs. The data within the financial reports of both Manitoba farms and the Hutterite colonies should first be subjected to detailed study to make certain that all entries are completely comparable. This was attempted in the present study and apparently the data are comparable, but this should nevertheless be investigated more fully.[1] If the major data are correct, it is obvious that some Hutterite enterprises must be extremely expensive to operate, hence reducing the overall net income of the colonies. On the basis of this study, the writer has no cause to suspect any enterprise of being fundamentally inefficient. On the contrary, throughout the years of field work, he was impressed with the seeming efficiency of Hutterite operations. Hence the whole problem of Hutterite economic efficiency must be a subject of further research.

The Hutterite Colony and the Hutterite Family as Units of Production

An average Manitoba Hutterite colony has 15 families and a total population of about 100. The colony operates on a communal basis and is under the direction of a single management. Although the colony itself is an obvious economic unit, the Hutterite family is seldom considered as a unit of production. However, it is one of the conclusions of this study, that for some purposes, it is appropriate to consider both the colony and the family as legitimate production units.

The Hutterite colony hardly needs any justification to be considered as a production unit. Nevertheless, its key characteristics should be pointed out. Although each enterprise has its own manager, the operation of the entire colony is under a central management. All activities are coordinated by an executive who are responsible for the overall welfare and development of the colony. Each colony is a legal entity and it keeps a single set of accounts for all its enterprises, and in every way functions as a single economic unit. For accounting and other comparison purposes, all enterprises and all types of production can be considered on a per colony basis. However, for certain production purposes and for certain types of comparisons, the colony as a production unit has limitations. For instance, it is impossible to make a meaningful comparison between a Hutterite colony and an average Manitoba farm. The scale of production on the two is so different that comparisons are almost meaningless.

Because the colony is such an obvious unit of production, the fact that the colony consists of individual families is often not appreciated. Yet it is the labour force of the families that makes the colony function. It is the labour and the overall contribution of each family that makes up the total production of the colony. Although the Hutterites operate on a communal basis and although the families may often live in multiple dwellings, each family is nevertheless an entity in itself. Furthermore, if for some reason, the Hutterites ceased to live on colonies, and the individual families wished to remain in farming, they would have no recourse but to establish individual farms. On this basis the present 48 colonies would split up into approximately 650 farms (the approximate number of families in 1971). Therefore, on the basis of this reasoning, it is not at all inappropriate to consider the Hutterite family as a production unit, particularly for comparison purposes with average Manitoba farms. This was done throughout this study and the comparison in almost all instances has proven meaningful.

The consideration of the Hutterite family as a production unit has far greater implications than simply its use for comparison purposes with Manitoba farms. For very practical purposes, the Hutterites in recent years have been agitating to have their families recognized as individual production units. Amongst their most recent efforts is a letter in this regard addressed to Premier Schreyer of Manitoba dated April 20, 1972.[2] The letter requested the recognition of family production units in five different areas. It pointed out that the revenue department of the federal government accepts the Hutterites as family production units and the Hutterites thus pay income tax on a family basis. However, apparently in all other instances it is the colony that is considered as the production unit and the families are disregarded.

With reference to Manitoba school tax rebates which are made on family ownership of land, the letter stated that the Hutterites receive a single rebate of $50 per colony, rather than $50 per family. Another issue is that farmers in Manitoba have been receiving a special subsidy grant of $1 per acre up to a maximum of $100 per farm. As in the case of the school issue, the Hutterites have been receiving $100 per colony rather than $100 per family.

A third area of grievance dealt with federal hog deficiency payments. Although this is not a provincial matter, the point was made nevertheless. The federal government recently made payments of $5 per hog up to a maximum of $1,000 per producer. However, each Hutterite colony was considered as a single producer, and on this basis each family received only 45 cents per hog.

The final two matters dealt with producer and marketing boards. Whereas each individual farmer or producer gets a vote on these boards, the Hutterites have only one vote per colony. The other matter dealt with restrictions on scale of operations. So far, each Hutterite colony is considered as a single producer, regardless of the fact that each colony supports approximately 15 families, while an average Manitoba farm supports only one family. Because their basic family production units are not being recognized, the Hutterites are being seriously affected by certain producer and marketing board regulations which were primarily designed to limit the operations of large "agribusiness" commercial corporations.

In conclusion, on the basis of this study there appear to be sufficient grounds to consider both the Hutterite colony and the Hutterite family as legitimate units of production, depending on the circumstances involved.

Areas for Further Research

In this pioneer study the main objectives were to compile reliable data on each Hutterite enterprise, compare the operations with Manitoba farms, and determine the overall Hutterite contribution to the Manitoba agricultural economy. In addition, an attempt was made to acquaint the reader with the operation of the colonies themselves and the life style of the Hutterite people. It is felt that these basic objectives have been accomplished, but in the course of the study other areas of possible investigation became apparent. With the experience gained from this study, the writer feels that several areas of further research can now be discussed profitably.

1. The Relative Efficiency and Profitability of each Hutterite Enterprise

Almost at the very beginning of the present study it became apparent that this topic, important as it is, could not be investigated because neither the resources nor the time were available for the compilation of the appropriate data. Furthermore, this is a major research topic in itself. As already discussed, research in this area is essential if the apparent lower economic efficiency of the Hutterite colonies is to be properly understood.

It is obvious that to be able to assess fully the efficiency and profitability of any enterprise, it is essential to take account of all the operating expenses. However, up to the end of 1971 not one Hutterite colony in Manitoba kept accurate accounts for each enterprise. On some colonies, especially in the last two or three years, efforts have been made to establish proper accounting systems, but so far these have not been extended to all operations. Very often practical problems are involved in some of the enterprises and proper accounting procedures are difficult to introduce without considerable expense and perhaps a restructuring of the operations. By and large, the problem centres on measuring the exact amount of colony-produced grain used by each enterprise. Many colonies have a central grain elevator which is used for the storage of grain for several departments. Often a system of augers conveys the grain directly from the storage bins to the various enterprise facilities. Under these conditions, without going to considerable expense, it is difficult to measure the amount of grain that was distributed to the various departments. Therefore, if the colonies themselves do not have reliable information on the exact amount of grain used by each enterprise, this poses a serious problem for research on the profitability of each operation.

Since some colonies now keep reasonably accurate records for some of their operations, by checking all the colonies it could be possible to find enough colonies with adequate accounting systems to cover every sphere of work. However, the operations of certain enterprises vary considerably from colony to colony, and therefore, it would be necessary to have several truly representative colonies for each enterprise.

As discussed in the previous chapter, the list of expenses that the colonies submit to their accountant is often very generalized. The financial reports that are prepared on the colonies are primarily for tax purposes, and because of grouping and generalization it is impossible to apply most of these data to individual enterprises.

This is not to say that it is impossible to collect a sufficient amount of appropriate data to assess the relative efficiency and profitability of each Hutterite enterprise, however, it will be a major task.

2. The Economic Effect of Hutterite Colonies on Local Regions

Although it is not a difficult area of research, this particular topic was not entirely relevant to the present study. Nevertheless, a considerable amount of data were collected which would be useful for such a suggested study. Complete data were collected on the cost and the place of purchase of all farm machinery for all colonies in 1968. Since the cost and the servicing of farm machinery is such a major expenditure, such data are essential for any study of this type. In other words, part of the research for this suggested study has already been done and the data are available.

Indications of Future Trends

Although this is basically a study of the agricultural operations of Hutterite colonies, a considerable part of this work was devoted to an analysis of the colonies themselves in order that the agricultural operations would be viewed not in isolation but as an integral part of Hutterite life. Viewed in this context, it should be apparent that changes or technical innovations would not be introduced into the agricultural sector if these in any way threatened or were damaging to Hutterite values or their pattern of life. It is fundamental to understand that the various agricultural enterprises are not conducted for the sole sake of profit or as ends in themselves. This is completely at variance with the agricultural operations of the average Manitoba farm. Admittedly, some farmers still operate their land as a way of life, but the majority operate their farms strictly as business operations. In the case of the Hutterites, the agricultural operations are conducted for the prime purpose of maintaining their way of life.

The continuance of Hutterite agricultural operations in Manitoba cannot be taken for granted. Significant as these operations are to the Manitoba economy, it is conceivable that other factors, totally apart from the realm of agriculture, could eliminate the entire Hutterite economic contribution. If circumstances arose that fundamentally threatened the Hutterite way of life, there is little doubt that the farmlands would be sold and the Hutterites would leave the province. There is sufficient precedent in their history of almost 450 years to support such a viewpoint. Throughout this period they have travelled from country to country, leaving after many years of permanent residence whenever their way of life was seriously challenged. After all, the only reason they are in Canada, and they have not been here very long, is because of persecution in the U.S.A. during the First World War. At that time the Americans could not accept the Hutterite pacifist philosophy, and the resulting actions brought about the sale of the Hutterite lands and their emigration to Canada in 1918.

Their sojourn in Canada has not been entirely without problems and pressures. During the Second World War they experienced some persecution because of their pacifist stand, and for years they have faced serious discrimination in Alberta concerning land purchase and colony expansion. Similar attempts were made in Manitoba by the rural municipalities, but these did not receive the sanction of the government and it seems highly unlikely that any Manitoba government would enact such legislation against them in the future. However, the school question is an entirely different matter. Until the introduction of the large school units the Hutterites had relatively few problems. They operated their own schools on the colonies, using the standard provincial curriculum. With the introduction of the large school division, some districts took advantage of the legislation limiting the small one-room schools and discontinued the education grants to the colonies. In these districts the colonies continue to pay their school taxes, but they themselves must now finance the entire operation of their own schools. There does not seem to be any question that this is fundamentally an attempt by these districts to force the Hutterites to send their children to large composite schools. Any acquaintance with Hutterite tradition would indicate that this is a completely unrealistic move. The blunt fact of the matter is that there is no foreseeable possibility that the Hutterites would ever send their children to outside schools. With their children going to outside schools, it is highly probable that in one generation the Hutterite mode of life would be totally undermined and the colonies would eventually disappear. The Hutterites realize this and they are not prepared to compromise on the issue. The withholding of education grants causes hardship for some colonies, but it is fairly certain that the Hutterites will endure this providing they are still able to operate their own schools. On the other hand, if legislation should ever be enacted forcing them to close their schools and send their children to outside schools, there seems little doubt that the Hutterites would sell their lands, and, in their traditional style, emigrate elsewhere.

Aside from the fundamental issue of the possibility of the Hutterites leaving the province at some time in the future, there are indications of certain trends, although these are not dramatic. When it comes to actual agricultural practices, the Hutterites are faced with the same basic issues that confront other farmers. *Statistics Canada*, in its latest release on the 1971 census, reports that between 1966 and 1971 the number Manitoba farms decreased from 39,747 to 34,981.[3] This is a reduction of 12 percent or a total of 4,766 farms in five years. However, the amount of farmland in production remained almost the same. In other words, there are now fewer farmers, but they are operating larger farms. Specifically, the average farm size in 1966 was 480 acres, while in 1971 it was 543 acres.[4] This study showed that in 1968 the average farm size in Manitoba was 500 acres, while the average amount of land owned by a Hutterite family was 250 acres, or exactly 50 percent of the average family farm (Table 7-3). There is no reason to suppose that the economic forces that gradually bring about an increase in the size of the average Manitoba farm do not apply with equal force to the Hutterite colonies. In fact, it is a certainty, considering the high operating expenses on the colonies, that the Hutterites will have to expand their operations in much the same way that other farmers are doing. Since on a per family basis they own only 50 percent of the land of an average family farm, it is one of the conclusions of this study that in order to remain economically viable the Hutterites will eventually be forced to acquire almost as much land per family as the average Manitoba farm. This of course means that the colonies of the future will be much larger, but if they continue to be as productive as they are at present, this should mean a corresponding increase in the agricultural output of the province.

It seems very unlikely that any future Manitoba government would enact discriminatory legislation against the Hutterites, thereby forcing them out of the province. Rather, it seems almost a certainty that the Hutterite colonies will continue to be a part of the Manitoba scene. However, the Hutterites will have to contend with the inevitable social pressures from the outside society. These are the forces that will bring about the greatest challenge to the Hutterite way of life. How they will cope with these problems remains to be seen.

Significance of the Study to the Field of Geography

The study makes available detailed production data not only on total Hutterite farm production, but also on the individual Hutterite production units, i.e., the individual colonies and family work units. These data were then used in a variety of ways to show how the Hutterite utilization of farmland compares with average farm operations, in the province as a whole and for individual agricultural regions. In addition, an analysis and explanation was made of the various comparisons and appropriate generalizations were advanced.

Although such research procedures have long been recommended, such as, ''sound generalizations about a region should be based on intensive studies of typical small areas,''[5] this approach has seldom been followed in studies on agricultural geography. For example, of the 47 papers submitted to the 22nd International Geographical Congress in Montreal in 1972, very few show any evidence of detailed field work on small areas.[6] Instead, most recent studies in agricultural geography deal with large regions or are based on the manipulation of standard census data. This is not to say that such an approach is in any way inappropriate, and certainly worthwhile contributions are being made. However, it seems that studies based on detailed field work are very seldom produced. In fact, it would appear that at present little research work is being done on regions or activities which lack official census data. This may explain the paucity of studies in agricultural geography relating to Manitoba. Because it is so completely based on new field work, the present study makes a significant contribution to agricultural geography in general, and to Manitoba in particular.

The specific findings and contributions of this study have already been enunciated in the foregoing sections of this concluding chapter. Where their geographic significance is not stated explicitly, it is nevertheless implicit in the context.

Notes and References

1. The comparability of data in the financial reports and this whole problem in general was discussed in a lengthy telephone interview on May 26, 1972 with Mr. Dave Norris, the accountant for the Hutterites at Brandon. Furthermore, the problem was discussed at considerable length on June 5, 1972 with Mr. Metro Daciw, Agricultural Statistician of the Manitoba Department of Agriculture. On the basis of these discussions, the data in the reports appear to be comparable, but at this stage of research, the fundamental problem of the apparent lack of economic efficiency of the Hutterite colonies is as inexplicable to Mr. Norris and Mr. Daciw as it is to the writer.
2. The letter to Premier Schreyer was made available to the writer by Reverend Jacob Kleinsasser of Crystal Spring Colony and permission was granted to discuss its contents.
3. Statistics Canada, *1971 Census of Canada: Agriculture— Number and Area of Census-Farms* (Advance Bulletin), April 1972, p. 3.

4. *Ibid*.

5. W. D. Jones and V. C. Finch, "Detailed Field Mapping in the Study of the Economic Geography of an Agricultural Area," *Bulletin of the American Geographical Society*, Vol. 15 (1925), pp. 148-57.

6. *International Geography 1972 La géographie internationale* (Papers submitted to the 22nd International Geographical Congress, Canada. Edited by W. Peter Adams and Frederick M. Helleiner. Vol. 2. Toronto: University of Toronto Press, 1972), pp. 695-787.

EPILOGUE*

Four years have elapsed since this study was completed and the text written. In our present rapidly changing world, it would be surprising to observe no significant changes in that time, but in the basically stable Hutterite society, it is change itself that would be surprising in such a relatively short period. When revisiting some of the colonies, the author was quickly reassured of the durability, permanence, and the seemingly changeless nature of the Hutterite economy and culture.

In revisiting the colonies there was no attempt to conduct a systematic study of any of the agricultural enterprises. Instead, a general inquiry was made about any significant events or changes that may have occurred in the intervening years. From all appearances, surprisingly little has changed. Moreover, all the new colonies that have been established since the completion of the original study have apparently adopted the same basic pattern of production as the previously existing colonies. True to Hutterite tradition, change is not something that occurs in a matter of a few years.[1]

Number of Colonies in 1975

By the end of 1975 there were a total of 60 colonies established in Manitoba. This is an increase of 12 colonies from the 48 that had been established by the end of 1970, which represents a 25 percent increase in five years. Table E-1 lists the new colonies, the parent colonies, and the years of establishment. Table E-2 shows the growth of colonies from 1918 to 1975. The latter table indicates that in the 10-year period between 1960 and 1970 the number of Manitoba colonies had increased by 50 percent; hence, the increase from 1970 to 1975 is essentially in line with the rate of increase during the previous decade. Actually when the increases are calculated at average annual compound rates, Table E-2 shows that colonies increased at 4¼ percent per annum between 1960 and 1970, but the increase was slightly higher between 1970 and 1975 (4½ percent) per year. However, this is overshadowed by the fact that the rates of increase from 1960 to 1975 are significantly lower than the increases during the previous years, for instance, a compound rate of 5¾ percent during the 1940's.

*The epilogue was written in March of 1976.

TABLE E-1

MANITOBA HUTTERITE COLONIES

NEW COLONIES, FOUNDING COLONIES, AND DATES OF

ESTABLISHMENT, 1971-1975

	Colony Founded	Parent Colony	Year Founded
1.	Mayfair	Riverside	1971
2.	Airport	New Rosedale	1972
3.	Grass River	Grand	1972
4.	Marble Ridge	Bloomfield	1972
5.	Newdale	Bon Homme	1972
6.	Baker	Rainbow	1973
7.	Pine Creek	Deerboine	1973
8.	Plainview	Waldheim	1973
9.	Broad Valley	Lakeside	1974
10.	Cypress	Homewood	1975
11.	Evergreen	Rose Valley	1975
12.	Holmfield	Riverdale	1975

Source: Meyers, Norris, Penny and Company, Chartered Accountants, Brandon, Manitoba

At the end of 1975 there were 8 colonies in the process of buying land and establishing facilities for the purpose of setting up new colonies.[2] In addition to these, it appears that there are 4 other colonies that are likely to establish new colonies within the next five years.[3] Hence by 1980 there could be an additional 12 new colonies established, making a total of 72 in the province. If this turns out to be the case, it would mean a 50 percent increase in colonies between 1970 and 1980, which would be the same increase as occurred between 1960 and 1970. As such, it seems that since 1960 colony expansion is stabilizing at a rate of about 50 percent per decade.

TABLE E-2

GROWTH OF MANITOBA HUTTERITE COLONIES, 1918-1975

Year	Total No. of Manitoba Colonies	Period of Increase	No. of new colonies formed	Per cent increase during period	Average annual increase during period (compound rate)
1918	6				
1930	9	1918-1930	4[1]	66 2/3%	4.5%
1940	14	1930-1940	6[2]	66 2/3%	5.25%
1950	20	1940-1950	10[3]	71%	5.75%
1960	32	1950-1960	13[4]	65%	5.25%
1970	48	1960-1970	16	50%	4.25%
1975	60	1970-1975	12	25%	4.5%

[1] Of the 4 new colonies, 1 was established in the U.S.A.

[2] Of the 6 new colonies, 1 was established in the U.S.A.

[3] Of the 10 new colonies, 4 were established in the U.S.A.

[4] Of the 13 new colonies, 1 was established in the U.S.A.

Source: Compiled from data acquired form the colonies by the author.

From 1918 to 1970 the average time interval between colony divisions was approximately 14 years. An examination of the 1971 to 1975 period indicates that the 14-year division interval has been essentially maintained. Appendix H shows the colony division intervals from 1918 to 1975 and Table E-3 summarizes these data. The most significant observation that can be made from Table E-3 is that there has been little variation in the colony division intervals from the time the Hutterites first settled in Manitoba to the present period. However, it appears that for the first time there may be a significant change in the next five-year period. At the beginning of 1976 for the 8 colonies that are in the process of establishing new colonies, the time interval since their initial establishment or previous subdivisions is 16.5 years (median) and 15.9 years (mean).[4] Furthermore, it will take some of these colonies a few more years before they are ready to subdivide, and so the time interval will be further extended. The inclusion of the 4 additional colonies that are likely to establish new colonies within the next five years should not affect the prospects of a much longer division interval in the next

TABLE E-3

COLONY DIVISION INTERVALS FROM 1918 TO 1975

Dates	No. of colonies that subdivided during the period	Division interval (median no. of years)	Division interval (Mean or average no. of years)
1918 - 1940	7*	15*	13.6*
1941 - 1950	10	13.5	15.2
1951 - 1960	13	14	14.6
1961 - 1970	16	15	14.3
1971 - 1975	12	13.5	14.2
1918 - 1975	61	14	14.4*

*excludes the first 3 divisions because they were at intervals of 1, 2, and 4 years during the initial settlement period (see Appendix H).

Source: Compiled from Appendix H.

period. It is difficult to account for this particular longer division interval, but it is much more likely that it is a coincidence rather than the beginning of a new trend.

Manitoba Hutterite Population in 1975

At the end of 1975 the Hutterite population in Manitoba totalled 5,191, and consisted of 850 families. Appendix I shows the population and the number of families on each of the 60 colonies. The population at the end of 1970 was 4,666, and so in the five-year period there was an increase of 11.25 percent (or an increase of 2.2 percent per year at a compound rate). The average number of families per colony was 14.2 and this compared with 14.8 families per colony in 1968. Although the number of families per colony has decreased slightly, the total population per colony shows a somewhat greater decrease. In 1975 the average number of persons per colony was 86.5 as compared to 97 in 1970 (the median was 87 in 1975 and 95 in 1970).

Although a couple of colonies had a population of over 160 in 1970, the largest population in 1975 was only 130 (on 3 colonies). On the other hand, while the smallest population in 1970 was 48, in 1975 one colony had a population of only 30 (with six families), and two others had a population of less than 50. However, there were unusual circumstances with regard to the formation of these 3 small colonies, and they are not really representative of the average colonies. Nevertheless, the average colony has a somewhat smaller population in 1975 than it did in 1970.

A point of considerable significance is the fact that of the 12 new colonies that were formed since 1970, only 6 were formed on the basis of almost equal population division. This had been the rule in the past and few colonies were ever established otherwise. However, in the past five years several colonies divided their assets and populations at ratios of approximately 45:55, plus one instance of a 35:65 division and one of a 30:70 division.[5] This indicates greater flexibility and adaptability in colony division.[6] At the present time it is not unusual to have new colonies being established with smaller amounts of land and fewer enterprises together with appropriately smaller populations. In time these colonies will gradually acquire additional amounts of land and will build up their enterprises to match those of the other colonies. It should be noted though that this is a new development.

Distribution and Location of New Colonies

The 12 new colonies as well as their founding colonies are shown on Map 19. Several significant observations can be made from a study of this map. One is that the average distance between a new colony and its parent colony is much greater now than at any period in the past—the present distance is approximately 100 miles. In two instances new colonies were established about 190 miles from the parent colonies, i.e., Bloomfield and its offspring Marble Ridge as well as Waldheim and its new colony Plainview. Only two colonies managed to buy land and established new colonies reasonably closeby, i.e., New Rosedale and Rose Valley, with their new colonies at distances of about 20 miles. With the exception of these two, for all others it meant that the parent colonies could not readily be used as the base of operations during the period of construction and small settlements had to be established on the new colonies almost immediately.

Map 19 shows that Hutterite colonies have now spread into almost every agricultural district of the province. The two notable exceptions are the Swan River-Roblin-Dauphin area and the extreme southwest of the province. The bulk of the new colonies were established in the productive south-central part of Manitoba. Only two colonies were

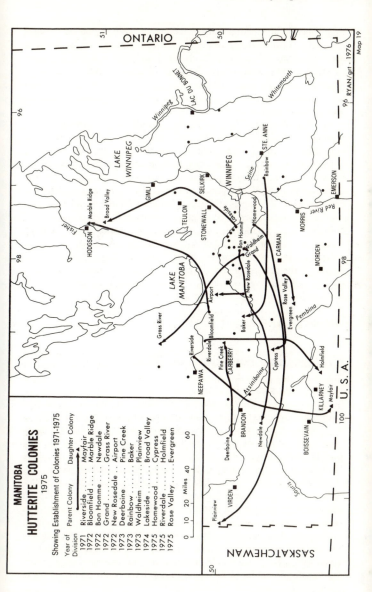

MANITOBA
HUTTERITE COLONIES
1975

Showing Establishment of Colonies 1971-1975

Year of Division	Parent Colony	Daughter Colony
1971	Riverside	Mayfair
1972	Bloomfield	Marble Ridge
1972	Bon Homme	Newdale
1972	Grand	Grass River
1972	New Rosedale	Airport
1973	Deerboine	Pine Creek
1973	Rainbow	Baker
1973	Waldheim	Plainview
1974	Lakeside	Broad Valley
1975	Homewood	Cypress
1975	Riverdale	Holmfield
1975	Rose Valley	Evergreen

0 10 20 40 60 Miles

RYAN/grt - 1976   Map 19

established in an area that is in general not noted for good agricultural land—the northern Interlake region. However, even here the colonies are located on pockets of relatively good land.[7] No new colonies were established in the area between Portage la Prairie and Winnipeg which already has a high concentration of colonies. Likewise no new colonies were set up in the Red River region nor in the agriculturally marginal area in the eastern part of the province.

In 1971 Manitoba Hutterite colonies could be grouped into eight reasonably distinct regions (Map 15, page 49). By 1975, with the establishment of 12 new colonies plus the prospect of another 12 colonies in the next five years, regionalization was no longer practical, especially in the central part of the province. Map 20 shows the distribution of the 60 Manitoba colonies in 1975. Although the heaviest concentration of colonies still occurs between Winnipeg and Portage la Prairie, the region west of Portage now contains the largest number of colonies. They are fairly evenly spread out from Lake Manitoba to the Saskatchewan border and then south to the U.S.A. border.

Map 21 shows the locations where 8 colonies have purchased land and are in the process of setting up new colonies. It is noteworthy that 6 of these areas are west of Portage la Prairie, adding to the concentration of colonies in this region. A further point that is made evident is the long distances between some of the new colony sites and their parent colonies.

Changes in Economic Conditions

Since 1972 significant changes have occurred in farm income not only for Manitoba Hutterites but for all farmers in Canada. This period has been among the best on record, and most farmers have been able to recoup losses and setbacks from previous lean years. This has been especially significant for the Hutterites because 1971, with its low prices for hogs, eggs, and poultry, proved to be the worst year that the Hutterites have had since the depression of the 1930's.

Although no new detailed data were gathered on Hutterite agricultural enterprises and income for the period since 1968, it is nevertheless reasonable to assume that Hutterite colonies have prospered at least as well as other Manitoba farmers. In fact, because of their scale of operations, they may have done considerably better than the average Manitoba farmer. In any event, an analysis of changes in economic conditions since 1968 for Manitoba farms in general should give a reasonable indication of the changes that have occurred on Hutterite colonies.

TABLE E-4

MANITOBA FARMS

GROSS SALES INCOME, EXPENSES, AND NET INCOME, 1968-1974

Year	Gross Sales Income[1] $	Expenses $	Net Income[3] $	Average Net Income
1968	364,816,000	288,814,000	76,002,000	
1969	350,409,000	279,979,000	70,430,000	78,937,000
1970	340,363,000	267,413,000	72,950,000	
1971	378,415,000	282,051,000	96,364,000	
1972	487,863,000	310,576,000	177,287,000	
1973	621,113,000	378,126,000	242,987,000	254,606,000
1974	819,981,000	476,436,000	343,545,000	

[1]Yearbook of Manitoba Agriculture 1974, p. 105

[2]Yearbook of Manitoba Agriculture 1974, p. 199.

[3]Compiled by subtracting Expenses from Gross Sales Income.

Table E-4 shows the gross sales income, expenses, and the net income of Manitoba farms for the years 1968 to 1974. The most striking feature revealed by this table is that the net income from 1968 to 1971 remained relatively stable (averaging 79 million dollars per year), but from 1972 to 1974 net income increased dramatically each year, and the average for this period more than tripled the average for the previous four-year period.

Table E-5 shows that although gross sales income increased by 125 percent from 1968 to 1974, expenses increased by only 65 percent, and this helps to account for the large increase in net income during this period—352 percent. Even allowing for the inflationary spiral of the last few years, it is nevertheless apparent that the real net income of farmers has increased very significantly, especially since 1972.

An analysis of various capital improvements on Hutterite colonies since 1968 is perhaps one of the best indicators of changes in general

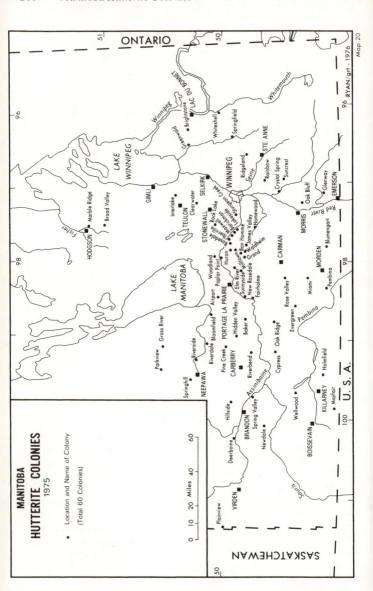

MANITOBA
HUTTERITE COLONIES
1975

•   Location and Name of Colony
(Total 60 Colonies)

0   10   20   40   60

Miles

Map 20

RYAN, grt - 1976

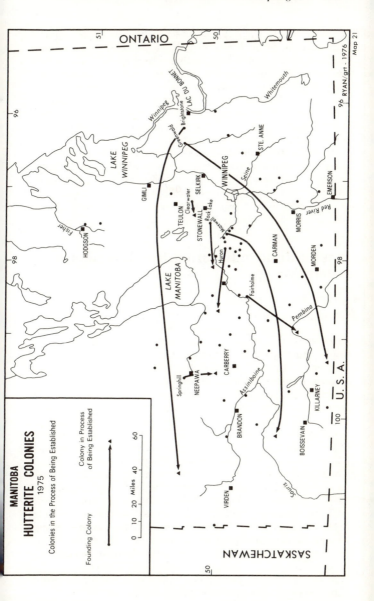

MANITOBA
HUTTERITE COLONIES
1975

Colonies in the Process of Being Established

■ Founding Colony

▲ Colony in Process
of Being Established

0 10 20 Miles 40 60

Map 21

economic conditions. Since 1968 most colonies have made significant investments in the modernization of hog and chicken barns and other facilities. Most colonies have purchased large amounts of new farm machinery, including expensive tractors and combines. In recent years many colonies have installed modern hot water or electric heating systems in all their dwellings. A further indication of improved conditions is that at the present time about 85 percent of the colonies have modern indoor plumbing systems, whereas back in 1968 only about 15 percent of the colonies had these facilities.[8]

By almost any standard there is no question whatever about the general improvement in the overall economic conditions of the Hutterite colonies. Although the Hutterites are somewhat concerned about the present problems of inflation and increasing costs of production, they do not appear to have any major economic problems and they are confident about the future.

Present Relative Importance of Agricultural Enterprises

The relative importance of each Hutterite agricultural enterprise appears to be basically the same as it was in 1968 (Appendix G). For the colonies as a whole, hog production is still unquestionably the most important activity, while the chicken enterprise, with its sale of eggs mainly, remains next in importance. These two enterprises accounted for almost 70 percent of the total gross sales income in 1968, and apparently this has not changed significantly since.

Grain sales appear to be in third place as before, but are probably of greater relative importance. This is largely because the price of wheat has gone up dramatically in the last few years, e.g., from $1.36 per bushel in 1968 to $4.30 in 1973 and $3.75 in 1974.[9] However, in terms of total bushels sold per colony, wheat sales have not increased significantly because the Hutterites have always sold their full quota of wheat. Since each colony's land holdings are still basically the same, the amount of wheat sold remains almost the same as well, regardless of the price that could be obtained. Although hog and egg prices have not gone up as much as wheat, the price increases have been significant nevertheless. Therefore, considering these factors, grain sales may have increased in relative importance, but in all likelihood there would not be a marked difference, and grain sales would still remain definitely in third place.

As for the remaining enterprises, indications are that their relative importance remains the same now as in 1968 (Appendix G). This seems

TABLE E-5

MANITOBA FARMS

1968 AND 1974 COMPARISON OF

GROSS SALES INCOME, EXPENSES, AND NET INCOME

Category	1968 $	1974 $	Per cent Increase from 1968
Gross Sales Income[1]	364,8.6,000	819,981,000	124.8%
Expenses[2]	288,814,000	476,436,000	65.0%
Net Income[3]	76,002,000	343,545,000	352.0%

[1]Yearbook of Manitoba Agriculture 1974, p. 105.

[2]Yearbook of Manitoba Agriculture 1974, p. 99.

[3]Net Income compiled by subtracting Expenses from Gross Sales Income.

to be the case because all new colonies have apparently adopted the same basic pattern of production as the old established colonies, and in these latter colonies there does not appear to have been any significant change in either the emphasis or the scale of operations.

Resolution of Contentious Issues

Throughout their history the Hutterites have always had to contend with a variety of problems that they felt were imposed on them by their surrounding society. In one way or another they managed to survive these problems, but for the Hutterites in Manitoba there were still a number of contentious issues circa 1970.

At that time they were still not entirely sure if the Manitoba Union of Municipalities had given up its efforts to impose restrictions on Hutterite land purchases. In Alberta the restrictions on land purchases and location of colonies remained in force, and until the question of restrictions became totally resolved in Manitoba it remained a worrisome issue. Another problem in Manitoba was that a number of School

Divisions had refused to provide grants for Hutterite schools, and in this way they hoped to force the Hutterites to send their children to public schools. This was an issue that was not negotiable for the Hutterites—they continued to operate their colony schools and paid the full costs for them, but they also had to pay the local school and municipal taxes as well. This proved to be a heavy financial burden for some of the colonies, and they persisted in their appeals to rectify what they considered to be a system of double taxation. A further area of concern for the Hutterites was their inability to establish the principle that in certain instances each Hutterite family on a colony should be considered as a separate production unit rather than having the whole colony considered as a single production unit. This was important in all cases where quotas, grants, or subsidies were based on production units by government departments or marketing boards. As was mentioned in the conclusion, at the time that this study was being completed the Hutterites had forwarded a brief to Premier Schreyer on this issue.

Remarkable as it may seem, by the end of 1975 each of these contentious issues had been resolved. The Manitoba government had made it known that it would not sanction any restrictions against any residents of the province with regard to land purchases. As such the Hutterites now feel free to buy land wherever they desire. With regard to the school question, every School Division now provides appropriate grants to every Hutterite colony, and so this issue has been resolved as well. The problem of classifying a Hutterite colony as a single production unit or alternatively considering it as a composite of separate family production units has also been resolved. It has been recognized that although a colony operates as a single production unit, it nevertheless supports a certain number of families, and that in many instances each of them should be considered as separate production units. In addition, Hutterites now have appropriate representation on agricultural marketing boards.

This is surely a sign of good times because it seems that reason has prevailed and the Hutterites in Manitoba have finally arrived at a stage where apparently they have no major conflicts with their surrounding society.

The Hutterite Strategy of Survival

The Hutterites are a remarkable people. Living as they do is almost being in two different worlds at the same time. One world is that of a twentieth century modern farm with the latest farm machinery and equipment. The other world is a lifestyle as it was practised about 450 years ago, including the clothing styles of that period. How is it possible for a group of people to live partly in the twentieth century and partly in the sixteenth century? How is it possible for a people to retain, almost totally intact, certain centuries-old beliefs, values, and traditions, but at the same time, and apparently with ease and without contradictions, to adopt various features of contemporary styles of life? The ability of the Hutterites to maintain their unique way of life is indeed remarkable.

The survival of the Hutterites and their unique way of life is the result of a combination of strategies. These have been operative through the years and they include uncompromising religious beliefs, a system of comprehensive socialization, the acceptance of human frailty, the development of a strong economic base, and an unrestricted demographic increase.

Perhaps the key to their survival has been their uncompromising religious doctrine. Religion is their raison d'être. History has shown that, if need be, Hutterites are prepared to die rather than change their religion or their social institutions. As John Hostetler, a noted authority on Hutterite society, put it:

> It is not simply "beliefs" which makes a Hutterite. To be a Hutterite is to participate in a religious experience, a group-related experience in which the spiritual nature rules over the carnal. The efficiency, motivation, and material prosperity of the colonies would collapse without the mystical qualities in the experience of community.[10]

Their basic ideology is learned from infancy and is supported by constant teaching and appropriate ritual.

Their religion, based on early Christian teachings, included a form of communal living as well as communal ownership of all property, opposition to military service and war, adult baptism, and fundamentalist practices. This alienated the Catholic and Protestant churches, and throughout history Hutterites have been persecuted by both. Being pacifists, their refusal to participate in military service resulted in persecution by governments. From their very beginnings, on no account would they compromise any of their basic beliefs, and in the early years when faced with "extermination by fire and sword" they fled from one European region to another (Map 22). Their migrations eventually led them to the United States and then Canada. Even now, firmly established as they are, there is little doubt that if their way of life should once again become seriously threatened, they would not hesitate to sell their farmlands and migrate to an area which would seem to offer a better chance of survival.

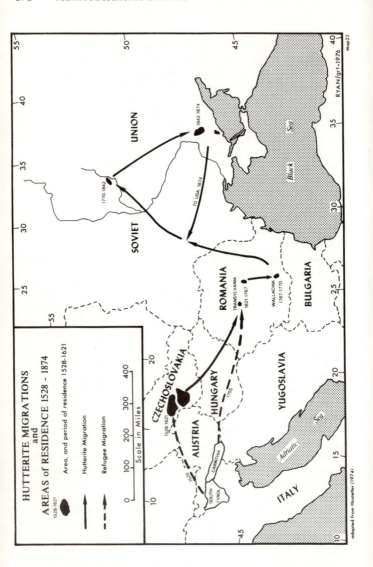

RYAN/grt-1976

Map 22

UNION

SOVIET

1842-1874

1770-1842

TO USA, 1874

Black Sea

ROMANIA

BULGARIA

TRANSYLVANIA
1621-1767

WALLACHIA
1767-1770

CZECHOSLOVAKIA
1528-1621

HUNGARY
1795

AUSTRIA

YUGOSLAVIA

CARINTHIA

SOUTH TYROL
1530

ITALY

Adriatic Sea

HUTTERITE MIGRATIONS
and
AREAS of RESIDENCE 1528 - 1874

1528-1621   Area, and period of residence 1528-1621

Hutterite Migration

Refugee Migration

Scale in Miles

0   100   200   300   400

adapted from Hostetler (1974)

A system of comprehensive socialization is another key factor in Hutterite survival. From early childhood and throughout adult life there is a consistent and continuous socialization process. Interaction with the outside world is minimized and dependency upon colony members is maximized. The Hutterite self-image demands identification with the colony. Each person is subservient to the colony at every stage of his life. The goals of each stage are attainable by virtually all Hutterites, and each person is rewarded by important work and is made aware of his contribution to the colony.

Each Hutterite is socialized and motivated to believe that the collective will is more important than the separate individuals who compose it. From infancy, he learns to fit into the group pattern and is treated as a member of the group rather than as an individual. He first identifies with his family, then with his peer group in school, and finally with his work group. At every stage there is a conscious effort to make group decisions, and to make all members aware of their responsibility to one another. The result is a firm sense of identity and a stable society.

Although Hutterite life demands total commitment, the system tends to be tolerant of deviance in its adolescent or immature members. Hutterites accept human frailty, and take the position that an individual is not perfect and cannot achieve perfection without aid from others. When a Hutterite youngster disobeys colony rules, he is punished but in such a way that he does not lose self-respect. Hutterites feel that immaturity will gradually be replaced by responsibility, and the whole system encourages rehabilitation with a minimum of condemnation. This is extended even to those who leave the colony for the outside world and afterwards return. This in particular seems to be a strong feature because it allows these "transgressors" to repent and in a sense to provide graphic evidence that colony life must be superior to the outside society.

Ultimately the whole Hutterite way of life depends upon its economic structure. For without this, they could not maintain their independent manner of living and Hutterite society would collapse. They have always been acutely aware of this, and some form of work is expected from everyone, including children (mainly to ingrain the virtue of work).

The Hutterites have always accepted as a basic premise that their way of life could best be preserved in a relatively isolated rural setting. Hence agriculture is a vital part of their lifestyle. As their population increases, they are forced to establish new colonies which must be financed from their agricultural operations. A modern colony with its land and facilities is a major expenditure by any standard, hence there is great pressure to be as economically efficient as possible.

Hutterites have always recognized that to be economically efficient they had to adopt the best technology available at any particular time. For this reason, they have never been hesitant to adopt modern farming techniques. This has been instrumental in their economic survival. In other words, Hutterites see no inconsistency in using twentieth century tools to achieve the basic objective of preserving their sixteenth century religious and social institutions.

Given the fact there is a basic necessity to adopt modern technology, not all innovation is accepted without qualification. In fact, certain common twentieth century features have not been accepted by the Hutterites, for instance, radios, television sets, automobiles. Wherever it is felt that certain innovations would threaten the social solidarity of colony life, they have been prohibited. Also prohibited are innovations that could be considered as mere luxuries without a utilitarian purpose. Consequently, innovations have not altered the basic social patterns of colony life.

The final feature that has been vital to Hutterite survival is the stability of the family institution along with unrestricted population growth. The family consists of a lifelong monogamous pair with their children, and this serves as a basic cohesive force within the colony. On the basis of their religious principles, no form of birth control has ever been practiced and large families have always been the norm.

Considering their history, unrestricted population growth has indeed been a factor in Hutterite survival. Starting with an initial population of approximately 200 in 1528, they expanded to over 20,000 by circa 1600.[11] However, disaster overtook them—through wars, religious persecution, plagues, and forced dispersion their numbers were reduced to about 2,500 by 1622 and to only 67 by 1767 (Diagram E-1). From the verge of extinction their numbers increased to 1,265 at the time they emigrated to the U.S.A. in 1874. Of these only 443 settled in colonies, and from this number they have grown to the present population of 21,521 in 1974.[12] Clearly, unrestricted population growth is one of their strengths and a significant factor in the survival of their society.

Although large population increase has helped to preserve Hutterite society, it creates an on-going problem for them. To maintain the Hutterian way of life it is necessary for them to keep colony populations to a manageable size. This has meant that on the average each colony has had to subdivide every 14 years. This in turn means that during this period enough capital has to be accumulated to purchase the land and establish the facilities for a new colony. Since the land and facilities of an average new colony are now worth over $1,500,000,[13] this is an awesome amount of capital to raise for an average colony of 15 families

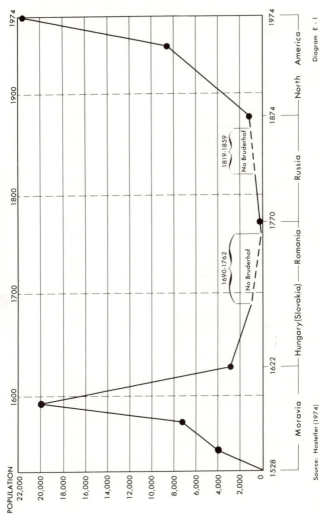

HUTTERITE POPULATION GROWTH, 1528-1974

Source: Hostetler (1974)

Diagram E - 1

in a matter of 14 years or so. Hence the colonies have no choice but to be efficient and to keep in the forefront of all agricultural developments. In the meantime, Manitoba should benefit from the agricultural produce, and as time goes along, the Hutterites will be producing a greater and greater proportion of total Manitoba agricultural output.

Notes and References

1. Although Hutterite tradition and culture appear to remain basically changeless throughout the years, much of modern technology is constantly being accepted and adopted. To vividly illustrate this point the author would like to relate an incident that occurred in February of 1976 when he visited Reverend Jacob Kleinsasser at Crystal Spring Colony. When asked about the availability of recent economic and population data, Reverend Kleinsasser, who at all times exudes an air of Hutterite tradition and culture, calmly and in a very matter-of-fact manner informed the author that all 1975 data would be available as soon as he received the latest computer printout from his accountant. He went on to add that he had phoned the accountant a number of days before and had requested that several additional variables should be added to the computer programme in order to obtain a more detailed breakdown of the past year's data. The author couldn't help but be amazed at the smooth integration and co-existence of basic traditional Hutterite values and the very latest developments in modern technology.
2. This information was provided by Meyers, Norris, Penny and Company, the accounting firm employed by the Hutterites. The 8 colonies involved are the following (shown on Map 21): Brightstone, Clearwater, Fairholme, Greenwald, Huron, Maxwell, Rock Lake, and Springhill.
3. Information on this was provided by Reverend Jacob Kleinsasser of Crystal Spring Colony. The four colonies are Elm River, Hillside, Milltown, and Parkview.
4. This was calculated from the data in Appendix H.
5. This information was provided by Meyers, Norris, Penny and Company. The population ratios may be calculated by reference to Table E-1 and Appendix I.
6. The author discussed this new development with Reverend Jacob Kleinsasser of Crystal Spring Colony, and this is the essence of his analysis.

7. According to the *Canada Land Inventory Soil Capability for Agriculture Map* (Manitoba South) the Marble Ridge and Broad Valley Colonies are located on the best soils in the northern Interlake, i.e., Class 3-2. Furthermore, the author grew up on a farm within a few miles of the present Marble Ridge Colony and knows from experience that this colony's area was considered to be good agricultural land.

8. Information on various colony changes and improvements was obtained from discussions with Reverend Jacob Kleinsasser and Mr. Dave Norris (accountant employed by the Hutterites), as well as from personal observation by the author.

9. *Yearbook of Manitoba Agriculture 1974*, p. 50.

10. John A. Hostetler, *Hutterite Society* (Baltimore: The Johns Hopkins University Press, 1974), p. 286.

11. *Ibid.*, p. 29.

12. *Ibid.*, p. 295.

13. This is an estimate made by the author from data provided by Mr. Dave Norris (accountant employed by the Hutterites) and Reverend Jacob Kleinsasser.

APPENDIX A

MANITOBA HUTTERITE COLONIES

DATES OF ESTABLISHMENT AND FOUNDING COLONIES

	Colony Founded	Parent Colony	Year Founded
1.	Bon Homme	original colony	1918
2.	Huron	original colony	1918
3.	James Valley	original colony	1918
4.	Maxwell	original colony	1918
5.	Milltown	original colony	1918
6.	Rosedale	original colony	1918
7.	Iberville	Rosedale	1919
8.	Barickman	Maxwell	1920
9.	Blumengart	Milltown	1922
10.	Elm River	Rosedale	1934
11.	Riverside	Iberville	1934
12.	Waldheim	Bon Homme	1935
13.	Poplar Point	Huron	1938
14.	Sturgeon Creek	Blumengart	1938
15.	Sunnyside	Milltown	1942
16.	New Rosedale	Rosedale	1944
17.	Riverdale	James Valley	1945
18.	Lakeside	Maxwell	1947
19.	Rock Lake	Iberville	1947
20.	Springfield	Poplar Point	1950
21.	Oak Bluff	Elm River	1953
22.	Crystal Spring	Sturgeon Creek	1954

	Colony Founded	Parent Colony	Year Founded
23.	Bloomfield	Riverside	1955
24.	Greenwald	Barickman	1955
25.	Spring Valley	James Valley	1956
26.	Hillside	Rosedale	1957
27.	Rose Valley	Waldheim	1957
28.	Brightstone	Maxwell	1959
29.	Deerboine	Riverdale	1959
30.	Fairholme	New Rosedale	1959
31.	Grand	Bon Homme	1959
32.	Clearwater	Poplar Point	1960
33.	Interlake	Rock Lake	1961
34.	Homewood	Lakeside	1962
35.	Pembina	Blumengart	1962
36.	Whiteshell	Iberville	1962
37.	Parkview	Huron	1964
38.	Rainbow	Elm River	1964
39.	Springhill	Sunnyside	1964
40.	Glenway	Milltown	1966
41.	Miami	James Valley	1966
42.	Ridgeland	Springfield	1967
43.	Wellwood	Spring Valley	1967
44.	Hidden Valley	Sturgeon Creek	1969
45.	Oak Ridge	Barickman	1969
46.	Riverbend	Oak Bluff	1969
47.	Suncrest	Crystal Spring	1969
48.	Woodland	Rosedale	1970

Source: Data compiled from field work by J. Ryan.

APPENDIX B

MANITOBA HUTTERITE COLONIES

NUMBER OF FAMILIES AND POPULATION PER COLONY

JULY 1, 1968

	Name of Colony	No. of Families	Population
1.	Barickman	18	168
2.	Bloomfield	18	118
3.	Blumengart	13	71
4.	Bon Homme	19	137
5.	Brightstone	12	90
6.	Clearwater	19	119
7.	Crystal Spring	20	158
8.	Deerboine	13	80
9.	Elm River	12	93
10.	Fairholme	15	110
11.	Glenway	12	54
12.	Grand	19	130
13.	Greenwald	11	78
14.	Hillside	14	130
15.	Homewood	19	89
16.	Huron	15	89
17.	Iberville	16	78
18.	Interlake	4	46
19.	James Valley	15	73
20.	Lakeside	12	92
21.	Maxwell	17	126
22.	Miami	12	82

	Name of Colony	No. of Families	Population
23.	Milltown	11	99
24.	New Rosedale	14	103
25.	Oak Bluff	22	119
26.	Parkview	14	101
27.	Pembina	15	78
28.	Poplar Point	12	98
29.	Rainbow	13	89
30.	Ridgeland	11	90
31.	Riverdale	12	107
32.	Riverside	20	116
33.	Rock Lake	15	112
34.	Rosedale	19	155
35.	Rose Valley	18	116
36.	Springfield	10	84
37.	Springhill	12	86
38.	Spring Valley	8	53
39.	Sturgeon Creek	24	151
40.	Sunnyside	14	75
41.	Waldheim	24	148
42.	Wellwood	9	85
43.	Whiteshell	13	86
	Total	635	4,362

Source:
Hutterian Brethren Genealogy Record, compiled by
Reverend Jacob Kleinsasser of Crystal Spring Colony.

APPENDIX C

MANITOBA HUTTERITE COLONIES

POPULATION PER COLONY, DECEMBER 31, 1970

	Name of Colony	Population		Name of Colony	Population
1.	Barickman	97	25.	New Rosedale	113
2.	Bloomfield	134	26.	Oak Bluff	74
3.	Blumengart	76	27.	Oak Ridge	87
4.	Bon Homme	161	28.	Parkview	117
5.	Brightstone	99	29.	Pembina	83
6.	Clearwater	127	30.	Poplar Point	104
7.	Crystal Spring	87	31.	Rainbow	95
8.	Deerboine	81	32.	Ridgeland	103
9.	Elm River	93	33.	Riverbend	61
10.	Fairholme	101	34.	Riverdale	113
11.	Glenway	55	35.	Riverside	128
12.	Grand	145	36.	Rock Lake	111
13.	Greenwald	94	37.	Rosedale	82
14.	Hidden Valley	70	38.	Rose Valley	124
15.	Hillside	121	39.	Springfield	97
16.	Homewood	107	40.	Springhill	98
17.	Huron	99	41.	Spring Valley	71
18.	Iberville	103	42.	Sturgeon Creek	76
19.	Interlake	48	43.	Suncrest	81
20.	James Valley	92	44.	Sunnyside	73
21.	Lakeside	84	45.	Waldheim	161
22.	Maxwell	127	46.	Wellwood	71
23.	Miami	83	47.	Whiteshell	88
24.	Milltown	81	48.	Woodland	90
				TOTAL	4,666

Source: Population data compiled from Hutterite
Income Tax records by Dave Norris, the
accountant employed by the Hutterite colonies.

APPENDIX D

INVENTORY OF FARM MACHINERY, 1968[1]

HUTTERITE COLONY "A"[2]

Colony "A" had the largest investment in farm machinery of all
colonies in 1968 -- $183,300. The colony owned 4,250 acres and
had a machinery investment of $43.13 per acre. However, the
colony had begun to purchase additional land at a different
site for a future subdivision and some machinery was purchased
for this purpose. Subdivision was not anticipated for a number
of years, but when it occurs some machinery will be allocated
to the new colony.

Description of machine, type, model, year, etc.	Year of purchase	New or Used	Place of Purchase	Amount Paid $	Estimated[3] value in 1968 - $
Caterpillar tractor-IHC, TD-14, 1952	1954	U	S. Dakota	6,500	4,500
Caterpillar tractor-IHC, D-6, 1947	1962	U	Winnipeg	2,700	8,000+
Caterpillar tractor-IHC, D-4, 1958	1961	U	*Elie	4,000	4,000+
Caterpillar Tractor-IHC, D-4, 1958	1963	U	S. Dakota	3,500	4,000+
Tractor - Versatile #145 4-wheel dr., 1968	1968	N	*Elie	11,500	11,500
Tractor - John Deere 50-20, 1967	1967	N	*St.Eustace	10,400	9,500
Tractor - John Deere 40-10, 1965	1967	U	*St.Eustace	3,200	3,200+
Tractor - John Deere 50-20, 1968	1968	N	*St.Eustace	10,400	10,400
Tractor - John Deere 30-20, 1967	1968	U	*Elie	3,200	3,200
Tractor - Case #930, 1964	1964	N	*Elie	8,000	5,500
Tractor - IHC WD6, 1954	1968	U	*Elm Creek	400	1,000+
Tractor - IHC,WD6,1954	1968	U	Manitou	300	300

Appendix D continued next page . . .

APPENDIX D - Continued

Description of machine, type, model, year, etc.	Year of pur- chase	New or Used	Place of Purchase	Amount paid $	Estimated[3] value in 1968 - $
Tractor - IHC, Farmall Model G, 1950	1953	U	Winkler	600	350
Tractor - IHC, Farmall Model H, 1952	1952	N	Winnipeg	1,200	500
Tractor - IHC, Farmall Model C, 1954	1954	N	Warren	1,300	300
Tractor - IHC, Farmall Model M, 1947	1957	U	*Portage la Prairie	400	400+
Combine - John Deere #95, 1961	1961	N	*St.Eustace	9,000	7,000
Combine -J.D.#95, 1961	1961	N	*St.Eustace	9,000	7,000
Combine - J.D.#95, 1961	1961	N	*St.Eustace	9,000	7,000
Combine - J.D.#95, 1961	1961	N	*St.Eustace	9,000	7,000
Combine - J.D.#95, 1967	1967	N	*St.Eustace	10,000	9,500
Combine - J.D.#95, 1967	1967	N	*St.Eustace	10,000	9,500
Combine - J.D.#95, 1967	1968	U	*St.Claude	8,500	8,500
Combine - J.D.#95, 1964	1967	U	S. Dakota	5,000	6,500+
Swather - Versatile self-prop. 18', 1968	1968	N	*Elie	3,100	3,100
Swather - Versatile pull-type 18', 1968	1968	N	*Elie	1,200	1,200
Swather - IHC, #200 pull-type 16', 1965	1965	N	*Elm Creek	1,200	800
Swather - IHC, #163 self-prop. 16', 1962	1962	N	*Oakville	2,700	800
Swather - Massey-Ferg. self-prop. 16', 1967	1967	N	**Glenella	2,800	2,500

Appendix D continued next page . . .

APPENDIX D - Continued

Description of Machine, type, model, year, etc.	Year of pur-chase	New or Used	Place of purchase	Amount paid $	Estimated[3] value in 1968 - $
Swather - Massey-Ferg. self-prop. 16', 1968	1968	N	**Glenella	2,800	2,800
Disk-drill - J.D. tandem 24', 1965	1965	N	*St.Eustace	3,700	3,000
Disk-drill - J.D. tandem 24', 1966	1966	N	*St.Eustace	3,700	3,000
Disk-drill - J.D. tandem 24', 1967	1967	N	*St.Eustace	4,000	3,500
Disk-drill - J.D. tandem 24', 1967	1967	N	*St.Eustace	4,000	3,500
Discer - IHC, 18',1965	1965	N	*Oakville	1,200	800
Discer - IHC,18', 1954	1954	N	*Oakville	900	600
Discer - IHC,18', 1958	1963	U	*Elm Creek	700	500
Drill - IHC, 12', 1962	1962	N	*Oakville	1,200	900
Drill - IHC, 12', 1962	1962	N	*Oakville	1,200	900
Drill - IHC, 12', 1962	1962	N	*Oakville	1,200	900
Cultivator - IHC, 13' chisel-plow, 1964	1964	N	*Elm Creek	800	500
Cultivator - IHC 19' chisel-plow, 1964	1964	N	*Elm Creek	1,300	800
Cultivator - IHC vibra-shank 26', 1965	1965	U	*Oakville	1,550	1,200
Cultivator - J.D. chisel-plow 24', 1968	1968	N	**Neepawa	2,300	2,300
Cultivator - IHC chisel-plow 13', 1964	1964	N	*Elm Creek	800	600
Cultivator - IHC chisel-plow 13', 1964	1964	N	*Elm Creek	800	600
Plow -IHC 6 bottom,1967	1967	N	*Oakville	1,500	1,200

Appendix D continued next page • • •

APPENDIX D - Continued

Description of machine, type, model, year, etc.	Year of purchase	New or Used	Place of Purchase	Amount paid $	Estimated value in 1968 - $ [3]
Plow - J.D. 5 bottom, 1954	1954	N	Winnipeg	900	400
Harrow - 20 sections	1955		hitch homemade; sections bought at Elie *		1,000
Harrow - 13 sections	1962		hitch homemade; sections bought at Elie *		400
Harrow - 18 sections	1967		hitch homemade; sections bought at Elie *		1,500
Sprayer - 30' Jeep-mount (Jeep not included)	1961	N	*Elie	700	400
Hay Mower - IHC 7',1961	1961	N	*Oakville	350	200
Rake- IHC side-delivery	1957	N	*Oakville	500	250
Hay Baler - IHC #47,1965	1965	N	*Oakville	1,200	900
Bale elevator J.D. 1962	1962	N	Winnipeg	350	200
Silage cutter - Allis-Chalmers, 1962	1964	U	*Oakville	750	500
Feed Wagon for geese	1965	N	Winnipeg	400	200
Manure spreader (liquid type) New Holland, 1965	1968	U	Manitou	350	400+
Manure spreader (liquid type) New Holland, 1965	1968	U	Manitou	350	400+
Manure spreader (solid type) Kilbury, 1964	1964	N	*Elie	850	400
Manure spreader (solid type) Kilbury, 1964	1964	N	*Elie	850	400
Grain Dryer - Hume,1968	1968	N	Manitou	8,500	8,500
Grain auger- 7" x 50' Scoop-a-Second, 1966	1966	N	Winnipeg	750	600

Appendix D continued next page . . .

APPENDIX D - Continued

Description of machine, type, model, year, etc.	Year of pur-chase	New or Used	Place of purchase	Amount paid $	Estimated[3] value in 1968 - $
Grain Auger- 7" x 50' Scoop-a-Second, 1967	1967	N	Winnipeg	750	650
Grain auger- 6" x 51' double-barrel	1961	N	*Portage la Prairie	750	400
Grain auger - 7" x 35'	1960	N	Winnipeg	600	400
Grain auger - 6" x 35'	1968	N	Winnipeg	580	550

Total value of machinery	$183,300
Value of machinery purchased locally	146,550
Machinery purchased locally as a % of total value	80.0%

---

[1]Data compiled from field work by J. Ryan.

[2]Name of colony not given to avoid revealing operation details.

[3]Value of machinery based on estimate by colony management.

*Purchased locally (within 25 miles) or from the closest dealer of a particular type of machinery.

**Purchased locally near the site of the proposed new colony.

+Machinery was repaired or rebuilt after secondhand purchase.

APPENDIX E

INVENTORY OF FARM MACHINERY, 1968[1]

HUTTERITE COLONY "B"[2]

Colony "B" was representative of the average Hutterite investment
in farm machinery in 1968. The colony's machinery totalled
$78,500, as compared to the average investment of $77,623.
Colony "B" had 3,520 acres and had a machinery investment of
$22.30 per acre.

Description of machine, type, model, year, etc.	Year of purchase	New or Used	Place of purchase	Amount paid $	Estimated [3] value in 1968 - $
Tractor- IHC,#806,1965	1965	N	*Morden	8,200	6,000
Tractor- IHC,#660,1961	1964	U	*Morden	9,200	5,000
Tractor-J.D. #420,1958	1960	U	S. Dakota	1,635	1,000
Tractor-J.D.#830, 1959	1959	N	**Winkler	6,000	3,000
Tractor- IHC,TD14,1956	1962	U	Elm Creek	4,200	3,000
Tractor- IHC,"M",1957	1962	U	*Morden	1,000	400
Tractor- IHC,#560, 1965	1968	U	Winkler	2,700	2,700
Combine- IHC,#403,1967	1967	N	*Morden	13,500	13,000
Combine- IHC,#403,1967	1967	N	*Morden	13,500	13,000
Combine- IHC,#151,1961	1961	N	*Morden	4,200	3,000
Combine - IHC,#151,1961	1966	U	N. Dakota	2,700	2,000
Swather- IHC, #175 self-prop. 16', 1967	1967	N	*Morden	1,800	1,400
Swather - Versatile pull-type, 18', 1967	1968	U	*Manitou	750	750
Swather- IHC, pull-type 16', 1967	1968	U	N. Dakota	800	800
Swather- IHC, p.t. 16'	1954	N	**Morden	850	150
Swather - IHC, p.t.16'	1954	N	**Morden	850	150

Appendix E continued next page . . .

APPENDIX E - Continued

Description of machine, type, model, year, etc.	Year of purchase	New or Used	Place of purchase	Amount paid $	Estimated[3] value in 1968 - $
Swather- IHC,p.t. 16'	1954	N	**Morden	850	150
Swather- IHC,p.t. 16'	1954	N	**Altona	850	150
Swather- IHC,p.t. 16'	1954	N	**Altona	850	150
Disk-drill - IHC 18'	1966	N	*Morden	1,800	1,600
Disk-drill - IHC 18'	1966	N	*Morden	1,800	1,600
Disk-drill - IHC 18'	1966	N	*Morden	1,800	1,600
Cultivator - IHC deep-tillage 20',1967	1967	N	*Morden	1,400	1,300
Cultivator - J.D. deep-tillage 14',1963	1963	N	*Manitou	960	600
Plow- IHC,5-bottom,1967	1967	N	*Morden	1,400	1,400
Sprayer- 52', 1968	1968	N	N. Dakota	3,100	3,100
Harrows- Ajax 15 sec.	1968	N	*Morden	900	900
Harrows - Fieldmaster 15 sections	1967	N	*Manitou	800	750
Hay Mower- IHC,7',1968	1968	N	*Morden	600	600
Rake- IHC, s.d., 1961	1968	U	N. Dakota	200	200
Hay Baler- IHC, 1968	1968	N	Winnipeg	1,000	1,000
Bale elevator	1968		Homemade		500
Stonepicker, 1961	1961	N	S. Dakota	800	700
Forage harvester- 1959	1968	U	N. Dakota	100	100
Bulk Feeder, 1961	1961	N	S. Dakota	790	300
Manure spreader- (liquid type) 1968	1968	N	*Morden	1,800	1,800
Manure spreader- (liquid type), 1968	1968	N	*Newton	2,300	2,300

Appendix E continued next page . . .

APPENDIX E - Continued

Description of machine, type, model, year, etc.	Year of pur-chase	New or Used	Place of purchase	Amount paid $	Estimated[3] value in 1968 - $
Manure spreader-"Farmhand", 1964	1964	N	*Brandon	1,400	1,000
Potato planter, 1958	1962	U	S. Dakota	150	100
Potato digger, 1958	1962	U	S. Dakota	150	100
Grain auger- 7"x35'	1968	N	*Morden	150	150
Grain auger- 6"x35'	1968	N	*Morden	100	100
Grain auger- 7"x50'	1968	N	*Manitou	350	350
Grain elevator, 1954	1968	U	N. Dakota	100	100
Road grader - 1949	1962	U	N. Dakota	400	150
3 Trailers	1965		Homemade		300

Total value of machinery	$78,500
Value of machinery purchased locally	$63,150
Machinery purchased locally as a % of total value	80.4%

[1]Data compiled from field work by J. Ryan.

[2]Name of colony not given to avoid revealing operation details.

[3]Value of machinery based on estimate by colony management.

*Purchased locally (within 25 miles) or from the closest dealer of a particular type of machinery.

**Purchased locally by parent colony prior to the founding of Colony "B".

APPENDIX F

INVENTORY OF FARM MACHINERY, 1968[1]

HUTTERITE COLONY "C"[2]

Colony "C" had the smallest investment in farm machinery of all
colonies in 1968 - $30,150. The colony owned 3,360 acres and
had a machinery investment of $8.96 per acre.

Description of machine, type, model, year, etc.	Year of pur-chase	New or Used	Place of purchase	Amount paid $	Estimated[3] value in 1968 - $
Tractor- IHC,WD-9,1953	1957	U	Elie	2,000	600
Tractor- IHC, WD-9,1956	1963	U	Killarney	1,000	600
Tractor- IHC, WD-9,1956	1967	U	*Neepawa	750	600
Tractor- Oliver 88,1957	1957	N	Portage la Prairie	5,600	1,200
Tractor- IHC "M", 1957	1962	U	Elie	750	400
Tractor- IHC "C", 1957	1961	U	Brandon	250	200
Tractor- IHC "A", 1960	1964	U	*Neepawa	640	400
Tractor- Ford "N", 1956	1958	U	Rapid City	450	250
Combine- John Deere #55, 1960	1960	N	*Gladstone	8,000	6,000
Combine- J.D. #55,1960	1960	N	*Gladstone	8,000	6,000
Swather- Versatile self-prop. 16', 1966	1966	N	*Neepawa	1,800	1,500
Swather- Versatile pull-type 18', 1966	1966	N	*Neepawa	1,300	1,000
Disk-drill - John Deere 16', 1964	1965	U	St.Eustace	1,300	1,000
Disker - Massey-Ferg. 16', 1965	1967	U	*A nearby Hutt. col.	1,600	1,200
Cultivator- Glencoe 14', 1967	1967	N	Plumas	1,200	900
Disk-drill - John Deere 16', 1963	1964	U	N. Dakota	800	600

Appendix F continued next page . . . .

APPENDIX F - Continued

Description of machine, type, model, year, etc.	Year of purchase	New or Used	Place of purchase	Amount paid $	Estimated[3] value in 1968 - $
Cultivator- Massey-Ferg. deep-tiller 14', 1956	1963	U	*Gladstone	450	350
Cultivator- Cockshutt 14', 1954	1958	U	*Langruth	400	250
Sprayer- 56', 1968	1968	N	*Gladstone	650	650
Hay mower - John Deere 7', 1960	1964	U	*Gladstone	350	300
Rake- Allis-Chalmers	1964	N	*Neepawa	500	300
Hay baler- J.D., 1965	1965	N	*Neepawa	1,200	1,000
Plow- Case, 6-bottom	1965	N	*Neepawa	1,500	1,200
Harrow - 12 sections	1960	hitch homemade; sections bought in Neepawa*			500
Manure spreader IHC,1967	1967	N	*Gladstone	960	800
Manure spreader IHC,1960	1964	U	*A nearby Hutt. col.	200	150
Liquid manure tank,1966	1966	N	*Newton	1,700	1,200
Grain auger, 7"x50'	1967	N	Winnipeg	750	700
Grain auger, 6"x35'	1964	N	*Gladstone	600	300
Total value of machinery					$30,150
Value of machinery purchased locally					$23,700
Machinery purchased locally as a % of total value					78.6%

[1] Data compiled from field work by J. Ryan.

[2] Name of colony not given to avoid revealing operation details.

[3] Value of machinery based on estimate by colony management.

*Purchased locally (within 25 miles) or from the closest dealer of a particular type of machinery.

APPENDIX G

MANITOBA HUTTERITE COLONIES

GROSS SALES INCOME, EXPENSES, AND NET SALES INCOME

TOTAL AND PER COLONY, 1968[1]

Enterprise	Total gross sales income	% of total	Average gross sales income per colony [2]
1. Hogs	$4,871,001.65	42.0%	$113,279.11
2. Chickens	3,241,275.67	27.9%	75,378.50
3. Grain	966,765.06	8.3%	22,482.91
4. Turkeys	908,694.94	7.8%	21,132.44
5. Cattle	701,776.29	6.1%	16,320.38
6. Geese & ducks	570,572.74	4.9%	13,269.13
7. Custom work	126,957.82	1.1%	2,952.51
8. Vegetables & potatoes	45,248.65	.4%	1,052.29
9. Honey	40,659.61	.4%	945.57
10. Miscellaneous	125,329.97	1.1%	2,914.65
Total/ Average	11,598,282.40	100%	269,727.40

	Total	Per Colony
Gross Sales Income	$ 11,598,282.40	$ 269,727.40
Expenses & depreciation	$ 10,224,120.37	$ 237,770.20
Net Sales Income	$ 1,374,162.03	$ 31,957.25

[1] Data compiled by J. Ryan from the financial reports on each colony for 1968, as prepared by Meyers, Dickens, Norris, Penny & Company, the accounting firm employed by the Hutterite colonies.

[2] Determined on the basis of the total 43 colonies in 1968.

APPENDIX H

MANITOBA HUTTERITE COLONIES

COLONY DIVISION INTERVALS FROM 1918-1975

	Name of founding colony[1]	Name of new colony formed	Year of division	Previous year of division	Colony division interval in years
1.	Rosedale (1)	Iberville	1919	1918	1
2.	Maxwell (1)	Barickman	1920	1918	2
3.	Milltown (1)	Blumengart	1922	1918	4
4.	Huron (1)	(U.S.A.)	1929	1918	11
5.	Maxwell (2)	(U.S.A.)	1932	1920	12
6.	Iberville (1)	Riverside	1934	1919	15
7.	Rosedale (2)	Elm River	1934	1919	15
8.	Bon Homme (1)	Waldheim	1935	1918	17
9.	Blumengart (1)	Sturgeon Creek	1938	1922	16
10.	Huron (2)	Poplar Point	1938	1929	9
11.	Barickman (1)	(U.S.A.)	1942	1920	22
12.	Milltown (2)	Sunnyside	1942	1922	20
13.	Rosedale (3)	New Rosedale	1944	1934	10
14.	James Valley (1)	Riverdale	1945	1918	27
15.	Iberville (2)	Rock Lake	1947	1934	13
16.	Maxwell (3)	Lakeside	1947	1932	15
17.	Bon Homme (2)	(U.S.A.)	1949	1935	14
18.	Huron (3)	(U.S.A.)	1949	1938	11
19.	Milltown (3)	(U.S.A.)	1950	1942	8
20.	Poplar Point (1)	Springfield	1950	1938	12
21.	Blumengart (2)	(U.S.A.)	1952	1938	14
22.	Elm River (1)	Oak Bluff	1953	1934	19

Name of founding colony[1]	Name of new colony formed	Year of division	Previous year of division	Colony division interval in years
23. Sturgeon Creek (1)	Crystal Spring	1954	1938	16
24. Barickman (2)	Greenwald	1955	1942	13
25. Riverside (1)	Bloomfield	1955	1934	21
26. James Valley (2)	Spring Valley	1956	1945	11
27. Rosedale (4)	Hillside	1957	1944	13
28. Waldheim (2)	Rose Valley	1957	1935	22
29. Bon Homme (3)	Grand	1959	1949	10
30. Maxwell (4)	Brightstone	1959	1947	12
31. New Rosedale (1)	Fairholme	1959	1944	15
32. Riverdale (1)	Deerboine	1959	1945	14
33. Poplar Point (2)	Clearwater	1960	1950	10
34. Rock Lake (1)	Interlake	1961	1947	14
35. Blumengart (3)	Pembina	1962	1952	10
36. Iberville (3)	Whiteshell	1962	1947	15
37. Lakeside (1)	Homewood	1962	1947	15
38. Elm River (2)	Rainbow	1964	1953	11
39. Huron (4)	Parkview	1964	1949	15
40. Sunnyside (1)	Springhill	1964	1942	22
41. James Valley (3)	Miami	1966	1956	10
42. Milltown (4)	Glenway	1966	1950	16
43. Springfield (1)	Ridgeland	1967	1950	17
44. Spring Valley (1)	Wellwood	1967	1956	11
45. Barickman (3)	Oak Ridge	1969	1955	14
46. Crystal Spring (1)	Suncrest	1969	1954	15
47. Oak Bluff (1)	Riverbend	1969	1953	16

	Name of founding colony[1]	Name of new colony formed	Year of division	Previous year of division	Colony division interval in years
48.	Sturgeon Creek (2)	Hidden Valley	1969	1954	15
49.	Rosedale (5)	Woodland	1970	1957	13
50.	Riverside (2)	Mayfair	1971	1955	16
51.	Bloomfield (1)	Marble Ridge	1972	1955	17
52.	Bon Homme (4)	Newdale	1972	1959	13
53.	Grand (1)	Grass River	1972	1959	13
54.	New Rosedale (2)	Airport	1972	1959	13
55.	Deerboine (1)	Pine Creek	1973	1959	14
56.	Rainbow (1)	Baker	1973	1964	9
57.	Waldheim (3)	Plainview	1973	1957	16
58.	Lakeside (2)	Broad Valley	1974	1962	12
59.	Homewood (1)	Cypress	1975	1959	16
60.	Riverdale (2)	Holmfield	1975	1959	16
61.	Rose Valley (1)	Evergreen	1975	1957	18

- Average number of years between colony divisions, 1918-1975
  (excluding the first 3 divisions of 1, 2, and 4 years during
  the initial settlement period) 14.4

- Median number of years between colony divisions (1918-1975).   14

[1]The number in parenthesis indicates the number of times a colony has
divided, e.g., (1) indicates that it is the colony's first division,
etc.

Source: Compiled by J. Ryan from data acquired from the colonies or
         from Meyers, Norris, Penny and Company, Chartered Accountants,
         Brandon, Manitoba.

APPENDIX I

MANITOBA HUTTERITE COLONIES

NUMBER OF FAMILIES AND POPULATION PER COLONY

DECEMBER 31, 1975

	Name of Colony	No. of Families	Population
1.	Airport	9	57
2.	Baker	8	45
3.	Barickman	13	107
4.	Bloomfield	11	86
5.	Blumengart	14	81
6.	Bon Homme	15	101
7.	Brightstone	18	111
8.	Broad Valley	7	37
9.	Clearwater	24	130
10.	Crystal Spring	13	101
11.	Cypress	15	62
12.	Deerboine	14	80
13.	Elm River	15	111
14.	Evergreen	10	67
15.	Fairholme	17	97
16.	Glenway	12	58
17.	Grand	15	84
18.	Grass	15	87
19.	Greenwald	18	113
20.	Hidden Valley	15	95

	Name of Colony	No. of Families	Population
21.	Hillside	17	116
22.	Holmfield	9	58
23.	Homewood	16	74
24.	Huron	18	105
25.	Iberville	18	111
26.	Interlake	9	57
27.	James Valley	19	108
28.	Lakeside	9	67
29.	Marble Ridge	11	67
30.	Maxwell	20	121
31.	Mayfair	9	57
32.	Miami	16	90
33.	Milltown	11	83
34.	Newdale	16	102
35.	New Rosedale	10	63
36.	Oak Bluff	17	87
37.	Oak Ridge	17	97
38.	Parkview	21	130
39.	Pembina	13	64
40.	Pine Creek	6	30
41.	Plainview	16	84
42.	Poplar Point	13	102
43.	Rainbow	9	59
44.	Ridgeland	18	118

Name of Colony	No. of Families	Population
45. Riverbend	14	77
46. Riverdale	8	60
47. Riverside	14	77
48. Rock Lake	18	130
49. Rosedale	12	88
50. Rose Valley	11	74
51. Springhill	19	116
52. Springfield	13	86
53. Spring Valley	16	87
54. Sturgeon Creek	14	95
55. Suncrest	13	88
56. Sunnyside	20	86
57. Waldheim	16	87
58. Wellwood	11	73
59. Whiteshell	20	110
60. Woodland	15	97
Total	850	5,191
Average no. per colony	14.2	86.5

Source:

Compiled by J. Ryan from population data prepared for computing 1975 Hutterite income tax returns by Meyers, Norris, Penny & Company, Chartered Accountants, Brandon, Manitoba.

SELECTED BIBLIOGRAPHY[1]

A. Books

Bennett, John W. *Hutterian Brethren: The Agricultural Economy and Social Organization of a Communal People.* Stanford: Stanford University Press, 1967.

———. *Northern Plainsmen: Adaptive Strategy and Agrarian Life.* Chicago: Aldine Publishing Company, 1969.

Deets, Lee Emerson. *The Hutterites: A Study in Social Cohesion.* Gettysburg: Time and News Publishing Company, 1939.

Eaton, Joseph W. *Exploring Tomorrow's Agriculture.* New York: Harper and Brothers, 1943.

———, and Albert J. Mayer. *Man's Capacity to Reproduce: The Demography of a Unique Population.* Glencoe: The Free Press, 1954.

———, and Robert J. Weil. *Culture and Mental Disorders: A Comparative Study of the Hutterites and Other Populations.* Glencoe: The Free Press, 1955.

Friedmann, Robert. "Hutterian Brethren," *The Mennonite Encyclopedia*, II, 854-865. Scottdale, Pennsylvania: Mennonite Publishing House, 1956.

Gregor, Howard F. *Geography of Agriculture: Themes in Research.* Englewood Cliffs, N.J.: Prentice-Hall, Inc., 1970.

Gross, Paul S. *The Hutterite Way.* Saskatoon: Freeman Publishing Company, 1965.

Hofer, Peter. *The Hutterite Brethren and Their Beliefs.* Starbuck, Manitoba: The Hutterite Brethren of Manitoba, 1955.

Hostetler, John A. *Amish Society.* Rev. ed. Baltimore: The Johns Hopkins Press, 1968.

———. *Hutterite Life.* Scottdale, Pa.: Herald Press, 1965.

———. *Hutterite Society.* Baltimore: The Johns Hopkins University Press, 1974.

———, and Gertrude Enders Huntington. *The Hutterites in North America.* New York: Holt, Rinehart and Winston, 1967.

[1]The writer obtained practically all the production data and information on the operation of Hutterite agricultural enterprises through interviews with the management personnel and the workers on each of the 48 Manitoba Hutterite colonies listed in Appendix C. Although there is extensive literature on the Hutterites, most of it is irrelevant or insignificant to the study, hence this is a selected bibliography.

Kleinsasser, Jacob, Jacob Hofer, Hardy Arnold, and Daniel Moody. *For the Sake of Devine Truth: Report on a Journey to Europe in the Summer of 1974*. Rifton, N.Y.: Plough Publishing House, 1974.

Peters, Victor. *All Things Common: The Hutterite Way of Life*. Minneapolis: The University of Minnesota Press, 1965.

Raber, Ben J. *The 43rd Year of the New American Calendar 1972*. Baltic, Ohio: published by Ben J. Raber and printed by the Gordonville Printshop, Gordonville, Pennsylvania, 1972.

Rideman, Peter. *Account of Our Religion, Doctrine, and Faith (1565)*. Translated by Kathleen E. Hasenberg. Suffolk: The Plough Publishing House, 1950.

Riley, Marvin P. *The Hutterian Brethren: An Annotated Bibliography with Special Reference to South Dakota Hutterite Colonies*. Rural Sociology Department, Project 255. Brookings: South Dakota State University, 1965.

————. *South Dakota's Hutterite Colonies: 1874-1969*. Rural Sociology Department, Bulletin 565. Brookings: South Dakota State University, 1970.

Ryan, John. *Mixed Farming Near Carman, Manitoba*. Toronto: Ginn and Company, 1968.

Smith, P. J. *The Prairie Provinces*. Toronto: University of Toronto Press, 1972.

Symons, Leslie. *Agricultural Georgraphy*. London: G. Bell and Sons Ltd., 1967.

B. Publications of the Government and Other Organizations

Alberta. *Report of the Legislative Committee Regarding the Land Sales Prohibition Act, 1944, as amended*. Edmonton: The Queen's Printer, 1947.

Alberta. *Report on Communal Property, 1972*. Select Committee of the Alberta Assembly. Edmonton: The Queen's Printer, 1972.

Barber, Clarence L. "Special Report on Prices of Tractors and Combines in Canada and Other Countries," *Royal Commission on Farm Machinery*. Ottawa: Queen's Printer for Canada, 1969.

Canada. Department of Regional Economic Expansion. *The Canada Land Inventory. Soil Capability Classification for Agriculture*, Report No. 2—1965, and maps Brandon-62G, Neepawa-62J, Selkirk-62I, Virden-62F, Winnipeg 62H. Ottawa: Queen's Printer and Controller of Stationery, 1966.

Canada. Dominion Bureau of Statistics. *1966 Census of Canada. Population: Age Groups*, Vol. I (1-10). Ottawa: Queen's Printer and Controller of Stationery, 1968.

Canada. Dominion Bureau of Statistics. *1966 Census of Canada. Households and Families: Household Composition*, Vol. II (2-4). Ottawa: Queen's Printer and Controller of Stationery, 1968.

Canada. Dominion Bureau of Statistics. *1966 Census of Canada. Agriculture: Manitoba*, Vol. V (5-1). Ottawa: Queen's Printer and Controller of Stationery, 1968.

Canada. Dominion Bureau of Statistics. *1970-71 Canada Year Book*. Ottawa: Information Canada, 1971.

Canada. Dominion Bureau of Statistics. *Estimated Value of Honey Production, 1969*, No. 23-007. Ottawa: Queen's Printer and Controller of Stationery, 1970.

Canada. Dominion Bureau of Statistics. *Report on Livestock Surveys—Hogs, June 1, 1968*, No. 23-005. Ottawa: Queen's Printer and Controller of Stationery, 1968.

International Geography 1972 La géographie internationale. Papers submitted to the 22nd International Geographical Congress, Canada. Edited by W. Peter Adams and Frederick M. Helleiner. Volume 2. Toronto: University of Toronto Press, 1972.

Manitoba. *Meeting of the Select Special Committee of the Manitoba Legislature on Hutterite Legislation*. Winnipeg: The Queen's Printer, July 23, 1948.

Manitoba Department of Agriculture, Economics and Publications Branch. *Yearbook*(s) *of Manitoba Agriculture 1966, 1967, 1968, 1969, 1970, 1971, 1974*. Winnipeg: Queen's Printer for Province of Manitoba.

Ryan, John. *The Economic Significance of Hutterite Colonies in Manitoba*. Background Papers for the Southern Prairies Field Excursion published by the 22nd International Geographical Congress, Montreal, 1972.

Statistics Canada. *1971 Census of Canada. Agriculture: Number and Area of Census-Farms*, Advance Bulletin No. 96-727. Ottawa: Information Canada, April 1972.

Statistics Canada. *Farm Input Price Indexes*. Ottawa: Information Canada, December 1971.

Statistics Canada. *Vital Statistics. Preliminary Annual Report 1970*, No. 84-201. Ottawa: Information Canada, May 1972.

Stothers, S.C., and J. C. Brown. *Guide to Practical Swine Rations in Manitoba*. Manitoba Department of Agriculture. Winnipeg: Queen's Printer for the Province of Manitoba, (n.d.).

United Nations. *United Nations Demographic Yearbook 1970*. New York: United Nations, 1971.

Warkentin, J. *Manitoba Settlement Patterns*. Papers published by the Historical and Scientific Society of Manitoba. Series 3, No. 16. Winnipeg, 1961.

Weir, Thomas R. *Economic Atlas of Manitoba*. Winnipeg: Manitoba Department of Industry and Commerce, 1960.

C. Periodicals and Newspapers

Allard, William A. "The Hutterites: Plain People of the West," *National Geographic*, (July, 1970), 98-125.

Barkin, David, and Bennett, J. W. "Kibbutz and Colony: Collective Economies and the Outside World," *Comparative Studies in Society and History*, XIV (September, 1972), 456-83.

Carillon News, Steinbach, Manitoba, September 30, October 7, 14, 21, 28, and November 4, 1965.

Clark, Bertha W. "The Hutterian Communities," *Journal of Political Economy*, XXXII (June, 1924), 357-374; XXXII (August, 1924), 468-486.

Cook, Robert C. (ed.). "The North American Hutterites: A Study in Human Multiplication," *Population Bulletin*, X (December, 1954), 97-107.

Dunlop, J. S. "Changes in the Canadian Wheat Belt, 1931-1969," *Geography*, LV (April, 1970), 156-168.

Fried, Morton H. "Land Tenure, Geography, and Ecology in the Contact of Cultures," *American Journal of Economics and Sociology*, XI (1952), 391-412.

Friedmann, Robert. "Bibliography of Works in the English Language Dealing with the Hutterite Communities," *Mennonite Quarterly Review*, XXXII (July, 1958), 237-238.

———. "A Hutterite Census for 1969: Hutterite Growth in One Century, 1974-1969," *Mennonite Quarterly Review*, XLIV (January, 1970), 100-105.

———. "Comprehensive Review of Research on the Hutterites 1880-1950," *Mennonite Quarterly Review*, XXIV (October, 1950), 353-363.

Hostetler, John A. "A Bibliography of English Language Materials on the Hutterian Brethren," *Mennonite Quarterly Review*, XLIV (January, 1970), 106-113.

———. "Hutterite Separatism and Public Tolerance," *Canadian Forum*, XLI (April, 1961), 11-13.

———. "The Communal Property Act of Alberta," *University of Toronto Law Journal*, XIV, 1961, 125-128.

————. "Total Socialization: Modern Hutterite Educational Practices," *Mennonite Quarterly Review*, XLIV (January, 1970), 72-84.

Jones, W. D., and V. C. Finch. "Detailed Field Mapping in the Study of the Economic Geography of an Agricultural Area," *Bulletin of the American Geographical Society*, XV (1925), 148-157.

Laatsch, William G. "Hutterite Colonization in Alberta," *The Journal of Geography* (September, 1971), 347-359.

Reeds, L. G. "Agricultural Geography: Progress and Prospects," *Canadian Geographer*, VIII (1964).

Steele, C. Frank. "Canada's Hutterite Settlement," *Canadian Geographical Journal*, XXII (June, 1941), 308-314.

Warkentin, J. "Mennonite Agricultural Settlements of Southern Manitoba," *Geographical Review*, XLIX (1959), 342-368.

Winnipeg Tribune, August 25, 1971.

File of magazine and newspaper clippings on Hutterites at the Manitoba Department of Agriculture Library, Norquay Building, Winnipeg.

D. Unpublished Materials

Daciw, M. "The Livestock Situation in Manitoba." Statistician's report, Economics and Publications Branch, Manitoba Department of Agriculture, September 27, 1971. (Mimeographed.)

Davies, Percy G. "Submission to the Agricultural Committee of the Legislature of the Province of Alberta on behalf of the Hutterite Colonies." March 29, 1960. (Mimeographed).

Drumheller (City of), Alberta. "A report concerning the spending habits of a typical colony of Hutterites as compared to those of the individual farmers that would be displaced in the founding of a colony on their land, and an evaluation of the economic impact this colony is expected to have on the City of Drumheller." Report prepared by Bogehold, Jensen and Lefebure Consultants Limited in association with Mack and Shield, Chartered Accountants. Calgary, Alberta. August 24, 1960. (Mimeographed.)

Fletcher, E. A. "Constitution of the Hutterian Brethren Church and Rules as to Community of Property." Winnipeg, Manitoba, 1950. (Mimeographed.)

Fordham, Richard C. "The Structure of Manitoba's Agricultural Geography, 1951-1964." Unpublished Master's thesis. University of Manitoba, 1966.

Friesen, John. "The Manitoba Sugar Beet Industry—A Geographical Study." Unpublished Master's thesis. University of Manitoba, 1962.

Hostetler, John A. "The Hutterians in Perspective." Paper based on an address to the Humanities Association of Canada, University of Alberta, Edmonton, October 20, and to the University of Alberta in Calgary on November 29, 1960. (Mimeographed.)

Katz, Saul M. "The Security of Cooperative Farming." Unpublished Master's thesis. Department of Sociology and Anthropology, Cornell University, 1953.

Manitoba Department of Agriculture, Technical Services Branch, Entomology Section. "1968 Apiary Inspection List." Unpublished report, 1969. (Mimeographed.)

Peters, Victor. "All Things Common—the Hutterians of Manitoba." Unpublished Master's thesis. University of Manitoba. 1958.

———. "A History of the Hutterian Brethren, 1528-1958." Unpublished Ph.D. thesis. University of Gottigen, Germany, 1960.

Pitt, Edwin L. "The Hutterian Brethren in Alberta." Unpublished Master's thesis. Department of History, University of Alberta, 1949.

Ryan, John. "The Agricultural Operations of Manitoba Hutterite Colonies." Unpublished Ph.D. thesis. McGill University, 1973.

Smith, D. L., A. J. Kolach and D. G. McRory. "1968 Annual Report of the Entomology and Apiculture Division." Unpublished report, Manitoba Department of Agriculture, Technical Services Branch, Entomology Section, 1969. (Mimeographed.)

Thompson, William Paul, "Hutterite Community: Artifact for Order—A Study of Hutterite Settlement Patterns and Architecture." Unpublished Ph.D. thesis. Cornell University, 1975.

Union of Manitoba Municipalities and The Hutterian Brethren of Manitoba. An untitled document commonly referred to as "the gentlemen's agreement" between the Union of Manitoba Municipalities and the Hutterian Brethren of Manitoba, signed April 12, 1957.

Warkentin, John H. "The Mennonite Settlements of Southern Manitoba." Unpublished Ph.D. Thesis. University of Toronto, 1960.

E. Other Sources

Kleinsasser, Jacob. "Hutterian Brethren Genealogy Record." Crystal Spring Colony, Ste. Agathe, Manitoba.

Meyers, Dickens, Norris, Penny & Company, Chartered Accountants, Brandon, Manitoba. Financial records of the Hutterian Brethren of Manitoba.

Production and operation records at each of the 48 Manitoba Hutterite colonies listed in Appendix C.

Note on the Author

John Ryan is a professor of geography at the University of Winnipeg. He received a B.A., B.Ed., M.Ed., and M.A. at the University of Manitoba and a Ph.D. in Geography at McGill University. He has been a professor at the University of Winnipeg since 1964. His experience includes early years on a farm, construction, factory, and railway jobs, school teaching, and participation in politics. Dr. Ryan's major academic interests are in agricultural geography, resource development, energy, and the regional geography of Canada, the USSR, and Cuba.

Being born and having grown up on a Manitoba farm proved to be an invaluable experience for Dr. Ryan in this type of study. He finds it easy to relate to farm people and has an intuitive feeling for farming problems and a rural lifestyle. An in-depth study of the Hutterite agricultural economy required the total cooperation of the Hutterites. A friendly rapport was maintained throughout the years of field work, and for the Hutterites, Dr. Ryan remains as "the friendly visiting professor."